the difference

더 디퍼런스

더 좋은 책을 만들기 위한 남다른 열정

Just
READING

HR·3

신석영 지음

더디퍼런스

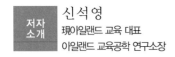

신석영
現아이랜드 교육 대표
아이랜드 교육공학 연구소장

주요저서
Just Reading 1, 2, 3 (전 3권)
Just Grammar Starter 1, 2, 3 (전 3권)
I can Reading 1, 2, 3, 4 (전 4권)
I can Grammar 1, 2, 3, 4 (전 4권 / 메가스터디 Mbest 인터넷 강의교재)
Easy I can Grammar 1, 2, 3, 4 (전 4권)
한국에서 유일한 중학 영문법 (전 6권)
한국에서 유일한 고교 영문법 (전 2권)
Easy I'm your grammar (원서 전 3권 / 대만 수출 / 메가스터디 Mjunior 인터넷 강의교재)
Easy I'm your grammar Workbook (전 3권)
You're my grammar (원서 전 3권)
You're my grammar Workbook (전 3권)

Just Reading HR•3

지은이   신석영
발행인   조상현
발행처   더디퍼런스

등록번호   제2015-000237호
주소   서울시 마포구 마포대로 127, 304호
문의   02-725-9988
팩스   02-6974-1237
이메일   thedibooks@naver.com
홈페이지   www.thedifference.co.kr

ISBN 979-11-86217-21-4 (53740)

빠르고 정확한 독해를 위한

Just READING

3

신석영 지음

더디퍼런스

PROLOGUE

"꿈에 젖은 수년보다 강렬한 한 시간이 더 많은 것을 이룬다"라는 말이 생각납니다. 지금 누구보다도 강렬한 인생을 살고 있는 학생들이 아닌가 싶습니다. 대학을 목표로 열심히 공부하는 학습자들에게는 공부를 잘하는 방법과 어떻게 준비하고 대처를 해야 좋은 점수를 받을 수 있을까? 하는 의문과 절실함은 항상 변함이 없습니다. 똑같은 노력과 주어진 시간이 같다면 좀 더 효과적으로 공부할 수 있도록 도움을 줄 수 있는 안내자와 같은 좋은 책과 선생님들이 절실히 필요할 때입니다. "한 권의 책이 사람의 인생을 바꿀 수도 있다"는 말이 있습니다.

이 책은 저자들이 직접 현장에서 오랜 세월동안 직접 가르치며 만들었습니다. 아이들과 함께 울고, 웃고, 기뻐하며 힘들고 행복했던 시간들을 함께 하면서 조금씩 다듬어 나갔습니다.

힘든 곳과 아픈 곳을 직접 어루만지며 또한 학생들에게서 더 많은 가르침을 받은 저자들이 그것을 해소할 수 있도록 심혈을 기울였습니다.

영어를 잘 듣고, 말하고, 쓰기 위해서는 많이 읽어야 합니다. 영어는 읽어 이해할 수 있는 속도와 정확도의 범위만큼만 들리며, 읽은 내용이 숙지되면 회화가 이루어지고, 글로 표현하면 영작이 따라오게 됩니다. 독해영역이 상당히 별개의 분야처럼 이해되어 회화와 영작도 별도의 훈련이 필요한 것처럼 여겨져 왔는데, 이와 같은 고정관념을 깨는 대수술이 필요합니다. 크라센(Crashen)이라는 언어학자는 '많이 읽을 것'을 강조합니다. 그는 배경지식을 알고, 읽어서 이해할 수 있는 영문을 많이 읽는 것이 영어 정복의 지름길임을 지적합니다. 오늘날 싱가포르의 영어 실력이 이를 증명하는데, 싱가포르의 리관유 전 총리는 학교 교실 뒤에 영문서적을 수십, 수백 권을 비치해 두고 읽기 교육을 시켰습니다. 우리나라는 우선 말해야 한다는 강박관념에 사로잡혀 읽기 교육이 안 되고 있는 현실입니다.

대학 수학능력 시험과 토플, 토익과 같은 시험에서의 관건은 다양한 지문을 얼마나 많이 접하고 또 얼마나 빨리 이해하느냐에 달려 있습니다. 가장 좋은 방법은 쉬운 지문부터 단계별로 공부하면서 영어 독해와 영작 그리고 듣기에 대한 자신감을 가지도록 하는 것입니다. 그런데 현재 영어 교육은 학습자 중심이 아닌 현실과 동떨어져 있고 학습자에 대한 세심한 배려나 사랑이 없어 보입니다. 학습자들은 처음부터 어려운 지문을 접하게 되거나, 흥미없는 소재를 바탕으로 단계학습을 하게 되는데, 그런 이유로 영어를 몇 년을 배워도 투자한 시간과 노력에 비하여 드러나는 학습효과가 실로 미미합니다. 이에 따라, 학생들은 영어가 주는 재미를 느낄 수 없을 뿐 아니라, 오히려 스트레스만 늘어갈 뿐입니다. 당연히 학교시험과 '영어 자체'에는 늘 자신 없어합니다.

Just Reading 시리즈는 이런 학생들을 위해 정밀하게 제작된 Reading 교재입니다. 수능과 TOEFL, TOEIC에 맞춘 지문과 문제는 학생들에게 실제적인 도움을 줄 것입니다.

사실, 저자들의 목표와 이상은 더 높은 곳에 있습니다. 우리가 안고 있는 근본적인 문제는 학습분위기 저변에 깔린 비판적 성향과, 고정된 사고방식 그리고 검증되지 않은 낡은 선입견들입니다. 한 언어가 자리 잡기 위해서는 다양한 과정이 요구되는데 그 중 가장 중요한 부분은 실제 많은 훈련을 할 수 있는 기회와 학습자의 자신감입니다.

언어는 말이요, 말은 정신이요, 정신은 사상입니다. 사상은 인격을 만듭니다. 생소한 언어체계가 우리의 뇌에 자리 잡기까지는 많은 양의 독서를 필요로 합니다. 이 교재는 학습자들이 다양한 범교과서적인 소재를 읽고 즐기는 동시에 많은 도움 장치들로 구성되어 있음을 밝혀 둡니다. 단순한 대학입시가 목적이 아닌 하나의 과정으로 더 큰 꿈과 미래를 향해 나아갈 대한민국 모든 학생들에게 응원을 보냅니다.

마지막으로 이 책의 문법 설명 중 상당수는 김성은 님의 저서 '브릿지 베이직'에서 우수한 해석 원리 기법을 허락 하에 인용하였습니다. 현재도 영어교육을 위해 헌신을 하고 계시고 더 좋은 영어교육을 위해 해석 원리 기법 사용을 허락해 주셔서 다시 한번 깊은 감사를 드립니다.

대표저자   신 석 영

About **Reading** I
독해를 위한 공부 방법

독해력 이란? 독해력은 Reading Power, 즉 '읽어 이해할 수 있는 능력'을 말한다. 많은 학생들이 '독해' 가 무엇인지를 물어보면 십중팔구 읽고 해석하는 것, 읽고 번역하는 것이라 한다. 지금까지 수능, 토익, 토플 같은 시험에서는 한번도 '읽고 해석' 하는 시험을 낸 적이 없다. Reading Comprehension, 즉 읽고 이해하는 것이 독해이다. reading의 첫 출발은 '글을 쓴 작가의 의도'를 파악하는 것, 글을 통하여 작가의 중요한 생각(main idea)을 알아내는 것이다. 고난도 독해력 측정이라는 것은 이러한 글의 중요성을 파악하고 추론해내는 능력이 있는지를 측정하는 것을 가리킨다. 왜 main idea를 통해 독해력을 측정하는 것일까? 이는 이러한 정도의 수준 높은 문제를 풀 줄 아는 학생이 대학의 학문을 이해할 수 있을 것으로 판단하기 때문이다.

독해에 필요한 필수 요소는 무엇인가?

독해도 요령이 있어야 글 속에서 헤매지 않고 주제를 파악할 수 있다. 유명한 그리스 신화에서 테세우스는 동굴의 괴물을 죽이려고 들어갔다가 살아온 유일한 사람인데, 그는 연인이 준 실을 가지고 갔다가 나중에 그 실을 따라 나옴으로써 죽음의 미로에서 살아나왔다고 한다. 학생들이 지문을 대하면 미로와 같고 문장들은 복잡한 통로와 같을 것이다. 이때 실과 같은 요령을 터득한다면 미로와 같은 지문 속에서 명쾌한 해답을 찾을 수 있을 것이다.

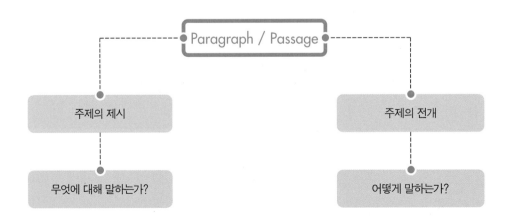

Paragraph / Passage

주제의 제시 — 무엇에 대해 말하는가?

주제의 전개 — 어떻게 말하는가?

1 이 글은 무엇에 관한 것인가?

주제 문장(Topic Sentence/Main idea)이란, 주제(Topic)가 포함된 문장으로, 그 글이나 단락의 내용이 무엇에 관한 것인가를 함축적으로 대변하는 문장이다. 따라서, 이 주제 문장을 통해 글을 읽는 독자는 그 글이 어떤 내용인가를 예상할 수 있고, 글을 쓰는 작가는 하나의 생각(idea)에 충실한 글을 쓸 수 있게 된다.

또한, 주제 문장은 사실(fact)보다는 대개 글쓴이의 견해(opinion)가 들어 있는 문장으로, 주제(topic)와 이에 대한 제한 진술(controlling statement)로 구성된다.

주제를 더욱 짧게 요약하면 그것이 제목(Title)이 된다. 그 외에 Topic/Key Point 등으로 표현할 수 있다. 제목은 어떠한 글에서든지 지문을 중요한 하나의 요소로 통합시키는 것이 된다. 따라서 제목은 간단한 몇 단어로 나타내야 한다.

2 작가는 제목에 대해서 어떤 생각을 말하려고 하는가?

제목, 즉 글쓴이가 어떠한 것에 대해 말하려고 할 때, 그 말하려는 자신의 생각이 곧 주제(Main idea)가 된다. 이것은 주제문으로 표현이 되는데, 제목을 문장으로 나타내는 것이 주제문이다. '무엇이 어떠하다' 라고 표현한다. 제목을 묻는 문제가 중요한 이유는 제목을 옳게 파악할 수 있다면 글의 중요한 요소를 파악하고 있는 것으로 볼 수 있기 때문이다.

3 자신의 생각을 어떻게 표현하는가?

글쓴이는 주로 글의 첫머리 부분에 '화젯거리' 를 제시한다. '화젯거리(Controlling Statement)' 는 마찬가지로 주제에 해당되는데 자신의 주장을 화젯거리로 제시하고 이를 논리적으로 납득할 수 있는 다양한 설명으로 주제를 뒷받침해 주는 문장들로 구성된다. 이러한 문장 구성 요소들을 Supporting Sentences라고 한다. 주제를 뒷받침해 주는 보충, 부연 설명이 연이어 나오는데, 흔히 독해 문제에서 본문의 내용과 일치/불일치를 물어보는 문제는 이러한 세부적인 보충설명을 올바로 이해하는지를 측정하는 문제이다.

전체 Supporting details(보충 · 부연 설명 문장)가 글의 주제와 논리적으로 잘 구성되어 하나의 흐름으로 연결이 잘 되었다면 이것을 우리는 '통일성' 을 잘 갖춘 글이라고 한다. 문단은 하나의 주제문(Topic sentence)을 중심으로 하여 각 문장들이 주제문을 뒷받침하도록 관련성 있게 구성되어 있어야 한다. 비약을 하거나 논지에 어긋나는 문장이 나오는 경우가 있다. 이러한 문장은 제거하거나 수정해야 한다. 글쓰기와 교정 능력을 간접 평가하기 위해 자주 출제되고 있다.

4 내가 읽은 내용을 통해 어떤 결론을 추론해낼 수 있는가?

글의 도입부분에서 화젯거리, 즉 작가의 main idea를 파악하고 이것을 뒷받침해 주는 보충 · 부연 설명글을 모두 이해했다면 그 글에 대한 결론(Concluding Sentence)을 내릴 수 있어야 한다. 이때 결론은 글속에 제시되어 있을 수도 있고, 결론을 추론해내야 하는 경우도 있다. 결론을 묻는 문제는 파악했던 주제와 내용과 의미가 같아야 한다. 내가 읽은 내용과 거리가 멀다면 주제에서도, 결론에서도 벗어나 있다고 판단해야 한다. 함정 문제에서는 일반적인 타당성 있는 결론을 제시하기도 하는데, 반드시 글의 주제와 관련된 결론을 유추해내는 것이 중요하다.

About **Reading** II
독해 원리 정리

Paragraph 구성 원리

Main Idea / Controlling Statement 주제문

Support sentence

Support sentence

Support sentence

Support sentence

Support sentence

Concluding Sentence 결론 문장

❶ 하나의 단락(문단)은 몇 개의 문장이 모여 하나의 주제(핵심사상)를 다룬다.

❷ 단락은 일관된 하나의 주제와 그것을 보충 설명하는 문장들로 구성된다.

❸ 보충 설명하는 문장을 다시 세부적으로 보충하거나, 예를 드는 문장이 있다.

●●● 어떤 글에서, 글쓴이가 말하거나 설명하려는 것이 그 글의 주제(main idea)가 된다. 이것은 글을 쓰는 사람의 입장에서 보면 글쓴이가 말하고자 하는 것이 무엇인지를 전달하고 독자의 입장에서 보면 이 글이 무엇에 관한 것인지를 알게 한다.

About **Just Reading Series Ⅰ**

1 각 Level별 65개의 실생활과 관련된 재미있는 독해 지문

각 Level별로 65개의 지문으로 구성되어 있으며, 5개의 지문이 하나의 Chapter로 이루어져 있다. 재미있는 주제와 다소 딱딱한 역사, 인물에 대한 지문까지 세밀화 된 단계에 맞는 수준의 지문을 실었다. 유익한 지문을 통해 학생들은 다양한 시사, 문화, 역사, 인물, 사회, 과학 분야를 모두 배울 수 있도록 균형 있게 배치되어 있어, 어떠한 유형의 독해 문제라도 당황하지 않고 대처할 수 있는 자기훈련의 기회를 제공하여 재미있게 공부할 수 있다.

2 수능 기출 문제 수록

각 Chapter 별로 수능 기출 문제와 응용 문제가 수록되어 있다. 특히 독해력을 측정하는 문제가 큰 비중을 차지하면서, 문제 출제도 사고력을 배양할 수 있도록 응용문제를 실어 원하는 대학 진학을 희망하는 학생들에게 도전정신과 자신감을 심어줄 수 있도록 구성되었다.

3 종합적 사고력, 분석력, 이해력을 획기적으로 길러 줄 참신한 문제

화제와 주제 파악에 중점을 두되, 본문 내의 빈칸 추론하기, 요약하기, 어법(어휘) 문제, 논술형 문제, 결론 문제의 출제의도를 밝혀 놓아 독해력 측정의 여러 문제 유형에 자신있게 대처할 수 있도록 하였다. 수능에 출제되는 모든 영역과 영어 제시문을 통해 각종 영어 시험에 대비할 수 있도록 구성되었다.

4 지문을 난이도에 따라 적절히 배열

각 Level을 세밀하게 나누어 영어에 대한 두려움을 쉽게 극복하도록 하였다. 각 Chapter 별 마지막 지문은 200자 이상의 장문으로 구성하여 지문에 대한 종합적인 분석이 가능하게 하였고, HR • 3에서는 장문이 2개씩 구성되어 풍부한 읽을 거리를 통해 단계적인 실력 향상에 도움이 될 것이다.

5 선생님 · 학생 · 학부모 모두가 참여할 수 있는 교재

기존의 교재들은 항상 집필자가 이끌어가는 단방향적인 교재였으나 본 교재는 위 삼자가 교재 중심으로 들어와서 서로 대화할 수 있도록 Check Box를 Chapter 별로 두어 학습의 효과를 높이도록 하였다.

About **Just Reading Series** Ⅱ
구성의 특징

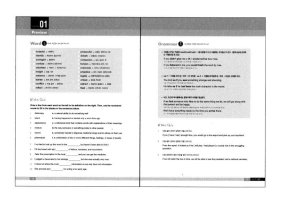

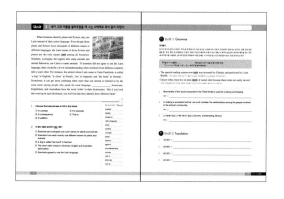

Drill 2 • Translation

본문 속에 있는 핵심 문장을 미리 한글로 해석 연습을 하는 코너
이다. 번역가가 될 필요는 없지만, 고민하면서 해석해보는 연습이
정확한 독해에 상당한 도움이 될 것이다.

Review Test

각 Chapter에서 배운 어휘와 구문, 문법을 복습, 확인하는 코너
이다. 현장수업에서는 Weekly 테스트 또는 Daily 테스트로 활용
하여 학생들의 실력과 복습 정도를 확인, 점검할 수 있다.

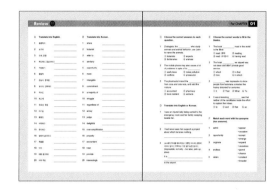

Check Box

부모의 학습 참여가 학생들의 학습에 상당한 긍정적 영향이 있다
는 연구 결과가 있었듯이, 본 교재에서는 숙제 및 학습 과정 이수
를 반드시 학부형 사인을 받아 선생님께 확인 받도록 하여 학생들
의 학습 효과를 극대화하도록 하였다.

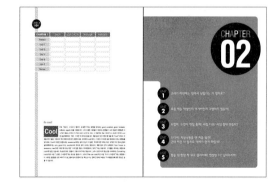

CHAPTER 01

Word 🏠 단어도 모르면서 영어 한다 하지 마!

- botanist *n.* 식물학자
- identify *v.* 확인하다, 동일시하다
- zoologist *n.* 동물학자
- confuse *v.* 혼동하다, 혼란시키다
- volunteer *n.* 지원자 *v.* 자진하여 하다
- insight *n.* 통찰, 식견
- enhance *v.* 강화하다, (가격을) 올리다
- barrier *n.* 장애, 장벽, 경계(선)
- conflict *n.* 투쟁, 충돌 *v.* 충돌하다
- reflect *v.* 반사하다, 반영하다

- prosecutor *n.* 검찰관, 실행하는 사람
- disturb *v.* 방해하다, 어지럽히다
- companion *n.* 동료, 동반자, 짝
- horizon *n.* 지평(수평)선, 범위, 시야
- overcome *v.* 이기다, 극복(정복)하다
- prejudice *n.* 편견, 선입관, (법적인) 침해
- legally *ad.* 법률적(합법적)으로, 법률상
- unique *a.* 유일한, 특이한
- extract *v.* 추출하다, 발췌하다 *n.* 추출물
- treat *v.* 취급하다, 간주하다, 치료하다

∷ Mini Quiz

Draw a line from each word on the left to its definition on the right. Then, use the numbered words to fill in the blanks in the sentences below.

1　dictionary　　　**a.** a natural ability to do something well

2　talent　　　**b.** having happened or started only a short time ago

3　appearance　　　**c.** a reference book that contains words with explanations of their meanings

4　mixture　　　**d.** the way someone or something looks to other people

5　recent　　　**e.** somebody trained to dispense medicinal drugs and to advise on their use

6　pharmacist　　　**f.** a combination of two or more different things, feelings, or types of people

7　I've tried to look up this word in the _____, but haven't been able to find it.

8　Fill the bread with a(n) _____ of lettuce, tomatoes, and cucumbers.

9　Take this prescription to the local _____ and you can get the medicine.

10　I judged a classmate by her strange _____ but she was actually very nice.

11　It does not show the most _____ information so we only have old information.

12　She showed a(n) _____ for acting at an early age.

Grammar 👤 기본 문법도 모르면서 독해한다 하지 마!

★ 가정법 과거는 주절에 〈would/could/might + 동사원형〉이 오고 if절에는 과거동사가 온다. (현재사실에 반대되는 가정을 할 때 쓰임)

If you **didn't give** me a lift, I **would not be** here now.
네가 나를 태워 주지 않았더라면 지금 여기에 올 수 없었을 것이다.

If you **listened** to me, you **could finish** the work by now.
네가 나의 말을 들었더라면 지금쯤 그 일을 끝냈을 것이다.

★ 〈as if + 가정법 과거〉는 '마치 ~인 것처럼' 〈as if + 가정법 과거완료〉는 '마치 ~이었던 것처럼' 이다.

You look **as if** you *saw* something strange and shocking.
너는 이상하고 놀라운 무엇인가를 본 것처럼 보인다.

He talks **as if** he *had been* the main character in the movie.
그는 그가 마치 그 영화의 주인공이었던 것처럼 말을 한다.

★ 시간, 조건의 부사절에서는 현재시제가 미래를 대신한다.

If we **find** someone who likes to do the same thing we do, we will get along with that person and be happy.
우리가 하는 같은 일을 하는 것을 좋아하는 누군가를 찾는다면, 우리는 그 사람과 친하게 지낼 것이고 행복할 것이다.

We'll have everything ready by the time you **arrive** there.
네가 거기에 도착할 때쯤 우리는 모든 것을 준비해 놓고 있을 것이다.

:: Mini Quiz

1   다음 괄호 안에서 알맞은 것을 고르시오.

If you [have / had] enough time, you would go to the airport and pick up your boyfriend.

2   다음 괄호 안에서 알맞은 것을 고르시오.

From the report, it looked as if he [will play / had played] a crucial role in the smuggling operation.

3   다음 문장에서 <u>틀린</u> 부분을 찾아 바르게 고치시오.

If we will catch the bus in time, we will be able to see the president visit a national cemetery.

[1] When botanists identify plants and flowers, they use Latin instead of their native language. Even though those plants and flowers have thousands of different names in different languages, the Latin names of those flowers and plants are the only names used among all botanists. Similarly, zoologists, the experts who study animals and animal behaviors, use Latin to name animals. [2] If scientists did not agree to use the Latin language, there would be a lot of misunderstanding when scientists from different countries talk to each other. For instance, the animal whose Latin name is Canis Familiaris, is called 'a dog' in English; 'le chien' in French; 'inu' in Japanese; and 'der hund' in German. [3] Sometimes, it can get more confusing when more than one animal is referred to by the same name among people who speak the same language. _____, Americans, Englishmen, and Australians have the word 'robin' in their dictionaries. [4] But if you look this word up in each dictionary, you will find that they identify three different birds!

1 **Choose the best phrase to fill in the blank.**

① In contrast
② For example
③ In consequence
④ That is
⑤ In addition

2 이 글의 내용과 일치하지 <u>않는</u> 것은?

① Botanists and zoologists use Latin names for plants and animals.
② Scientists from each country use different names for plants and animals.
③ A dog is called 'der hund' in German.
④ The word 'robin' exists in American, English and Australian dictionaries.
⑤ Scientists agreed to use the Latin language.

단어 조사해 오셔~ **Word**

botanist

identify

instead of

native language

similarly

zoologist

expert

behavior

agree to

misunderstanding

confuse

refer to

dictionary

look up

 **Drill 1** Grammar

과거분사

분사가 명사의 앞이나 뒤에서 꾸며 줄 때 형용사가 아닌 분사로 수식해 주는 이유가 무엇일까? 형용사는 명사의 '상태' 만을 설명 해 줄 뿐 '동작, 행위' 를 표현해 줄 수 없다. 따라서 명사가 행위의 주체가 아닌 객체, 즉 동작이 필요하나 동작의 행위를 받는 경 우에 과거분사를 사용한다. 분사와 관련된 대부분의 어법 문제는 이 차이를 알고 있는지를 물어 보는 것을 목적으로 한다.

> N(명사) + -ed/en .....   (뒤에 딸린 어구가 있을 때 명사 뒤에 위치)
> └─────────┘ 우리말 "~된, ~진, ~하여진"을 붙여 해석한다.

- The special reading system now used was invented by Charles, and perfected by Louis Braille. 지금 사용되는 특별한 읽기 시스템은 Charles에 의해 발명되어 Louis Braille에 의해 완성되었다.
- Desert tribes often live in tents made of camel skin because these tents are easily moved.
  사막의 부족은 종종 낙타 가죽으로 만들어진 텐트에서 사는데 그 이유는 텐트들이 이동하기 쉽기 때문이다.

---

1 Nine-tenths of the wood consumed in the Third World is used for cooking and heating.

해석 ◉ _____

2 In making a successful school, we must consider the relationships among the people involved in the school's community.

해석 ◉ _____

3 도서관에서 빌린 그 책은 재미가 없었다. (borrow, uninteresting, library)

영작 ◉ _____

Drill 2 Translation

1 1번 문장 ◉ _____

2 2번 문장 ◉ _____

3 3번 문장 ◉ _____

4 4번 문장 ◉ _____

[1] Volunteering can help you gain the experience that provides you with the opportunity to give time and energy towards meeting human needs, while learning about yourself, the community and world in which you live. Volunteering can take very little time and commitment on the part of the volunteer, but its effects can be felt by many. [2] There are opportunities to use your special talents in many different settings for a variety of causes. Through volunteering you can learn new skills and gain insights. You can also explore career possibilities, hence, enhance the job search. Many employers are often impressed by volunteer work. Volunteering has many other intangible benefits. [3] It can help you give back to society, break down barriers of misunderstanding or fear, explore personal issues, and even have fun. [4] _____, your volunteering will work not only to increase your personal satisfaction but also to build a better society.

1 Choose the best answer to fill in the blank.

① Because of this   ② For example
③ On the other hand   ④ Consequently
⑤ In addition

2 Choose the best main idea for the paragraph.

① Volunteering is a good opportunity to impress employers.
② Volunteering is a warm-hearted thing to do and it gives self-satisfaction.
③ There are many benefits people may get through volunteering.
④ People may find their talents or learn new skills through volunteering.
⑤ It's important to volunteer in many areas of volunteering.

단어 조사해 오셔~ **Word**

volunteering

provide

opportunity

meet

commitment

on the part of

talent

insight

career possibility

enhance

be impressed

intangible

barrier

issue

satisfaction

 **Drill 1** Grammar

전치사 + 관계대명사

관계대명사가 자신이 데리고 있는 절 속에 있는 전치사의 목적어로 쓰일 때 전치사를 관계대명사 바로 앞에 두거나 맨 끝에 둔다. 전치사를 맨 뒤로 보낼 경우 관계대명사는 생략할 수 있다. 〈전치사+관계대명사〉를 한 단어로 취급하여 앞에 있는 명사를 꾸미면 서 우리말 '~하는, ㄴ, ~했던' 을 붙여 해석한다. 전치사의 의미가 강할 경우 전치사의 의미만을 살려 주면 된다.

- The group to which Harry belongs encourages individual members to think creatively.

  Harry가 속해 있는 집단은 구성원 각각이 창조적으로 생각하도록 장려한다.

- The way in which we spend our own money must be learned from our parents.

  우리가 우리 자신의 돈을 쓰는 방법은 우리 부모님으로부터 배워져야 한다.

---

1   She wrote on a topic about which she knew almost nothing.

    해석 ◐ _____

2   Language is the means by which people communicate with other people.

    해석 ◐ _____

3   사람들이 자기의 두려움을 통제하는 방법을 배우는 특별한 수업이 있다.
    (how to control, special, in which, their fear, learn)

    영작 ◐ _____

Drill 2 Translation

1   1번 문장 ◐ _____

2   2번 문장 ◐ _____

3   3번 문장 ◐ _____

4   4번 문장 ◐ _____

According to a recent survey, at least five out of ten Korean people are mobile phone users. Mobile phones can be used to solve conflicts. [1] In a recent political struggle between politicians and prosecutors, the two sides were able to solve their problems over mobile phones. However, the mobile phone may also cause a lot of problems. [2] A majority of car-related accidents these days are caused by people who talk on the phone while driving, or crossing a busy street. [3] In Korea, it is very common to see old people as well as children talking on their mobile phones regardless of time or place. The ring tones of mobile phones are often terribly sharp and annoying. Even if the phone has a musical ring tone, it is still disturbingly noisy. When it rings in a movie theater, or in a concert hall, the lousy ringing sounds disturb and annoy the public. [4] Those problems caused by mobile phones reflect the endless needs of Korean people to be connected with others.

1 **According to the passage, what is a disadvantage of the mobile phone phenomenon?**

① Children talk on their mobile phones instead of studying.

② Mobile phones can cause brain cancer.

③ Mobile phones can cause car accidents.

④ It is difficult to talk to somebody when you can't see his or her face.

⑤ Mobile phones cause a lot of diseases.

2 **Why are mobile phones popular in Korea?**

① Korean people have endless reasons to be connected with others.

② People like to talk to their friends when they are stuck in traffic.

③ Mobile phones are not very expensive.

④ There are few public phones in Korea.

⑤ They are important in case of an emergency.

단어 조사해 오서~ **Word**

survey

mobile phone

conflict

political

struggle

politician

prosecutor

a majority of

car-related accident

noise pollution

regardless of

disturbingly

disturb

reflect

endless

 **Drill 1** Grammar

가주어, 진주어 구문 〈It + V ~ + to do …〉

영어는 주어와 동사를 가급적 가까이 위치해야 핵심적인 말을 빨리 전달할 수 있다. 그래서 주어가 조금이라도 길어지면 그 자리에 'it'을 쓰고 전부 뒤로 보낼 수 있다. 주어가 To부정사로 시작되면 어쩔 수 없이 주어가 길어질 수밖에 없다. 이 때 현대영어에서는 가급적 It을 그 자리에 두고 모두 뒤로 보내버린다. it은 우리말 '그것'이란 말을 꼭 붙이고 'to do'는 우리말 '~것, ~기' 정도로 해석하면 된다.

- **It is important for a journalist to be honorable and to write about both sides of a problem.**
  그것은 중요하다 언론인이 명예를 지키는 것 그리고 문제의 양측 면에 대해서 글을 쓰는 것. (언론인이 명예를 지키고 문제의 양측 면에 대해서 글을 쓰는 것은 중요하다.)

- **Because women were weaker physically than men, the knights believed that it was their duty to protect them.** 여자들은 신체적으로 남자보다 더 약하기 때문에, 기사들은 여자를 보호하는 것이 자기들의 의무라고 믿었다.

---

1 Because the student has short legs and is not strong, it is difficult for him to be an excellent soccer player. As a result, he is learning golf and table tennis.

   해석 ○ _____

2 During our trip to Rome, it was difficult to see all the sights that we had hoped to see. There just was not enough time, so we hope to go again in the future.

   해석 ○ _____

3 아이들에게 그들이 원하는 모든 것을 주는 것은 잘못이다. (wrong, it, everything, want, give)

   영작 ○ _____

 Drill 2 Translation

1 1번 문장 ○ _____

2 2번 문장 ○ _____

3 3번 문장 ○ _____

4 4번 문장 ○ _____

(A)

You drive through a town and see a drunken man on the sidewalk. A few blocks further on you see another. You turn to your companion: "Nothing but _____ in this town!" Soon you are out in the country, driving at 80 kilometers per hour. A car passes you as if you were parked. On a curve a second whizzes by. Your companion turns to you: "All the drivers in this state are crazy!" Here we start at the level of facts properly enough, but we do not stay there. <u>A case</u> or two and on we go to an over-simplification about _____ and speeders.

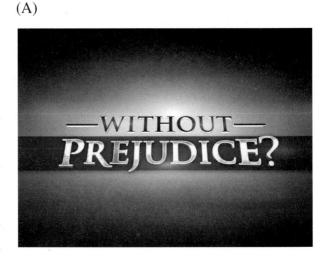

(B)

I try very hard to _____, because I realize it limits me. Several years ago, I judged a classmate by her strange appearance and possibly missed the chance to make a good friend. Now, I no longer judge people according to what is on the outside, but instead pay attention to what is on the inside. I have widened my horizons to include many delightful people whom I might have never known if I had maintained my original judgment.

기출

1 글 (A)와 (B)를 통하여 얻을 수 있는 교훈으로 가장 적절한 것은?

① 난폭한 운전을 고발하자.
② 친구를 골라 사귀자.
③ 판단을 신중하게 하자.
④ 용모를 단정히 하자.
⑤ 창의적인 사고력을 키우자.

2 글 (A)의 밑줄 친 <u>A case</u>에 상응하는 단어를 (B)에서 고른다면, 가장 적절한 것은?

① chance
② attention
③ horizons
④ years
⑤ appearance

3 글 (A)의 빈칸에 공통으로 들어갈 수 있는 단어는?

① men
② beggars
③ drivers
④ strangers
⑤ drunks

4 **Choose the best answer to fill in the blank in paragraph B.**

① overcome my prejudice
② succeed my career
③ be generous to people
④ be fashionable with my appearance
⑤ make friends

단어 조사해 오세요~ **Word**

drunken man

sidewalk

companion

park

pass

whizz by

properly

over-simplification

speeder

overcome

prejudice

limit

judge

appearance

no longer

pay attention to

widen

horizon

delightful

maintain

original judgment

Coca-Cola (a) must be the world's most popular soft drink. In May, 1886, John Pemberton, a pharmacist living in Atlanta, Georgia, invented the drink. He mixed the extracts from coca and cola nuts, and sold the mixture, (b) which contained cocaine, at his pharmacy as a drug. Until 1905, cocaine was legally used to treat headaches. Frank M. Robinson, Pemberton's accountant at the pharmacy, was the person who first came up with the name "Coca-Cola" and also the distinctive script. "Coca-Cola" has became the famous logo of today.

What made today's Coca-Cola company (c) is the original shape of the coca cola bottle. The bottle's shape was invented by professional designer Earl R. Dean and Alexander Samuelson, who were members of a design team working for the Root Grass Company. Dean and his team were inspired by a picture of a gourd-shaped cocoa pod. Later, after they mass-produced the bottles, they learned that the shape was not only unique but also good for sales. Interestingly, the curvy shape (d) made people thirsty!

Without the help of the U.S. army, Coca-Cola could not (e) have been spread throughout the world so fast and widely. Everywhere U.S. soldiers went, Coca-Cola was with them. Factories were built in Europe and in Asia to provide the soldiers with their Coca-Cola. After the soldiers left, the factories kept running for the local residents.

Right now, 5,214 cans of Coca-Cola are sold every second all over the world. Once, the company tried to change the taste of Coca-Cola, but too many people fought against it. As a result, Coca-Cola still has its original taste. That's how much we're used to Coke!

1 **What was a surprising factor in the success of the Coca-Cola company?**

① the particular taste
② the pharmacist
③ the Coca-Cola company
④ Frank M. Robinson
⑤ the shape of the bottle

2 밑줄 친 (a)~(e) 중, 어법상 틀린 것을 찾아 바르게 고치시오.

3 이 글에서 주로 사용한 서술 방식으로 알맞은 것은?

① 사실 묘사
② 정의와 분석
③ 시간의 흐름에 대한 설명
③ 비교와 대조
⑤ 원인과 결과

4 **What was the inspiration for the bottle's shape?**

① The curviness of the cola nuts
② John Pemberton's accountant
③ A picture of a gourd-shaped cocoa pod
④ The curvy figure of a woman's body
⑤ An idea of the Coca-Cola factory

단어 조사해 오셔~ **Word**

pharmacist

Atlanta

extract

coca

cola nut

mixture

contain

cocaine

pharmacy

legally

treat

headache

come up with

distinctive

script

be inspired by

gourd-shaped

pod

accountant

mass-produce

unique

interestingly

spread throughout the world

provide

local resident

fight against

original taste

Review 😊

A **Translate into English.**

1 동물학자 _____

2 모국어 _____

3 오해, 분쟁 _____

4 확인하다, 동일시하다 _____

5 자원봉사 _____

6 통찰력 _____

7 관심사, 문제점 _____

8 높이다, 강화하다 _____

9 적어도 _____

10 최근의 _____

11 유효성, 유용 _____

12 이기심 _____

13 동행인 _____

14 극복하다 _____

15 유지하다 _____

16 씽하며 날아가다 _____

17 추출물 _____

18 약국 _____

19 대량 생산하다 _____

20 지역 주민 _____

B **Translate into Korean.**

1 share _____

2 botanist _____

3 refer to _____

4 similarly _____

5 opportunity _____

6 meet _____

7 intangible _____

8 commitment _____

9 a majority of _____

10 struggle _____

11 regardless of _____

12 annoy _____

13 judge _____

14 delightful _____

15 over-simplification _____

16 properly _____

17 accountant _____

18 treat _____

19 provide _____

20 interestingly _____

C **Choose the correct answers to each question.**

1   Zoologists, the _____ who study animals and animal behavior, use Latin to name the animals.
    ① botanists   ② experts
    ③ dictionaries   ④ animals

2   The mobile phone may also cause a lot of problems in spite of its _____.
    ① usefulness   ② noise pollution
    ③ conflicts   ④ prosecutor

3   The pharmacist mixed the _____ from coca and cola nuts, and sold the mixture.
    ① accountant   ② pharmacy
    ③ local resident ④ extracts

D **Translate into English or Korean.**

1   I saw an injured lady being carried to the emergency room and her family weeping beside her.

    _____

2   I had never seen him support a project about which he knew nothing.

    _____

3   Jim에게 우리를 데리러오는 것뿐만 아니라 공항에 태워다달라고 부탁하는 것은 불가능한 일이다.
    (impossible, not only ~ but also, pick up, drive)

    It is _____

    _____

    to the airport.

E **Choose the correct words to fill in the blanks.**

1   The book _____ most in the world is the Bible.
    ① read (현재)   ② reading
    ③ read (과거분사)   ④ having read

2   The hotel _____ we stayed was not clean and didn't provide good service.
    ① which   ② in that
    ③ how   ④ in which

3   _____ was impressive to show people how historians corrected the history distorted for centuries.
    ① It   ② That   ③ What   ④ To

4   It was interesting _____ see that neither of the candidates made the effort to explain their ideas.
    ① to   ② and   ③ that   ④ so

F **Match each word with its synonyms (two answers).**

1   admit   • appear
                         • occasion
2   opportunity   • accept
                         • emerge
3   originate   • expand
                         • ceaseless
4   endless   • permit
                         • chance
5   widen   • constant
                         • broaden

CHECK
BOX

CHAPTER 1	DATE	SELF CHECK	TEACHER	PARENTS
Preview				
Unit 1				
Unit 2				
Unit 3				
Unit 4				
Unit 5				
Review				

So cool!

 주로 '멋있다, 근사하다, 캡이다, 끝내준다' 라는 표현을 영어로는 good, excellent, great, fantastic, brilliant, superb 등을 사용합니다. 젊은 사람들이 사용하는 표현들이 그리 점잖은 표현들은 아니지만 때로는 오히려 더 자연스럽게 쓰이기도 하죠. 그 대표적인 예로 시원하거나 신선한 의미의 cool은 일상 대화에서 '멋진, 근사한' 의 의미로 통합니다. 예를 들어 멋진 비행기를 봤을 때 "Cool!" 이라고 외쳤을 때 이 말을 '시원하다' 라고 해석하면 웃긴 표현이 되죠. 영어에서 cool(멋진, 근사한)과 비슷한 말로 통용되고 있는 표현들을 알아보 죠. cool과 비슷한 표현으로는 awesome이라는 말이 있는데 이 말은 '무시무시한' 이라는 뜻도 있지만 미국 청소년들의 일상대화 에서는 very good 또는 excellent의 의미로 많이 쓰이는 말입니다. 예를 들어 만약 상대방이 Your house is awesome, man! 이란 이야기를 듣는다면 "너의 집은 정말 근사해(캡이야, 멋져)!" 라는 뜻입니다. 근사함을 나타내는 표현으로 rock이란 말도 있습 니다. Rock은 원래 '흔들나, 진동시키나' 라는 뜻입니다. 그러나 요즘 미국 청소년들 사이에서는 Something rocks!라고 하면 "그 물건 근사한데!" 라는 뜻으로 통합니다. 그래서 This car rocks!라고 하면 "이 차 근사한데!" 라는 표현입니다. 이러한 표현들 은 요즘 미국 TV프로그램에 많이 등장하므로 책으로 하는 공부도 좋지만 때로는 TV 시청을 통해 많은 정보도 얻을 수 있습니다.

CHAPTER 02

Word 🏠 단어도 모르면서 영어 한다 하지 마!

- **creature** *n.* 창조물, 생물, 동물
- **surface** *n.* 표면, 수면 *a.* 외관의
- **evolve** *v.* 발전시키다, 진화시키다
- **breathe** *v.* 호흡하다, 숨을 쉬다
- **tremendous** *a.* 거대한, 대단한, 무서운
- **puberty** *n.* 사춘기, 성숙기, 개화기
- **limit** *n.* 한계, 범위 *v.* 제한하다
- **awkward** *a.* 어색한, 서투른, 힘든
- **durability** *n.* 내구성, 내구력
- **fibrous** *a.* 섬유의, 섬유질의

- **material** *n.* 재료, 도구, 자료 *a.* 물질적인
- **block** *n.* 덩어리, 블록 *v.* 막다, 방해하다
- **incredible** *a.* 놀라운, 대단한, 믿기 힘든
- **ease** *n.* 안정 *v.* 진정시키다, 늦추다
- **urge** *v.* 몰아대다, 강요하다 *n.* 충동
- **irresistible** *a.* 저항(억제)할 수 없는
- **fit** *v.* 알맞다 *a.* 적당한 *n.* 꼭 맞음
- **adjustment** *n.* 조정, 조절, 수정
- **route** *n.* 길, 수단, 방법, 항로
- **priority** *n.* 상위, 우위, 우선권

∷ Mini Quiz

Draw a line from each word on the left to its definition on the right. Then, use the numbered words to fill in the blanks in the sentences below.

1 huge   **a.** the circular path of a planet, satellite, or moon

2 mature   **b.** move safely down onto the ground

3 available   **c.** fully developed and balanced in personality and emotional behavior

4 orbit   **d.** able to be used or can easily be bought or found

5 attentive   **e.** extremely large in size, amount, or degree

6 land   **f.** behaving toward somebody in a way that shows special regard or affection

7 We're _____ enough to disagree on this issue and to take the responsibility for that.

8 This makes a(n) _____ difference, especially in the high school years.

9 The space shuttle is now in _____.

10 There are plenty of jobs _____ in this area.

11 Flight 846 _____ five minutes ago.

12 Customers want companies that are _____ to their needs.

Grammar 🎯 기본 문법도 모르면서 독해한다 하지 마!

★ 의미상 목적어가 필요 없는 자동사 occur, appear, seem, remain, happen 등은 수동태로 쓸 수 없다.

Researchers said the maximum number of all eclipses that can **occur** in a year is five. 연구원들이 말하길 일 년에 일어날 수 있는 최대의 일식 수는 5번이라고 했다.

People often find their dreams **remain** unaccomplished and give up.
사람들은 종종 자신들의 꿈이 이뤄지지 않은 채로 있는 것을 발견하고 포기한다.

★ 수동태에서 by 대신 다른 전치사를 사용하는 경우를 주의해야 한다.

*be covered **with** / be filled **with** / be made **of** / be satisfied **with** / be disappointed **in** / be surprised **at*** ...

Terrorists will use anything that they can cause people to *be scared **of*** something actual or fictional.
테러리스트는 실제 사실 또는 허구적인 일로 사람들을 무서워하게 만들기 위해 어떤 것이든 사용할 것이다.

★ 비교문에서 비교대상은 어법상 동일 어구를 사용해야 한다.

My family prefers **eating outside** to **eating at home** on special occasions like Christmas. 크리스마스 같은 특별한 때에 우리 가족은 집에서 먹는 것보다 외식하는 것을 더 좋아한다.

To evaluate each student is more efficient than **to evaluate the group of students**. 학생 개개인을 평가하는 것은 학생들 그룹을 평가하는 것보다 더 효과적이다.

:: Mini Quiz

1 다음 괄호 안에서 알맞은 것을 고르시오.

When you send an e-mail to your friend, your nickname will [appear / be appeared] in the "From" field.

2 다음 문장에서 틀린 부분을 찾아 바르게 고치시오.

I remember being surprised on how good the pictures we had taken actually came out.
  ①   ②   ③   ④

3 다음 문장에서 틀린 부분을 찾아 바르게 고치시오.

How you see yourself is different from others see you when you talk with people.

A whale is a huge creature living in the ocean. [1] A blue whale can grow up to 100 feet long, and a newborn blue whale is bigger than a full-grown elephant. There are many types of whales like the sperm whale, humpback whale, Sei Whale, great blue whale, California Grey Whale, and Greenland Right Whale. [2] A whale is a mammal, because it is a warm-blooded

animal, and the young are born out of their mother's womb and fed with the mother's milk. [3] Since whales are mammals, they breathe through lungs, unlike fish that use gills for breathing. _____, whales must come up to the surface every half hour to breathe air. But isn't it strange that whales don't live on land like other mammals but live in water? [4] According to zoologists, ancestors of whales used to live on land in very ancient times, but they evolved and became fishlike after they started living in water.

1   이 글의 내용과 일치하는 것은?

① Dolphins and porpoises aren't part of the mammal family.
② Whales breathe through gills.
③ Whales must breathe air every hour or so.
④ All baby whales are born through their mother's womb.
⑤ Zoologists believe that whales were fishlike in ancient times.

2   **Choose the best word to fill in the blank.**

① Amazingly   ② Therefore   ③ In contrast
④ Likewise   ⑤ To begin with

단어 조사해 오셔~ **Word**

huge

creature

newborn

full-grown

mammal

warm-blooded animal

womb

breathe

gill

surface

zoologist

ancestor

used to do

evolve

fishlike

 **Drill 1** Grammar

가주어 진주어 it ~ that 구문

주어가 길어지면 그 자리에 it 쓰고 모두 뒤로 보낼 수 있다고 했다. 주어 자리에 명사절 접속사 that이 오면 그 덩치는 정말로 클 수 있다. 이 때도 마찬가지로 it을 쓰고 모두 뒤로 보내는데, 이를 가주어, 진주어라 한다. 이때, it은 우리말 '그것' 을 붙여 해석하고 that은 우리말 '것, 기' 로 해석하면 된다.

• [That people live longer than they did before] *is* true.
  S는~~~~~~~~~~~~~~~~~~~~~~~~~~~~~ 사실이다. (주어가 너무 길다.)

• It *is* true that people live longer than they did before.
  그것은 사실이다 사람들이 예전보다 더 오래 산다는 것. (사람들이 예전보다 더 오래 산다는 것은 사실이다.)

---

1 It is very surprising that many of the most educated people in our society know so little of our country's history.

해석 ◎ _____

2 It is natural that people will always want to have holidays.

해석 ◎ _____

3 신이 천지를 창조했다는 것은 확실하지 않다. (it, clear, the whole world, create, God)

영작 ◎ _____

 **Drill 2** Translation

1 1번 문장 ◎ _____

2 2번 문장 ◎ _____

3 3번 문장 ◎ _____

4 4번 문장 ◎ _____

[1] Some adolescents experience tremendous changes as early as fourth or fifth grade, while others may not begin developing until their high school years. In general, girls develop and mature earlier than boys. [2] In girls, the growth spurt begins in early puberty, while in boys, the growth spurt usually begins in mid to late puberty. The growth spurt usually _____. For example, first the hands and feet begin to grow

longer, then the arms and legs, and finally the trunk of the body catches up. This may seem awkward, but it is perfectly natural. [3] You may worry that your body is developing too slowly or too fast or that your shape is different from that of your friends or people you see on television or in magazine ads. Remember, your body has its own limits and its own growth schedule. [4] Rather than worrying too much about outer appearances, focus your energy on participating in fun activities with friends in everyday life.

1 이 글의 빈칸에 들어갈 내용으로 가장 적절한 것은?

① grows rapidly in a short time ② occurs in sequence
③ doesn't happen until puberty ⑤ maintains a healthy body
⑤ occurs in difference

2 이 글의 내용과 일치하지 <u>않는</u> 것은?

① 성장 스케줄에 따라 청소년들은 비슷한 시기에 성장변화를 겪는다.
② 어떤 청소년들은 고등학교 때까지도 성장이 시작되지 않기도 한다.
③ 소녀들은 소년들보다 더 일찍 성장변화를 겪는다.
④ 성장변화는 처음에 손과 발이 먼저 성장한다.
⑤ 소녀들에게 성장변화는 사춘기 초기에 시작된다.

단어 조사해 오세요~ **Word**

adolescents

tremendous

growth spurts

mature

puberty

in sequence

trunk

awkward

shape

magazine ads

limit

appearance

focus A on B

 **Drill 1** Grammar

명사절 접속사 that

접속사 that은 명사절을 이끌어 문장에서 목적어 역할을 할 수 있다. 기능에 따라서는 주어와 보어 역할도 할 수 있다. 우리말 '~것, ~라고'를 붙여 명사절 전체를 해석하면 된다.

• Experts point out that a labor shortage is a serious problem.
전문가들은 노동력의 부족이 심각한 문제라고 지적하고 있다.

• I believe that success is a journey, not a destination. 나는 성공은 여정이지, 목적지가 아니라고 믿고 있다.

---

1 The problem is that he does not want to go to the university his father attended.

해석 ◯ _____

2 Though he was a child, Franz knew that Germany had been in a brutal war with France and that his country, France, had been beaten.

해석 ◯ _____

brutal 잔인한, 심한 | beat 이기다

3 그 점쟁이는 그 커플이 결혼하지 말아야 한다고 충고했다. (get married, the couple, advise)

영작 ◯ The fortune teller _____

Drill 2 Translation

1 1번 문장 ◯ _____

2 2번 문장 ◯ _____

3 3번 문장 ◯ _____

4 4번 문장 ◯ _____

Around the world, the ways to construct a house usually depend on the _____ of building materials. [1] For instance, people who live in fertile regions, use the most available materials, mud or clay, which block out the heat and solar radiation. They also provide good insulation and durability from the heat. [2] On the other hand, the Eskimos,

living in some parts of the Arctic, build their houses with thick blocks of ice because they live in a treeless region of snow and ice. [3] In Northern Europe, Russia, and other areas of the world where people have easy access to forests, houses are usually made of wood. Also, in the islands of the South Pacific, there grow bamboos and palm trees. [4] So, people use these tough, fibrous plants to build their houses.

1 Choose the best word to fill in the blank.

① size   ② availability   ③ price
④ demand   ⑤ kinds

2 이 글의 내용을 다음 한 문장으로 요약하고자 한다. 빈칸 (A)와 (B)에 들어갈 말로 가장 적절한 것끼리 짝지은 것은?

➡ The paragraph shows that people are _____(A)_____ enough to adapt to their environment because they have been _____(B)_____ in various environments throughout history.

	(A)		(B)
①	idle	···	hard working
②	noxious	···	constructing
③	intelligent	···	surviving
④	inane	···	creating
⑤	sedate	···	engaging

단어 조사해 오세요~ **Word**

construct

material

fertile region

available

block out

solar radiation

insulation

durability

Arctic

access to

be made of

bamboo

palm tree

fibrous

 **Drill 1** Grammar

관계사 who

관계대명사가 선행사를 수식하는 경우는 어떨 때 가능한가? 관계사의 역할을 하려면 who 또는 that, which도 모두 똑같이 앞에 반드시 '명사'가 위치해야 한다. 이때 관계사의 역할은 우리말 '하는, ~ㄴ, ~했던'으로 해석하여 앞에 명사를 꾸며 주고, 특별한 의미나 해석을 갖지 않는 기능적인 역할만을 하게 된다. 어법에서는 주어를 수식하는 경우에 동사의 '수일치'와, '시제일치'에 대해 자주 물어 보게 된다.

• The child who doesn't make the baseball team feels terrible.

  야구팀에 합류하지 못한 그 아이는 기분이 몹시 좋지 않다.

• I saw the musician who electrified the audience on TV last night. His name is Rain.

  나는 지난밤에 TV에서 청중을 전율시킨 음악가를 보았어. 그의 이름은 비야.

1 They look for employees who support each other, take pride in their work, and encourage maintenance of a pleasant working environment.

  해석 ⊙ _____

2 Those who cannot achieve success in their business or profession are the ones whose concentration is poor.

  해석 ⊙ _____

3 자신에게 신뢰를 갖고 있는 사람이 다른 사람들에게 충실할 수 있다. (person, others, faithful, faith, in himself)

  영작 ⊙ _____

Drill 2 Translation

1 1번 문장 ⊙ _____

2 2번 문장 ⊙ _____

3 3번 문장 ⊙ _____

4 4번 문장 ⊙ _____

(A)

"There is a good reason to make this trip to the Island of Paradise," Captain Koppe told himself as he stepped out of the elevator car into (i) the covered rooftop hangar of his house. The journey itself would be of use. There were times (ii) when it was important to be alone, to have time to think. Alone even from one's personal robot, from one's trusted wife.

(B)

The outer doors opened, and the aircar slowly eased out into the driving rain. Suddenly, (a) it was in the middle of the storm, jumping and swinging in the darkness, the rain crashing down on the windows with incredible violence. The storm boomed and roared outside the long-range aircar as (b) it fought for altitude, the banging and clattering (iii) getting worse with every moment.

(C)

Smooth sailing after the storm, the aircar arrived at the orbit of the Island of Paradise. Captain Koppe looked out at the island through the window. He had been longing for (c) it since his childhood. At that moment, his family picture (iv) posted on the inside of the aircar came into his eyes. All of a sudden, he had an irresistible urge to go to see his beloved wife and his two sons. He turned his back on the Island of Paradise and directed (d) it toward the homeland.

(D)

Captain Koppe sensed that this was one of those times when he had to be alone – if for no other reason than to remind himself that he (v) should have to make his decision alone. And he would have the duration of the flight all to himself. The thought appealed to him as he powered up the aircar and (e) it lifted a half-meter or so off the deck of the hangar.

hangar 격납고

기출

1 글 (A)에 이어질 내용을 순서에 맞게 배열한 것으로 가장 적절한 것은?

① (B) – (C) – (D)
② (C) – (B) – (D)
③ (C) – (D) – (B)
④ (D) – (B) – (C)
⑤ (D) – (C) – (B)

2 이 글의 내용과 일치하는 것은?

① 비행선에는 로봇 승무원들도 탑승하였다.
② 비행선이 낙원의 섬에 비상 착륙했다.
③ Koppe 선장은 낙원의 섬에서 친구를 만났다.
④ Koppe 선장은 가족이 몹시 보고 싶어졌다.
⑤ Koppe 선장은 우주 비행단과 함께 여행했다.

3 밑줄 친 (a)~(e) 중에서 가리키는 대상이 나머지 넷과 <u>다른</u> 것은?

① (a) ② (b) ③ (c) ④ (d) ⑤ (e)

4 밑줄 친 (i)~(v) 중에서 어법상 <u>어색한</u> 것은?

① (i) ② (ii) ③ (iii) ④ (iv) ⑤ (v)

단어 조사해 오셔~ **Word**

rooftop

of use

aircar

ease

swing

crash

incredible

boom

roar

long-range

altitude

bang

clatter

duration

power up

deck

orbit

long for

irresistible

urge

(A)

Usually it is important not to stick to _____. (a) Especially in a hospital when emergency situations happen, Dr. Neal Flomenbaum says, team leaders are required not to be overly attentive to medical procedures, but to find the best ways to handle the situation and supervise others. (b) Also, they should ignore

other emergency patients because there are many other doctors available to take care of them. (c) "It's important to have someone who stands back and keeps the whole situation under control," he says. (d) "Otherwise a patient's life can be at risk." (e) My friend Schorn, an Aloha pilot, once told me, "When you land a plane, the most important thing is to remember what your priority is. It is landing."

(B)

Sometimes, we struggle over _____ at the cost of larger objectives. In order not to make a mistake of losing the whole forest while saving one tree, we should keep asking ourselves whether the details we are working on fit into the larger picture or not. If they don't, we should stop and move on to something else. For example, the Apollo 11 mission couldn't have been possible if the astronauts had lost sight of the big picture. When the spacecraft was coming back to Earth, it was not exactly following its route. However, it could successfully land on the ground because the astronauts knew exactly where they were headed. Therefore, they could make the necessary adjustments instead of changing the whole route. There is no difference in daily life: knowing what we want to achieve in our lives helps us judge the importance of every task we undertake.

1 (A), (B)의 빈칸에 공통으로 들어가기에 가장 적절한 것은?

① details
② aims
③ results
④ plans
⑤ directions

2 글 (A)와 (B)가 공통으로 시사하는 바로 가장 적절한 것은?

① We should not overlook details.
② We should keep our composure in emergency situations.
③ Your sincere efforts will be paid off sooner or later.
④ Teamwork is very important when you perform a difficult task.
⑤ We should be able to see the bigger picture.

3 이 두 글의 내용과 일치하지 <u>않는</u> 것은?

① In (A), all doctors must always be very meticulous in medical procedures.
② In (A), it is significant for a leader to manage the situation.
③ In (B), it is suggested that we should always look ahead.
④ In (B), the Apollo 11 mission was successful.
⑤ In (B), it is important to know what we want to accomplish in our lives.

4 글 (A)에서 전체 흐름과 관계 <u>없는</u> 문장은?

① (a)   ② (b)   ③ (c)   ④ (d)   ⑤ (e)

Word

stick to

emergency situation

overly

attentive

procedure

supervise

under control

priority

struggle

larger objective

fit (into)

route

land (on)

adjustment

achieve

undertake

Review 😊

A **Translate into English.**

1 충분히 성장한 _____

2 생물, 동물 _____

3 동물학자 _____

4 조상 _____

5 성숙하다 _____

6 이상한 _____

7 외모 _____

8 몸매, 체격 _____

9 재료, 원료 _____

10 북극 _____

11 섬유의, 섬유가 많은 _____

12 내구성(력) _____

13 비행선 _____

14 범위, 궤도 _____

15 고도 _____

16 장거리의 _____

17 ~를 고수하다, 얽매이다 _____

18 감독 하에, 지시 하에 _____

19 감독하다, 관리하다 _____

20 ~에 적합하다 _____

B **Translate into Korean.**

1 surface _____

2 used to do _____

3 mammal _____

4 gill _____

5 growth spurts _____

6 limit _____

7 tremendous _____

8 adolescents _____

9 insulation _____

10 palm tree _____

11 access to _____

12 solar radiation _____

13 clatter _____

14 duration _____

15 incredible _____

16 of use _____

17 adjustment _____

18 treat _____

19 land (on) _____

20 procedure _____

C **Choose the correct answers to each question.**

1 The ancestors of whales used to live on land in ancient times, but they _____ and became fishlike.
① involved   ② evolved
③ breathed   ④ full grew

2 Eskimos, living in some parts of the Arctic, build their houses with thick _____ of ice.
① bamboos   ② palm trees
③ brock   ④ blocks

3 A whale is a _____, because it is a warm-blooded animal, and the young are born out of their mothers' womb and fed with their mothers' milk.
① ancestor   ② cold-blooded animal
③ mammal   ④ fishlike

D **Translate into English or Korean.**

1 It was shocking that nobody stood up and helped the old woman.

_____

2 He predicted not only that war would break out in 2010 but also who would win.

_____

3 이 게임의 법칙은 사람들이 질문을 하면 그 대답을 아는 사람들이 그것을 설명하는 것이다. (people, questions, other people, who, explain)

The rule of this game is that _____

and then _____

_____.

E **Choose the correct words to fill in the blanks.**

1 _____ is very surprising that people on the beach fed fish and the fish came up to the beach.
① What   ② That   ③ Which   ④ It

2 A doctor advised _____ she should not get up.
① that   ② and   ③ so   ④ it

3 Those people _____ were severely injured in the accident were carried to the emergency room.
① why   ② who   ③ where   ④ what

4 These are the products _____ were made in China and should be refunded right away.
① where   ② who   ③ which   ④ what

F **Match each word with its synonyms (two answers).**

1 huge
2 material
3 durability
4 orbit
5 achieve

a. stuff
b. course
c. endurance
d. magnificent
e. accomplish
f. resources
g. conclude
h. enormous
i. sturdiness
j. path

CHAPTER 2	DATE	SELF CHECK	TEACHER	PARENTS
Preview				
Unit 1				
Unit 2				
Unit 3				
Unit 4				
Unit 5				
Review				

청량음료 브랜드

청량음료의 브랜드. 북미에서는 캐드베리-스윕스 아메리카스 베버리지스(Cadbury Schweppes Americas Beverages: 줄여서 CSAB)가, 그 외의 나라에서는 펩시코(PepsiCo)가 소유하고 있습니다. 1920년에 미국인 찰스 그리그(Charles L. Grigg)가 세인트루이스에 청량음료 회사 '하우디 코퍼레이션 (Howdy Corporation)'을 설립했습니다. 그는 1929년 10월 월스트리트 주가대폭락이 있기 2주 전에 레몬라임맛의 탄산음료 '빕-라벨 리티에이티드 레몬-라임 소다(Bib-Label Lithiated Lemon-Lime Soda)'를 출시했죠. 당시 미국의 청량음료 시장은 코카콜라가 장악하고 있었고, 600 종류가 넘는 레몬라임맛 음료가 나와 있었어요. 그러나 카페인이 없고 조울증 치료제로 쓰이는 구연산 리튬(lithium citrate)을 함유한 이 신제품은 건강음료로 부각되어 경제적으로 어려운 시기에도 크게 성공할 수 있었습니다.

브랜드명은 후에 '세븐업 리티에이티드 레몬소다(7Up Lithiated Lemon Soda)'를 거쳐 1936년에 '세븐업(7Up)'으로 변경되었고, 같은 해에 회사명도 '세븐업 컴퍼니(Seven Up Company)'로 변경되었습니다. 세븐업이란 브랜드명의 유래는 정확히 알려져 있지 않으나 제품에 들어간 성분 7가지와 탄산방울이 위로 올라오는(up) 모습에서 유래되었다는 설, 초기 제품의 7온스짜리 포장용기에서 유래되었다는 설, 7음절로 이루어진 초기 제품의 이름에서 유래되었다는 설 등이 있죠. 1961년에 경쟁사 코카콜라 회사는 세븐업과 비슷한 '스프라이트(Sprite)'를 출시했으나 1980년 이전까지는 세븐업의 아성을 무너뜨리지 못했습니다. 2000년에 세븐업 브랜드 마스코트 '피도 디도(Fido Dido)'를 만들었습니다. 2006년에 고과당 콘시럽(HFCS)으로 단맛을 내고 구연산나트륨을 첨가한 100% 천연성분의 신제품을 출시했습니다.

1978년 6월에 필립 모리스(Philip Morris)가 세븐업 컴퍼니를 인수했습니다. 1986년에 개인투자그룹(Private Investment Group)이 필립 모리스로부터 세븐업을 인수했어요. 그리고 닥터페퍼 컴퍼니(Dr Pepper Company)와 세븐업을 합병하여 텍사스주의 댈러스에 본사를 둔 '닥터페퍼/세븐업(Dr Pepper/Seven Up, Inc.: 줄여서 DPSU)'을 설립했죠. 두 회사의 합병 후 세븐업의 북미 지역 이외에서의 판매권은 펩시코가, 닥터 페퍼의 북미 지역 이외에서의 판매권은 코카콜라가 인수했습니다. 1995년에 영국의 제과, 음료 회사인 '캐드베리-스윕스 아메리카스 베버리지스'가 닥터페퍼/세븐업을 인수하여 세븐업과 닥터페퍼의 북미 판매권을 소유하게 되었습니다.

CHAPTER 03

Word 🏠 단어도 모르면서 영어 한다 하지 마!

- **seem** *v.* ~처럼 보이다, ~인 듯하다
- **influence** *n.* 영향, 영향력 *v.* 영향을 끼치다
- **lighten** *v.* 밝게 하다, 명백히 하다
- **affect** *v.* 영향을 미치다, 감동시키다
- **point** *n.* 끝, 점, 점수, 요점 *v.* 가리키다
- **potential** *a.* 가능한, 잠재하는 *n.* 잠재(능)력
- **diffident** *a.* 자신 없는, 수줍은, 소심한
- **failure** *n.* 실패, 실수, 실패자, 낙오자
- **prophet** *n.* 예언자, 선지자
- **occur** *v.* 생기다, 발생하다, 떠오르다

- **hostile** *a.* 적의, 적대하는
- **threaten** *v.* 위협하다, 협박하다
- **originate** *v.* 시작하다, 비롯하다
- **admit** *v.* 수용하다, 인정하다, 허락하다
- **suspect** *v.* 짐작하다, 의심하다 *n.* 용의자
- **principle** *n.* 원리, 원칙, 신념
- **ordinary** *a.* 평상의, 보통의, 평범한
- **addictive** *a.* 습관성의, 중독성의
- **device** *n.* 장치, 설비, 고안, 방책
- **latest** *a.* 최신의, 최근의 *n.* 최신유행품

:: Mini Quiz

Draw a line from each word on the left to its definition on the right. Then, use the numbered words to fill in the blanks in the sentences below.

1 friendly   **a.** somebody born or brought up in a particular place

2 necessary   **b.** behaving towards someone in a way that shows you like them and are ready to talk to them or help them

3 native

4 unreasonable   **c.** not fair or sensible

5 convenient   **d.** useful or suitable, because it makes things easier

    e. extremely important and essential

6 Is it really _____ to call the police?

7 It's _____ to expect you to work 24 hours and seven days a week.

8 The Internet shopping malls are _____ for shopping.

9 He's been _____ to us since we moved in this building.

10 Canadian demographic statistics indicate that _____ people number 1.2 million, or 4% of the population.

Grammar 기본 문법도 모르면서 독해한다 하지마!

★ 주어 자리에 구나 절이 오면 동사는 단수형을 쓴다.

Choosing the perfect job for me **is** difficult. 나한테 꼭 맞는 직업을 고르는 것은 힘들다.

What he meant **was** that the schedule of the new project will be posted today.
그가 말하려 했던 것은 새로운 프로젝트의 스케줄이 오늘 발표될 것이라는 점이었다.

★ 같은 문장 안에서 주어가 의미상 다시 목적어로 쓰일 경우 재귀대명사를 사용한다.

When the silkworm matures, it spins a white cocoon around **itself** for protection.
누에가 다 자라면 방어용으로 자신의 주위를 감싸는 흰 누에고치를 만든다.

The new research says dolphins name **themselves** with distinctive whistles
that they use to identify each other.
새로운 연구는 돌고래들이 서로를 확인할 때 사용하는 특유의 소리로 자신들에게 이름을 짓는다는 사실을 보여 준다.

★ 다음 비교급, 최상급의 뜻을 주의하자.

- late - later - latest (시간)
- far - farther - farthest (거리)
- old - older - oldest (나이)
- late - latter - last (순서)
- far - further - furthest (정도)
- old - elder - eldest (손위)

*구어체에서는 공통적으로 older(oldest)를 많이 사용한다.

This computer, which is the **last** one we have, is the **latest** model.
이 컴퓨터는, 우리가 가지고 있는 마지막 물건인데, 최신 모델이다.

:: Mini Quiz

1 다음 괄호 안에서 알맞은 말을 고르시오.

Finding the difference between my twin brothers [make / makes] people puzzled.

2 다음 괄호 안에서 알맞은 말을 고르시오.

I found [me / myself / I] irritated by the fact that I mistakenly deleted the file I worked on all
day long.

3 다음 괄호 안에서 알맞은 말을 고르시오.

This magazine will provide you with a reliable analysis of the [last / latest] political and
economic trends.

The changes of weather seem to have an influence on our _____. [1] Some people feel gloomy when the sky gets dark, and some people even feel depressed during the rainy season. [2] It seems like rain or dark clouds make people sad and depressed for no reason. [3] People may have these negative

feelings, because they have to stay indoors too long during bad weather. In contrast, a sunny day can lighten one's mood. Most of us would agree that the sunshine makes us energetic and happy. When the weather is pleasant, people tend to be friendlier and more willing to help each other. For example, one study found that waiters and waitresses receive bigger tips on sunny days. [4] The most interesting fact that weather affects our mood is the relationship between how much one stays outside and what season it is. Some people are big summer fans because summer has more daylight and sunshine.

1 **Choose the best word to fill in the blank.**

① job   ② mood   ③ health
④ fashion   ⑤ lifestyle

2 이 글에서 글쓴이가 주장하는 바로 가장 알맞은 것은?

① All the people feel more cheerful on fine days.
② Many people's lives depend on the weather.
③ Weather can treat people's mental states.
④ Weather has a big effect on our everyday lives.
⑤ Some people become depressed in the rainy seasons.

단어 조사해 오셔~ **Word**

seem

influence

gloomy

depress

negative feeling

indoor

lighten

energetic

tend to do

friendly

be willing to

receive

affect

 **Drill 1** Grammar

동격절 that

특정명사가 명사절 앞에 올 때, 동격절이 되는 경우가 있다. the fact 뒤에는 현대영어에서는 'that' 만을 사용한다. 관계사절과 똑같이 해석해도 무관하나, 앞에 있는 명사를 꾸미면서 우리말 '~라는 ...' 으로 해석하면 된다.

• **The fact** that he is honest *is* clear. 그가 정직하다는 사실은 분명하다.

• **The news** that his son was killed *is* false. 그의 아들이 살해당했다는 소식은 거짓이다.

---

1   In fact, research confirms the popular wisdom that age is more a state of mind than of body.

   해석 ◯ _____

2   Our current difficulties and stress come from our thinking that there is not enough time.

   해석 ◯ _____

3   그 노인은 자신이 여전히 살아 있다는 그 사실에 대해 항상 신에게 감사했다.
   (for the fact, still alive, thanked, old man, God)

   영작 ◯ _____

Drill 2 Translation

1   1번 문장 ◯ _____

2   2번 문장 ◯ _____

3   3번 문장 ◯ _____

4   4번 문장 ◯ _____

[1] My point is that you feel diffident, stupid and unsuccessful right now because you are looking at your "failures" and focusing on them. [2] What you are missing is that things go wrong, even for successful, confident people. It happens to everyone. It happens equally to successful and unsuccessful people. It happens to young people and old. It happens constantly, no matter where you are, no matter what you are doing, and no matter how hard you try. Things go wrong. The difference between confident people and diffident people is how they react to problems. [3] Confident people dig through problems, rebuild and move on. Diffident people wallow in them, are miserable and die. It is as simple as that. That is why you need confidence. [4] Right now you are choosing to be diffident because you are looking at your failures rather than looking at your potential for success in the future. A confident person accepts failure and understands that it is a necessary part of success. You cannot be successful unless you fail and learn from your failures.

1 이 글의 내용을 요약하고자 한다. 빈칸 (A)와 (B)에 들어갈 말로 가장 적절한 것끼리 짝지은 것은?

> ➡ A person without self-confidence looks at the ____(A)____ and says, "All successful people are so lucky! I could never be like them. They have all natural talent but I am so stupid! I hate being me." The big difference between successful people and unsuccessful people is that the successful people ____(B)____ until they succeed.

	(A)		(B)
①	positive aspect	⋯	keep trying
②	negative aspect	⋯	keep trying
③	negative aspect	⋯	keep shopping
④	dreams	⋯	look at the bright side
⑤	positive aspect	⋯	try to be positive

단어 조사해 오셔~ **Word**

point

diffident

unsuccessful

failure

focus on

constantly

no matter where

wallow

miserable

potential

accept

necessary

 **Drill 1** Grammar

관계부사 why

관계부사 why는 그 앞에 오는 명사(선행사)를 꾸며주는 역할을 한다. 그러나 관계부사의 특징은 명사(선행사)를 생략할 수 있고, 또한 관계부사 자체를 생략할 수도 있다. why 앞에 명사(선행사)가 없을 경우 생략되어 있다고 봐도 무관하나 이때, 우리말 '왜 ~지'를 붙여서 해석하면 된다.

- I *don't know* (the reason) why she hates me. 나는 그녀가 나를 왜 싫어하는지를 모르겠다.

- One reason why folk stories are so popular in all cultures *is* that they are generally easy to follow. 민화가 모든 문화에서 아주 인기 있는 하나의 이유는 민화가 일반적으로 이해하기 쉽다는 것이다.

---

1 That is why the lines all over her face are so deep.

해석 ◯ _____

2 There are many reasons why people like to go to the mountains.

해석 ◯ _____

3 Angela는 왜 그녀가 그 모임에 늦었는지를 말했다. (for that meeting, late, said, Angela)

영작 ◯ _____

Drill 2 Translation

1 1번 문장 ◯ _____

2 2번 문장 ◯ _____

3 3번 문장 ◯ _____

4 4번 문장 ◯ _____

Once, Columbus saved his own life by using an almanac. [1] In 1504, Columbus was marooned on the island of Jamaica for a few weeks. The natives were hostile to him, and refused to share their food with him. [2] One day, Columbus remembered what he learned from an almanac: there would be a total lunar eclipse on February 29, 1504. [3] So Columbus threatened the natives that he would hide the moon unless they gave him supplies. The natives thought he was crazy. [4] But on the night of February 29th, the total eclipse of the moon did actually occur, and all Jamaicans were terrified. The poor people really believed that Columbus hid the moon since they hadn't fed him. They gave Columbus everything he needed and begged him, in return, to give them back the moon.

1 **What is the main idea of this paragraph?**

① Columbus was marooned on Jamaica for many weeks in the year 1504.

② Natives rarely owned almanacs or understood scientific facts.

③ Columbus once saved his life because he knew when there was going to be an eclipse of the moon.

④ On his arrival in Jamaica, Columbus had no food to eat.

⑤ The natives gave Columbus all the food he needed and begged him to give them back the light.

2 이 글의 분위기로 가장 적절한 것은?

① dark and gloomy

② scary and horrible

③ exciting and lively

④ humorous and funny

⑤ dynamic and spectacular

단어 조사해 오세요~ **Word**

almanac

maroon

native

hostile

refuse

total eclipse (of the moon)

threaten

hide

occur

be terrified

feed

in return

prophet

supernatural

Drill 1 Grammar

관계사 생략

which, that, who(m)가 목적격 관계대명사일 경우 거의 생략된다. 관계사가 생략되면 명사 뒤에 바로 주어, 동사가 이어진다. 즉 명사가 나오고 바로 명사가 연이어 나오는 경우 관계사가 생략된 경우가 많다. 앞에 있는 명사를 꾸며 주면서 우리말 '~하는, 했던'으로 해석한다.

> 명사 (관계사 생략) + (명사 ....)
> └_____┘ 앞에 있는 명사를 꾸며 주며 '~하는, 했던'을 붙여 해석

- Almost everyone *failed* the test the teacher gave last week.
  거의 모두가 선생님이 지난주에 내 주신 시험에 낙제했다.

- Parents *feel* a special kind of love for their own children they do not feel for other children.
  부모들은 다른 아이들에게서 느끼지 못하는 특별한 사랑의 감정을 자신의 아이들에게 느낀다.

---

1   Parents should be models for good behavior their children can be influenced by.

   해석 ◎ _____

2   She began to hum the song she had sung with her classmates, tears running down her cheeks.

   해석 ◎ _____

3   소설가 Poe가 읽고 있었던 그 이상한 편지들은 그녀의 다락방에서 발견되었다.
   (the novelist Poe, letters, be found, attic(다락방))

   영작 ◎ _____

Drill 2 Translation

1   1번 문장 ◎ _____

2   2번 문장 ◎ _____

3   3번 문장 ◎ _____

4   4번 문장 ◎ _____

(A)

Thus, the astronomy we know tells us that the UFO principle is unreasonable, not because we don't believe in aliens on other worlds, but because we suspect they could never visit us.

(B)

As astronomers, we know that life could be very common in the universe. Planets appear to be byproducts of star formation, and it does seem possible that life could originate on any world where conditions are right. Once active, life modifies itself to fit its environment, so, although we don't know how common suitable planets are, we must admit that our galaxy could be well populated. Could such worlds, however, send spacecraft to visit ours?

(C)

No other planet in our solar system is suitable for intelligent life, so any visitors to Earth must come from other planetary systems orbiting other stars. This argues against the UFO principle because of the difficulty in traveling between stars. Other creatures might be different from us, but they must still obey the same laws of physics, and that means that traveling from their star system to ours would be almost impossible. The stars are very, very far apart.

1 (A), (B), (C)를 이어 하나의 글로 구성할 때 가장 적절한 순서는?

① (C) - (B) - (A)
② (B) - (A) - (C)
③ (C) - (A) - (B)
④ (A) - (B) - (C)
⑤ (B) - (C) - (A)

2 글쓴이가 자신의 생각을 주장하기 위해 중요하게 생각하는 것은?

① 물리학적 법칙
② 천문학자의 양심
③ 지적 생명체의 존재
④ 우주의 생성 역사
⑤ 우리 은하계의 발생

3 이 글의 주제로 가장 적절한 것은?

① 사람들은 UFO의 존재를 입증하는 노력을 하고 있다.
② UFO의 존재는 과학적으로 인정하기 어렵다.
③ 은하수에는 아직 인간들이 연구해야 할 많은 것들이 있다.
④ 현대과학으로 모든 것들을 입증해낼 수 있다.
⑤ 외계인의 존재는 아직 수수께끼이다.

4 (C)의 밑줄 친 their가 가리키는 것으로 가장 적절한 것은?

① UFOs
② astronauts
③ creatures
④ planets
⑤ stars

단어 조사해 오셔~ **Word**

astronomy

principle

unreasonable

not because A but because B

alien

suspect

byproduct

star formation

originate

suitable planet

admit

populate

spacecraft

intelligent life

planetary system

orbit

laws of physics

far apart

Person A: In ordinary life, you can be very comfortable with modern technology. Just as people search for books in bookstores, you can find and select what you want with a computer. You have already seen how much modern technology has changed the world. You can talk to each other in real time, looking at each other on a palm-sized phone. In the near future, I believe that most people will

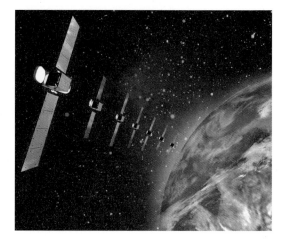

wear user-friendly computer equipment making their daily lives even more convenient. This would give us the chance to find information quickly and communicate with others, no matter where we are or what we are doing.

Person B: The latest devices are fun to use for many tasks like browsing cyber space, but it is important to keep your distance from them as well. The constant noises of electronic devices like computers, mobile phones, fax machines, stereos, and home appliances will drown out the sounds of the birds singing in the morning, the wind blowing through the trees, or a pencil drawing on rough paper. Modern technology is addictive, so be sure to plan days away from its electromagnetic fields. Go out into nature and leave your mobile phone behind. Or just turn everything off and _____.

기출

1 이 두 글의 핵심 쟁점으로 가장 적절한 것은?

① use of modern technology
② web-surfing for home appliances
③ increase in technological problems
④ sharing information in technical ways
⑤ buying a new mobile phone

2 Person B의 빈칸에 들어갈 말로 가장 적절한 것은?

① acquire computer skills
② enjoy the peace and quiet
③ learn how to access data
④ make the most of technology
⑤ get involved in the modern society

3 **What is the main idea of Person A?**

① Improved methods of finding books
② Communication of palm-sized phones
③ People's opinions of modern technology
④ Convenience of modern technology
⑤ Radical changes in communication

4 **What is the main idea expressed by Person B?**

① Importance of electronic devices
② Protection of the natural environment
③ Possibility of modern technology addiction
④ Pleasure of using latest devices
⑤ Not losing touch with the natural world

단어 조사해 오셔~ **Word**

ordinary

technology

search for

select

palm-sized

user-friendly

convenient

communicate with

no matter where

latest

device

home appliance

drown out

addictive

electromagnetic field

leave ~ behind

turn off

Review 😊

A **Translate into English.**

1 ~처럼 보이다 _____

2 우울하게 하다 _____

3 기운 나게 하다 _____

4 원기 왕성한 _____

5 요점 _____

6 받아들이다 _____

7 계속하여 _____

8 파묻히다 _____

9 발생하다, 일어나다 _____

10 답례로, 그 대신에 _____

11 협박하다, 위협하다 _____

12 예언자 _____

13 부산물 _____

14 원리 _____

15 궤도를 돌다 _____

16 인정하다 _____

17 일상적인, 보통의 _____

18 장치, 설비 _____

19 가전제품 _____

20 끄다 _____

B **Translate into Korean.**

1 influence _____

2 tend to do _____

3 affect _____

4 be willing to _____

5 failure _____

6 no matter where _____

7 potential _____

8 diffident _____

9 total eclipse _____

10 supernatural _____

11 native _____

12 hostile _____

13 populate _____

14 planetary system _____

15 suspect _____

16 unreasonable _____

17 search for _____

18 communicate with _____

19 latest _____

20 leave ~ behind _____

C **Choose the correct answers to each question.**

1 The UFO _____ is unreasonable, not because we don't believe in aliens on other worlds, but because we suspect they could never visit us.
  ① byproduct   ② alien
  ③ orbit   ④ principle

2 No other planet in our solar system is _____ for intelligent life.
  ① unreasonable   ② suitable
  ③ originate   ④ byproduct

3 In the near future, most people will wear user-friendly computer equipment making their daily lives more _____.
  ① electromagnetic ② ordinary
  ③ palm-sized   ④ convenient

D **Translate into English or Korean.**

1 The rumor that we don't have to take the entrance exam for the university was not true.

  _____

2 Finishing your homework is the first thing you should take care of.

  _____

3 심리학자들은 비디오게임을 그만두는 것이 왜 힘든 지에 대해 연구했다.
  (psychologist, study, reason, why)

  _____

  video games are hard to give up.

E **Choose the correct words to fill in the blanks.**

1 I don't agree with the idea _____ the law must be revised for certain.
  ① what ② that ③ of ④ it

2 The real reasons _____ stocks are plunging are the weak dollar, and recession risks.
  ① what ② why ③ so ④ it

3 He argued with the clerk over the extra ten cents _____ he had to pay for his new camera.
  ① where ② who ③ which ④ what

4 The opinion _____ he was a good president was supported by 75 percent of the votes.
  ① that ② who ③ of ④ whom

F **Match each word with its antonyms (two answers).**

1 hostile   a. old
                     b. hospitable
2 admit   c. bright
                     d. outdated
3 latest   e. deny
                     f. avoidable
4 gloomy   g. friendly
                     h. optional
5 necessary   i. cheerful
                     j. keep out

CHAPTER 3	DATE	SELF CHECK	TEACHER	PARENTS
Preview				
Unit 1				
Unit 2				
Unit 3				
Unit 4				
Unit 5				
Review				

청량음료 좋아하시나요? 우리의 것으로 마십시다!

1929년에 미국인 찰스 그리그(Charles L. Grigg)가 세인트루이스에 청량음료 회사 하우디 코퍼레이션 (Howdy Corporation)을 설립했습니다. 당시 청량음료 시장은 코카콜라가 장악하고 있었고, 600종류 가 넘는 레몬라임맛 음료가 나와 있었죠. 그러나 카페인이 없고 조울증 치료제로 쓰이는 구연산 리튬 (lithium citrate)을 함유한 이 신제품은 건강음료로 부각되어 경제적으로 어려운 시기에도 크게 성공할 수 있었습니다.

브랜드명은 후에 세븐업 리티에이티드 레몬소다(7Up Lithiated Lemon Soda)를 거쳐 1936년에 세븐업 7Up으로 변경되었고, 같은 해에 회사명도 세븐업 컴퍼니(Seven Up Company)로 변경되었죠. 몇 년간에 걸친 레몬향 음료수 시험 끝에 그리그는 일 곱까지 자연향을 혼합한 음료를 고안해냈습니다. 제품에 들어간 성분 일곱까지와 탄산방울이 위로 올라오는 Up 또는 이 음료수를 마셨을 때 기분이 Up된다는 것을 나타내기 위해 7Up이란 이름을 얻게 됐었죠. 2000년에는 세븐업 브랜드 마스코트 파이도 다이 도(Fido Dido)를 만들었습니다.

그럼 이제 한국에서 개발된 칠성사이다에 대해서 알아보죠. 국내 사이다 시장의 75%를 차지하고 있는 칠성사이다는 콜라를 상대 로 한 '사이다의 반란'을 이끌고 있습니다. 칠성사이다는 50년이 넘는 역사에도 불구하고 깨끗하고 시원한 그 맛처럼 변치 않는 젊음을 유지하고 있습니다. 칠성사이다는 1950년 첫 선을 보인 이후 100억 개(병, 캔, 페트병 포함) 이상이 팔린 국내 탄산음료의 대 명사입니다. 음료 브랜드가 1~2년 단위로 생기고 사라지는 가운데 칠성사이다는 54년 동안 변함없는 인기를 누려왔습니다. 롯데 의 인수로 진열을 재정비한 칠성사이다는 경쟁 브랜드의 도전을 물리치고 청량음료의 강자 자리를 지켰습니다. 킨 사이다, 7UP, 스프라이트 등이 칠성사이다에 지속적으로 도전했지만 모두 패하고 말았죠. 칠성사이다는 세계 청량음료 시장을 석권하고 있는 코 카콜라에도 밀리지 않고 맞대결을 시작했습니다. 칠성사이다는 1968년 국내에 수입된 코카콜라는 1980년대 국내 패스트푸드의 급성장에 힘입어 탄산음료 시장 1위 자리를 차지하기 전까지 선두 자리를 놓고 접전을 펼쳤죠. 한때 코카콜라가 브랜드 파워를 앞 세워 청량음료 시장의 40% 이상을 점유하기도 했지만 칠성사이다는 색소, 카페인, 인공향이 없다는 점을 강조하며 최근 코카콜라 와의 격차를 좁히고 있습니다. 전 세계적으로 음료 시장에서 토종 브랜드가 글로벌 브랜드를 이긴 경우는 흔치 않습니다. 7UP, 스 프라이트 같은 세계적인 브랜드도 칠성사이다를 꺾지 못했습니다.

CHAPTER

04

Word 🏠 단어도 모르면서 영어 한다 하지 마!

season *n.* 계절, 제철 *v.* 맛을 내다	**literary** *a.* 문학의, 문학에 능통한
claim *v.* 요구하다, 청구하다 *n.* 요구, 주장	**criticism** *n.* 비평, 평론, 혹평
pound *v.* 마구 치다, 두드리다	**nutritious** *a.* 영양분이 많은
soften *v.* 부드럽게 하다	**organic** *a.* 유기체의, 기관의, 타고난
gratitude *n.* 감사(하는 마음)	**contribute** *v.* 기부하다, 기증하다, 공헌하다
grateful *a.* 감사하는, 고마운, 쾌적한	**nonetheless** *ad.* 그럼에도 불구하고, 역시
express *v.* 표현하다 *a.* 급행의 *n.* 급행	**brutal** *a.* 잔인한, 난폭한, 혹독한
attention *n.* 주의(력), 배려, 차려 자세	**fame** *n.* 명성, 평판 *v.* 유명하게 하다
fragment *n.* 파편, 단편 *v.* 부서지다	**combatant** *n.* 투사, 격투자 *a.* 전투적인
naive *a.* 순진한, 소박한 *n.* 순진한 사람	**foundation** *n.* 창설, 창립, 기초, 재단

⠇ Mini Quiz

Draw a line from each word on the left to its definition on the right. Then, use the numbered words to fill in the blanks in the sentences below.

1   recipe   **a.** what something is intended to achieve

2   purpose   **b.** the skin of some fruits and vegetables, especially the thick skin of fruits

3   evidence   **c.** protective clothing of metal or leather worn in battle by soldiers in former times

4   peel   **d.** a set of instructions for cooking a particular type of food

5   armor   **e.** a large amount of money, property, etc. that a person or country owns

6   wealth   **f.** facts or signs that show clearly that something exists or is true

7   Apple _____ may be more nutritious than apple flesh for people trying to keep cancer at bay.

8   This _____ book was written by several famous cooks.

9   There was not enough _____ to show the cause of his death.

10 The country's _____ comes from its oil.

11 The knight wearing a suit of _____ in this movie is the main character.

12 The _____ of this meeting is to elect a new chairman.

Grammar 기본 문법도 모르면서 독해한다 하지 마!

★ not only가 문장 맨앞으로 올 때 그 절의 주어와 동사는 도치된다.

Not only **does he** solve a Rubik's Cube in a minute, but he does it blindfolded.
그는 짧은 시간 안에 루빅 큐브를 맞출 뿐 아니라 눈을 가리고도 그것을 한다.

Not only **does my keyboard** not work, but also I cannot use desktop short cuts.
내 키보드가 작동을 하지 않을 뿐 아니라 바탕화면에 바로가기도 사용할 수 없다.

★ 타동사 뒤에 목적어가 없으면 수동태 문장이므로 〈be + p.p.〉 형태로 써야 한다.

Go to a fairly quiet place where you are not likely to **be disturbed**.
당신이 방해받지 않을 것 같은 가장 조용한 장소로 가라.

When **asked** about the secret to her long life, Palmer says that learning
something new every day keeps a person young.
장수비결에 대한 질문을 받을 때, Palmer는 매일 새로운 것을 배우는 것이 사람을 젊게 유지시킨다고 말한다.

★ 분사가 명사를 수식하거나 보어 자리에 왔을 때 주어와 능동관계이면 현재분사를, 수동관계이면 과거분사를 사용
한다.

Talking to strangers is often a **pleasing** experience for me because I enjoy
meeting people. 나는 사람들을 만나는 것을 즐기기 때문에 낯선 사람과 이야기하는 것은 나에게는 즐거운 경험이다.

My experience with your company has been very **rewarding**.
당신의 회사와 함께 했던 경험은 매우 가치 있는 것이었다.

∷ Mini Quiz

1 다음 괄호 안에서 알맞은 것을 고르시오.

Not only [is / does] it taste good, it is good for you.

2 다음 괄호 안에서 알맞은 것을 고르시오.

People's goals often [are remained / remain] unfocused, and therefore unrealized.

3 다음 괄호 안에서 알맞은 것을 고르시오.

We are tired of looking for missing papers and [misplacing / misplaced] files.

(A)

[1] During a trip to Asia in the early 1800s, a German merchant noticed that the nomadic Tartars softened their meat by keeping it under their saddles. The motion of the horse pounded the meat to bits. [2] The Tartars would then scrape it together and season it for eating. The idea of pounded beef found its way back to the merchant's home town of Hamburg where cooks broiled the meat and referred to it as Hamburg meat. German immigrants introduced the recipe to the US. [3] The term "hamburger" is believed to have appeared in 1834 on the menu of Delmonico's restaurant in New York.

(B)

[4] However, there is another claim to that term. There is an account of Frank and Charles Menches who went to the Hamburg fair in the state of New York to prepare their famous pork sausage sandwiches. But since the local meat market was out of pork sausage, they used ground beef instead.

1 **What is the best title of this paragraph (A) and (B)?**

① The Origin of the Hamburger
② The Inventor of the Hamburger
③ The Recipe of the Hamburger
④ The First Hamburg Fair in the state of New York
⑤ The History of the Hamburger and Pork sausage sandwich

2 **What can be inferred about the hamburger?**

① The recipe for hamburger was a secret in the 17th century.
② The word hamburger actually originated from the city of Hamburg, Germany.
③ The German merchant ate the hamburger with vegetables.
④ It was a Asian immigrants who introduced the hamburger to the US.
⑤ The cooks in Germany scraped meat and seasoned it for eating.

단어 조사해 오세요~ **Word**

merchant

nomadic

Tartars

soften

saddle

pound

bit

scrape

season

find one's way

refer to A as B

recipe

broil

term

ground beef

 **Drill 1** Grammar

to have p.p.

부정사와 같은 준동사의 과거표현이 있을까? 본동사와 비교하여 먼저 발생한 동작, 행위를 표현할 때는 'to have p.p.' 를 사용한다. 흔히 여러분들이 전통문법에서 배울 때는 '완료 부정사' 라고 하는데 이는 'have p.p.' 가 들어갔다고 하여 영어를 정말 모르는 무식한 일본 사람들이 '완료' 라는 말을 붙인 것으로 잘못된 표현이다. 우리말에는 '했었다, 였었다' 를 붙여 '과거' 로 해석해 주면 된다.

- It is thought that he was (과거) rich.
  = He is thought to have been rich. 그는 부자였던 것으로 여겨진다.
- It is truly an honor to have received the Fisher Scholarship last year.
  작년에 Fisher 장학금을 받은 것은 정말 영광입니다.

---

1 He seems to have lived there for years.

 해석 ◎ _____

2 To pass through a landscape swiftly is almost the same thing as not to have traveled through it at all.

 해석 ◎ _____

3 그는 어제 숙제를 끝내서 행복하다. (finish, happy, his homework)

 영작 ◎ _____

 Drill 2 Translation

1 1번 문장 ◎ _____

2 2번 문장 ◎ _____

3 3번 문장 ◎ _____

4 4번 문장 ◎ _____

Once a week, write a heartfelt letter. [1] Taking a few minutes each week to do so does many things for you. (a) <u>Picking up a pen</u> slows you down long enough to remember the beautiful people in your life. The act of sitting down to write helps to fill your life with appreciation. [2] Once you decide to try (b) <u>this</u>, you'll probably be amazed at how many people appear on your list. The purpose of your letter is very simple: to express love and gratitude. Don't worry if you're not good at (c) <u>writing letters</u>. If you can't think of much to say, start with short little notes like, "Dear Jasmine, How lucky I am to have friends like you in my life! I am truly blessed, and I wish you all the happiness and joy that life can bring. Love, Richard." [3] Not only does the act of writing a note like this focus (d) <u>your attention</u> on what's right in your life, but the person receiving it will be touched and grateful. [4] Often (e) <u>this simple action</u> starts a chain of loving actions whereby the person receiving your letter may decide to do the same thing to someone else, or perhaps will act and feel more loving toward others.

기출

1 이 글의 제목으로 가장 적절한 것은?

① Love Letters and Dating
② How to Write Business Letters
③ How Letters Improve Life
④ Reasons for Writing to Yourself
⑤ Types and Purposes of Letters

2 이 글의 내용으로 보아, 밑줄 친 부분 중 나머지 넷과 가리키는 바가 <u>다른</u> 것은?

① (a)　　② (b)　　③ (c)　　④ (d)　　⑤ (e)

단어 조사해 오셔~ **Word**

heartfelt

act

appreciation

be amazed at

purpose

express

gratitude

be good at -ing

attention

be touched

grateful

whereby

 **Drill 1** Grammar

명사 + -ing

명사 뒤에서 명사를 수식하는 분사는 명사 다음에 '주격 관계사+be동사' 가 생략되어 있다. '-ing' 형태의 단어가 명사 뒤에 위치할 경우 우리말' ~하는, ㄴ, ~하고 있는' 을 붙여 해석한다. 어법상 판단 문제의 핵심은 현재분사와 과거분사의 의미 차이를 이해해야 풀 수 있는 문제가 출제된다. 분사와 관련된 문제는 대부분 이 차이를 알고 있는지를 테스트하는 것을 목적으로 한다.

- This *is* similar to people getting wiser by overcoming difficulties and hardships.
  이는 곤경과 역경을 극복함으로써 더 현명해지는 사람들과 비슷하다.

- The woman dancing in front of the mirror *is* a ghost. 거울 앞에서 춤을 추고 있는 여자는 귀신이다.

---

1 The men sleeping on the bench don't have family to look after them.

해석 ◑ _____

2 The man standing at the corner was reading a newspaper written in English.

해석 ◑ _____

3 손에 칼을 쥐고 있는 그 여자는 그 귀신을 기다리고 있다. (hold, in her hands, wait, a knife)

영작 ◑ _____

Drill 2 Translation

1 1번 문장 ◑ _____

2 2번 문장 ◑ _____

3 3번 문장 ◑ _____

4 4번 문장 ◑ _____

[1] The Greeks were great talkers and they must have, among other things, talked about poetry. ① Yet their words were carried away by the winds of the Mediterranean. [2] ② Before Plato, except for a line or two in the poets and a few fragments from philosophical writings, there was no real literary criticism in the sense of a theory of literature. ③ The Greeks were the first of the early Europeans to develop the arts, literature, philosophy and even science to a fairly high degree. [3] So if we want to begin with general ideas on literature, we must begin with Plato. ④ One could wish to begin elsewhere, for Plato, the most poetic of philosophers, was an enemy of poetry. ⑤ This fact is so shocking that many have refused to believe it. [4] Like overly naive lovers, they have refused the evidence of their own eyes. Honey-mouthed Plato could not be unfaithful.

1 이 글에서 전체 흐름과 관계 <u>없는</u> 문장은?

2 이 글의 내용과 일치하지 <u>않는</u> 것은?

① 플라톤은 시적이었지만 사실 시의 적이었다.
② 시에 대해서도 그리스인들은 굉장히 수다스러웠을 것으로 판단된다.
③ 플라톤 이전에는 진정한 문학비평이라는 것은 존재하지 않았다.
④ 플라톤은 일반적인 인식과는 달리 문학을 적대시했다.
⑤ 플라톤은 시에 대해 부정적인 의견을 가지고 있었다.

단어 조사해 오세요~ **Word**

great talker

poetry

word

be carried away

Mediterranean

fragment

philosophical

literary

criticism

in the sense of

refuse

naive

evidence

overly

honey-mouthed

unfaithful

🍴 Drill 1 Grammar

so ~ that 용법

> so + 형용사(부사) + that ... 너무 ~해서 ... 하다 〈결과, 정도〉
>
> such + 명사 + that ... ...할 정도로 ~하다 〈정도〉

• A cent is worth so little that we don't usually bother to pick it up on the street.
  1센트는 가치가 거의 없어서 우리는 대개 그것을 길에서 주우려고 수고하지 않는다.

• Hand gestures are such an important part of our speech that we sometimes use them even when we talk on the telephone.
  손짓은 우리 말의 아주 중요한 부분이어서 우리는 심지어 우리가 전화로 이야기를 할 때도 때때로 손짓을 사용한다.

---

1 The hummingbird is one of the most beautiful birds. It is so beautiful that it has been called a flying flower.

   해석 ◉ _____

2 He had such a fierce dog that no one dared to go near his house.

   해석 ◉ _____

3 그 돌은 너무 무거워서 나는 그것을 움직일 수 없었다. (heavy, move, stone, so, that)

   영작 ◉ _____

🍴 Drill 2 Translation

1 1번 문장 ◉ _____

2 2번 문장 ◉ _____

3 3번 문장 ◉ _____

4 4번 문장 ◉ _____

Person A: Most people agree that fruit is a valuable, healthy food. Nonetheless, they usually throw away a very nutritious part of the fruit – the peel. (a) Dietary fiber helps to lower the level of cholesterol and blood sugar, which reduces the risk of heart disease and diabetes. (b) Fiber also helps

to lessen calorie intake, because people don't feel hungry even though they eat less. Eating fruit peel can also help to decrease the amount of food waste which is a cause of pollution. (c) Finally, I think people who eat fruit peel prefer organic food, which encourages farmers to use less pesticide and thus to contribute to a cleaner environment.

Person B: Personally, I don't like the bitter taste and roughness of fruit peel, though I understand that it has some nutritious value and contains dietary fiber. (d) Even so, I don't think it is wise to eat fruit without peeling it. You might think you're removing all the pesticide on the fruit when you wash it, but some chemicals are bound to remain on the surface of the peel. The use of detergent to clean the fruit can also cause additional water pollution. (e) Another reason for removing the peel before eating is that some fruits such as apples, pears, and grapes have a tough skin, which can be harder to chew and to digest.

dietary fiber 식이 섬유 | pesticide 농약

(기출)

1 두 글의 핵심 쟁점으로 가장 적절한 것은?

① the use of pesticide
② the use of detergent
③ the eating of fruit peel
④ the nutrition in fruit peel
⑤ the recycling of food waste

단어 조사해 오셔~ **Word**

nonetheless

nutritious

peel

essential

dietary fiber

blood sugar

diabetes

organic

pesticide

contribute to

roughness

detergent

2 두 글의 내용과 일치하지 않는 것은?

① A는 식이 섬유 섭취가 콜레스테롤 수치를 낮춘다고 믿는다.
② A는 유기농 식품의 선호가 농약 사용을 줄일 수 있다고 본다.
③ B는 과일의 잔류 농약을 모두 제거할 수는 없다고 믿는다.
④ B는 세제 사용이 수질 오염의 원인이 된다고 생각한다.
⑤ B는 과일 껍질이 소화를 촉진시킨다고 생각한다.

3 글의 흐름으로 보아 (a)~(e) 중, 다음 문장이 들어가기에 가장 적절한 곳은?

> In fact, fruit peel contains essential vitamins and is a source of
> dietary fiber.

① (a)   ② (b)   ③ (c)   ④ (d)   ⑤ (e)

4 밑줄 친 a cleaner environment의 반대되는 견해를 Person B에서 찾아 한 문장으로 쓰시오.

In ancient Rome, there was one popular contest in which two combatants fought against each other until one was killed. It was the most brutal sport ever in history. The fighters in the contest were called 'gladiators.'

However, the Roman people were not the inventors of this contest. Etruscan people, the people (A) who / which lived in Italy prior to the foundation of Rome, forced the slaves to fight each other, and enjoyed watching the fight. The Romans adopted this sport in 264 B.C. First, it was a part of a funeral ceremony. Later, it became the most popular entertainment among the Roman people. (B) They / It was held in huge arenas.

Until one Emperor became interested in the sport, the combatants were mostly slaves or criminals. This emperor built a number of schools to train gladiators. Theatres and arenas were built to open more games. Soon, to become a gladiator was thought to be an honor among the people. It was the fastest way to have both wealth and fame.

Once the contest started, two gladiators wearing armor of gold and silver had a mock fight. Then the real fight began following the sound of trumpets. The combatants could use a variety of weapons. When one gladiator was wounded or fell down, the fight stopped. Then the audience decided the loser's fate. People expressed their decisions with their gestures. If they raised their handkerchiefs, the loser's life could be spared. If they (C) were held / held their thumbs down, the loser was to be killed.

After a while, _____. They changed the rules; the gladiators did not fight against each other any more, but fought with lions, tigers, and other wild beasts.

1 (A), (B), (C)의 각 네모 안에서 어법에 맞는 표현을 골라 짝지은 것은?

	(A)		(B)		(C)
①	which	⋯	They	⋯	were held
②	which	⋯	It	⋯	were held
③	who	⋯	They	⋯	held
④	who	⋯	It	⋯	were held
⑤	who	⋯	It	⋯	held

2 **What is the passage mainly about?**

① Description of gladiators' fighting in the old days

② Daily life of the combatants

③ Explanation of the funeral ceremony in ancient Rome

④ The origin of gladiators and their sport

⑤ The most popular amusement among Roman emperors

3 **Choose the best answer to fill in the blank.**

① gladiators took over the Romans

② people felt pitiful for the gladiators

③ romans became bored with this contest

④ gladiators were rewarded with treasures

⑤ new weapons were created

4 이 글의 내용과 일치하는 것은?

① 로마 사람들이 처음으로 노예들을 검투사로 만들어 게임을 즐겼다.

② 고대 로마의 노예들은 부와 명예를 얻기 위해 검투사를 스스로 지원했다.

③ 게임에서 진 검투사는 관중들의 반응에 따라 운명이 결정되었다.

④ 로마 황제는 노예들과 죄수자들을 모두 처형하기를 원했다.

⑤ 글래디에이터들은 선택한 무기 한 가지만을 사용해야만 했다.

단어 조사해 오셔~ **Word**

combatant

brutal

gladiator

Etruscan

prior to

foundation

force

adopt

funeral ceremony

entertainment

arena

wealth

fame

armor

have a mock fight

a variety of

fate

after a while

A **Translate into English.**

1 상인 _____

2 말 안장 _____

3 작은 조각 _____

4 조리법 _____

5 행위 _____

6 감동을 받다 _____

7 진정어린 _____

8 목적 _____

9 수다쟁이 _____

10 불충실한, 성실하지 않은 _____

11 비평 _____

12 순진한, 소박한 _____

13 그럼에도 불구하고 _____

14 없어서는 안 될 _____

15 세제 _____

16 유기체의, 유기 농법의 _____

17 (고대 로마의) 검투사 _____

18 부 _____

19 원형 투기장 _____

20 채택하다 _____

B **Translate into Korean.**

1 nomadic _____

2 broil _____

3 season _____

4 throne _____

5 attention _____

6 grateful _____

7 appreciation _____

8 express _____

9 honey-mouthed _____

10 refuse _____

11 philosophical _____

12 literary _____

13 nutritious _____

14 diabetes _____

15 dietary fiber _____

16 blood sugar _____

17 fate _____

18 have a mock fight _____

19 prior to _____

20 foundation _____

C Choose the correct answers to each question.

1 The nomadic Tatars _____ their meat by keeping it under their saddles.
① softened   ② broiled
③ referred   ④ claimed

2 People who eat fruit peel may prefer _____ food, which encourages farmers to use less pesticide.
① essential   ② detergent
③ diabetes   ④ organic

3 Once the contest started, two gladiators wearing _____ of gold and silver had a mock fight.
① fame   ② force
③ foundation   ④ armor

D Translate into English or Korean.

1 Letters carved on the stone seem to have been worn away by weather.

_____

2 This software analyzing the data is brand new.

_____

3 그 뮤지컬은 너무 형편없어서 우리는 중간에 걸어 나왔다. (musical, so ~ that, terrible, in the middle, walk out)

_____

_____

E Choose the correct words to fill in the blanks.

1 A child is said to _____ in the accident yesterday.
① be killing   ② have been killed
③ kill   ④ killed

2 The commission approved the policy _____ the recent technological developments.
① considered   ② considering
③ consider   ④ being considered

3 He drove _____ badly and dangerously that he had two accidents yesterday.
① lots   ② many   ③ so   ④ such

4 What he said to us was _____ a nice joke that everybody burst out laughing.
① lots   ② many   ③ so   ④ such

F Match each word with its antonyms (two answers).

1 refuse   a. noxious
                       b. accept
2 criticism   c. dishonor
                       d. obtain
3 nutritious   e. rotten
                       f. compliment
4 brutal   g. ignominy
                       h. caring
5 fame   i. praise
                       j. gentle

CHECK BOX

CHAPTER 4	DATE	SELF CHECK	TEACHER	PARENTS
Preview				
Unit 1				
Unit 2				
Unit 3				
Unit 4				
Unit 5				
Review				

국제소포, 보내 보신 적 있나요?

We ship via UPS

UPS, DHL, FedEx하면 떠오르는 단어는 국제소포죠. 이 중에서도 현재 미국 최대의 소포 배달업체는 우리에게도 친숙한 이름인 UPS입니다. UPS(United Parcel Service)는 창업자 James E. Casey가 1907년 친구에게 100달러를 빌려 시애틀에서 자전거 배달부 10명으로 시작한 소화물 소포 전문회사였습니다. 처음에는 American Messenger Company라는 조그만 민간 소포 배달업체로 시작했으나 2차 대전 이후 전국적인 소포 서비스망을 갖추게 되었고, 1988년부터 항공화물을 시작해 현재는 미국에서 9번째 큰 항공사를 보유하고 있습니다. UPS는 2007년, 100주년을 맞이하면서 약 475억 달러의 수익을 내는 대기업으로 성장했어요. 비록 FedEx나 DHL만큼 지명도가 우리나라에선 그다지 높진 않지만 특송업계 No.1으로 자리 잡았죠. 현재 UPS의 직원의 수는 미국에 약 35만 명과 국제적으로 6만 명으로 총 약 40만 명입니다. 이 회사는 미국의 500대 기업 중 43위를 차지했고, 조지아(Georgia)주에 본사를 두고 있는 기업 중에서 2위를 차지했습니다. UPS는 최대의 네트워크와 소비자 지향적인 영업전략 등으로 매년 시장의 평균 성장률보다 상회하는 성장률을 기록했지만, 저성장하는 시장에서 고성장을 유지하는 것이 갈수록 힘들다는 것을 깨달았습니다. 그 결과, 성장의 흐름을 계속 살리기 위해서 물류업이라는 사업을 확장하여 물류 금융, 물류 정보, 물류 컨설팅 등 인접 영역으로 범위를 넓혀나가기 시작했습니다.

UPS의 또 다른 성공비결은 직원들을 아끼는 마음에 있다고 하네요. 이 회사는 직원들의 건강, 안전, 웰빙에 각별히 신경을 더 쓰고 있습니다. 특히 배송 시 장거리 이동이 있는 직원들의 안전을 최우선으로 생각하고 있다고 합니다. 배송직원들뿐만이 아니라 사무실에서 업무를 보는 직원들까지도 사고를 예방하는 안전교육, 훈련, 프로그램을 만들고 안전성을 사수한 직원들에게 표창을 하기도 합니다. UPS 본사건물에서는 고객에게 신뢰 및 긍정적인 인상을 심어 주기 위해서 늘 깔끔한 외모와 의상을 유지하고 있습니다. 고객들이 한눈에 봐도 UPS라는 것을 인식하기 위해서 배송직원들은 사계절 모두 친근한 인상을 주는 갈색의 유니폼을 입습니다.

CHAPTER

05

Word 🏠 단어도 모르면서 영어 한다 하지 마!

- **awesome** *a.* 무시무시한, 아주 멋진
- **content** *n.* 내용, 목차
- **advertise** *v.* 광고하다, 선전하다
- **get over** ~에서 회복하다
- **value** *n.* 가치, 가격, 평가하다
- **taboo** *n.* 금기 사항, 금기의 *v.* 추방하다
- **forbid** *v.* 금하다, 허락하지 않다
- **thrive** *v.* 번영하다, 성장하다
- **consonant** *n.* 자음 *a.* 일치하는, 자음의
- **grocery** *n.* 식료 잡화점, 식품점
- **articulate** *a.* 명료한 *v.* 또렷하게 발음하다
- **drop** *n.* (한)방울 *v.* 떨어지다, 내려놓다
- **tempt** *v.* 유혹하다, 부추기다
- **acknowledge** *v.* 인정하다, 사례하다
- **overconfident** *a.* 자부심이 강한, 너무 믿는
- **fame** *n.* 명성, 평판 *v.* 유명하게 하다
- **appetite** *n.* 식욕, 욕구
- **deceive** *v.* 속이다, 사기 치다
- **screw up** 망치다, 엉망으로 만들다
- **concern** *v.* ~에 관계하다, 걱정하다 *n.* 관심

∷ Mini Quiz

Draw a line from each word on the left to its definition on the right. Then, use the numbered words to fill in the blanks in the sentences below.

1   detergent   **a.** to feel sorry about something you have done and wish you had not done it

2   nausea   **b.** the feeling that you have when you think you are going to vomit

3   vocabulary   **c.** a look on someone's face that shows what they are thinking or feeling

4   regret   **d.** a liquid or powder used for washing clothes, dishes, etc

5   pretend   **e.** all the words that someone knows or uses

6   expression   **f.** to behave as if something is true when in fact you know it is not, in order to deceive people or for fun

7   Are you sure it's all right to wash this skirt with regular _____?

8   Let's _____ we're on the moon.

9   He _____ having eaten so much at the party.

10   Reading is one of the best ways of improving your _____.

11   There was a blank _____ on her face.

12   Symptoms can include _____, stomach cramps, and headache with a low fever.

Grammar

기본 문법도 모르면서 독해한다 하지마!

★ 목적격 관계대명사 또는 〈주격 관계대명사 + be동사〉는 생략 가능하다.

We study philosophy because of the mental skills **(which or that)** it helps us develop. 우리는 우리를 발전하게 도와주는 정신적 기술 때문에 철학을 공부한다.

It is so easy to include hidden assumptions **(which or that)** you do not see but that are obvious to others. 당신은 알지 못하지만 다른 사람들에게는 명백한 숨겨진 가정들을 포함하는 것은 매우 쉽다.

★ 가정법 과거완료(과거사실의 반대) 〈If + 주어 + had + p.p. ~, 주어 + 조동사 과거 + have + p.p. ~〉

If you **had turned** a light toward Mars that day, it **would have reached** Mars in 186 seconds. 만약 당신이 그 날 화성을 향해 빛을 쏘았다면, 그것은 186초 만에 화성에 도달하였을 것이다.

If Clauss **hadn't reacted** so quickly and decisively, there **would have been** two drownings instead of one.
만약 Clauss가 빠르고 결정적으로 대처하지 않았다면 익사 사고가 하나가 아니라 둘이었을 것이었다.

★ 〈전치사 + 관계대명사〉의 형태의 관계대명사절에는 다른 관계대명사절과 달리 완전한 문장이 온다. that 앞에는 전치사가 올 수 없음을 주의하자.

The phrase "The Empire **on which** the sun never sets" was used to describe the Spanish Empire in the 16th century.
'해가 절대 지지 않는 제국' 이라는 문구는 16세기 스페인 제국을 표현하기 위해 사용되었다.

:: Mini Quiz

1　다음 중 생략 가능한 것은?

This is not the dish which I ordered ten minutes ago.
　　①　　②　　③　　　　　　　④

2　다음 괄호 안에서 알맞은 것을 고르시오.

If I had been able to reach the remote, I never [would see / would have seen] this movie

3　다음 괄호 안에서 알맞은 것을 고르시오.

This is the book in [that / which] I can find the clearest and most concise explanation.

One day, Jason found a small yellow bottle in his mailbox. [1] On the label of the bottle, there was a picture of two lemons with the words "with Fresh Lemon Juice." "Awesome!" said Jason. "This is a free sample of lemon dressing! I guess I should have a salad for dinner. Hopefully, the salad will taste good with this lemon dressing." Jason put the contents of the yellow

bottle on his salad. That night, he had a stomachache. [2] As a matter of fact, the bottle was a free sample from a soap company. The soap company mailed their new liquid dish detergent to millions of people. [3] It said "with Fresh Lemon Juice" on the label, because the company wanted to advertise that the detergent had a good smell. However, Jason was not the only person who read the label wrong. A lot of people thought it was lemon dressing. So they put the soap on dishes or on salads. Later they felt sick, too. [4] Most of the people had stomachaches; but got over their illnesses in a few hours. Luckily, no one died from eating the soap.

1   **What can you learn from this paragraph?**

① Strike the iron while it is hot.
② Nothing ventured, nothing gained.
③ Look before you leap.
④ The early bird catches the worm.
⑤ Don't put the cart before the horse.

2   이 글의 주인공 Jason의 심경 변화로 가장 적절한 것은?

① delighted → regretful
② unhappy → excited
③ unexpected → ecstatic
④ curious → calm
⑤ astonished → satisfied

단어 조사해 오셔~ **Word**

mailbox

label

awesome

content

stomachache

as a matter of fact

detergent

advertise

get over

Drill 1 Grammar

명사절 생략

명사절의 생략은 어떨 때 가능한가? 문법적인 여러 가지 설명에 귀 기울이다 보면 오히려 독해도, 문법도 둘 다 어려워질 때가 있다. 글을 읽다가 아무런 이유 없이 〈명사 + 동사 (that 생략) 명사 + 동사〉(즉, 명동 명동)가 연이어 나오는 경우 명사절 접속사 that이 생략되어 있다고 보면 된다. 명동, 명동이 연이어 나올 때 뒤에 연이어 나오는 명동을 우리말 '~것, ~라고'의 의미로 해석한다.

• The bank did not realize the clerk had secretly been stealing money.

그 은행은 그 직원이 몰래 돈을 훔쳐 왔다는 것을 알아차리지 못했다.

• Approaching Mr. Howard's, I at first thought the house was on fire. But as I turned the corner off the tree-lined street, I realized the whole house was shining with light.

Mr. Howard의 집에 가까워지자, 나는 처음에는 그의 집에 불이 났다고 생각했다. 그러나 가로수가 늘어선 모퉁이를 돌아서자, 그의 집 전체가 햇살로 빛나고 있음을 알아차렸다.

---

1 Many scientists believe the earth was created by something.

해석 ◯ _____

2 She knows there will never be another opportunity like this again.

해석 ◯ _____

3 대부분의 대학생들은 좋은 직업을 찾기가 어렵다는 것을 안다. (college, hard, to find, good jobs)

영작 ◯ _____

Drill 2 Translation

1 1번 문장 ◯ _____

2 2번 문장 ◯ _____

3 3번 문장 ◯ _____

4 4번 문장 ◯ _____

[1] Our values are determined by our parents, and in a larger sense, by the culture in which we live. [2] For example, the drinking of milk is forbidden in some regions of China. The natives of these areas may actually become sick if they are forced to drink a glassful of the beverage. Americans, _____, thrive on milk, although they have many taboos of their own.

Some years ago, I gave a dinner party during which I served a delicious hors d'oeuvre filled with a meat that tasted somewhat like chicken. [3] My guests wondered what the meat was, but I refused to tell them until they had eaten their fill. I then explained that they had just dined on the flesh of freshly killed rattlesnake. The reaction was nausea and in some cases violent vomiting. [4] If I had served rattlesnake to a Chinese, he or she would doubtless have requested a second helping, for in China the dish is considered a delicacy.

hors d'oeuvre 전채 요리 (식사 전에 입맛을 돋우려 가볍게 나오는 음식)

1 **What can be inferred from the passage?**

① Our values are determined by the way we are brought up.
② We respect our parents' values but wish to form our own values.
③ As we grow up and mature, we can choose our values.
④ Our values are determined by our own thinking.
⑤ Our values can be changed as fast as our beliefs.

2 **Choose the best answer to fill in the blank.**

① as a result
② on the other hand
③ for example
④ likewise
⑤ therefore

단어 조사해 오세요~ **Word**

value

determine

forbid

force

beverage

thrive

taboo

refuse to

eat one's fill

rattlesnake

nausea

vomit

helping

delicacy

Drill 1 Grammar

문장 중간에 오는 what

문장 중간에 접속사 what이 등장할 경우 이를 문법적으로 명사절로 쓰였는지, 의문사로 쓰였는지를 규명하는 것은 무의미한 일이다. 무엇보다 중요한 것은 문장에 대한 이해가 우선이다. 문장 중간에 등장하는 what은 우리말로 '~것' 을 붙이거나 또는 '무엇 ~지' 를 붙여 둘 중에 자연스러운 것을 선택해 해석해 주면 된다.

- When doing anything, just *focus* on what you are doing.   어떤 것을 할 때, 당신이 하고 있는 것에만 집중하시오.

- Have you ever *thought* about what you will major in at college?
  너는 대학에서 무엇을 전공할지 생각해 본 적 있니?

---

1 Poetry provides us with what is missing in our own lives – the experience of imaginative pleasure.

   해석 ⊙ _____

2 When arresting a person, the police officer must tell the suspect what his or her rights are.

   해석 ⊙ _____

3 미래에 무슨 일이 일어날지 아무도 모른다. (in the future, what, happen, nobody, will, know)

   영작 ⊙ _____

Drill 2 Translation

1 1번 문장 ⊙ _____

2 2번 문장 ⊙ _____

3 3번 문장 ⊙ _____

4 4번 문장 ⊙ _____

As we know, Americans and British both speak in English. [1] However, there are some important differences between British and American English, so they sometimes seem like totally different languages. First, the pronunciations are very different. Often, Americans tend to drop the consonant which comes right after certain consonants, which make sounds of /t/, /th/, /d/, etc. For example, when they say "I don't know", it sounds like "I dunno."

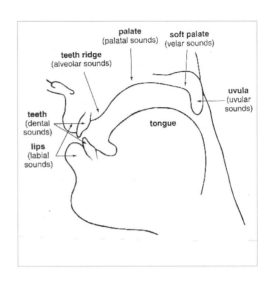

On the contrary, the British usually articulate all the letters without dropping any sounds. [2] Second, British and American English often use different words for the same things. For example, the vocabulary for cars and roads is very different. [3] While Americans use 'highway' to name a certain type of road, the British call the same road 'motorway.' While Americans drive trucks, the British drive lorries. [4] American people call the front of the car a hood, but the British call it a bonnet.

1 **Choose the best main idea of this passage.**

① the history of English
② two main dialects of English
③ the sound system of English
④ various sounds and meanings of English
⑤ the difference between American English and British English

2 American English와 British English의 구분이 <u>잘못된</u> 것은?

American		British
① highway	···	motorway
② I dunno	···	I don't know
③ hood	···	bonnet
④ truck	···	lorry
⑤ without dropping any sounds	···	to drop the consonant

 **Drill 1** Grammar

관계사 which

which가 명사 뒤에 위치하여 앞에 있는 명사를 꾸며 줄 경우 '~하는, 했던, 할' 으로 앞에 명사를 꾸며 주며 해석한다.

- Parents set the stage upon which the friendships of their children are played out.
  부모들은 자녀들의 교우관계가 이루어지는 무대를 마련한다.

- This is the taxi which hit the old man. 이것이 그 노인을 친 택시이다.

---

1 Wind power is a source of energy which people can depend on in the future.

해석 ◯ _____

2 A journey aboard the Sea Cloud which carries only 64 passengers is a special experience.

해석 ◯ _____

3 내 여자친구는 항상 나에게 싼 선물을 사주었다. (presents, cheap, bought, always, which)

영작 ◯ _____

Drill 2 Translation

1 1번 문장 ◯ _____

2 2번 문장 ◯ _____

3 3번 문장 ◯ _____

4 4번 문장 ◯ _____

I was an art student. Everybody told me I had a talent for painting. Tempted by fame, I told my art professor that I wanted to leave university to go to Paris, the home of many well-known artists. (a) Also, I was an acknowledged student by the professor of the university.

(b) "Jim," Professor Turner said, "I believe you've mastered the basic skills of painting, but there are many more things you need to learn about art and life. If you finish your studies at university, I will teach you all that you need."

I didn't listen to him, however, choosing the possibility of fame instead. Professor Turner said, "You are making a mistake, Jim, and perhaps some day _____."

(c) I went to Paris anyway. I was sure I'd become a famous artist quickly. Overconfident of my skills, I didn't work hard and too frequently went to the movies and to parties with my friends. One of them, who painted for art's sake alone, told me that I should work harder and quit painting for money. (d) Ignoring his advice, I wasted my time and continued to paint what I thought was popular. Gradually, however, people lost interest in my paintings. (e) I became penniless and finally stopped painting. Now I am working in an office but I still think about my art. All my life, I'll regret not taking <u>my teacher's advice</u> seriously.

기출

1 Jim에 관한 설명 중, 이 글의 내용과 일치하지 <u>않는</u> 것은?

① He was once expected to be a good painter.
② He went to Paris after getting his university degree.
③ He was overconfident in his ability to paint.
④ In Paris, he painted for money rather than for art's sake.
⑤ Now he is making a living as an office worker.

2 밑줄 친 <u>my teacher's advice</u>의 내용으로 가장 적절한 것은?

① 화가로서의 소양을 더 쌓아라.
② 귀국해서 후학 양성에 힘써라.
③ 자신의 개성을 최대한 살려라.
④ 대중 예술에 집착하지 말라.
⑤ 파리에서 화가로 성공하라.

3 (a)~(e) 중, 이 글의 전체 흐름과 관계 <u>없는</u> 문장은?

① (a)   ② (b)   ③ (c)   ④ (d)   ⑤ (e)

4 Choose the best answer to fill in the blank.

① you may become a famous artist
② you'll be better than me
③ you'll miss your friends a lot
④ you'll be homesick
⑤ you'll regret your decision

단어 조사해 오셔~ **Word**

talent

painting

tempt

fame

well-known

acknowledge

possibility

be sure

overconfident

frequently

penniless

regret

After watching television all day, Kelly remembered (A) what / that she was going to have a test at school the next day. She also remembered that she had not finished her homework. It was already midnight, so Kelly was too sleepy to do her homework and study for the test. However, she did not want to screw up on the test and be punished for

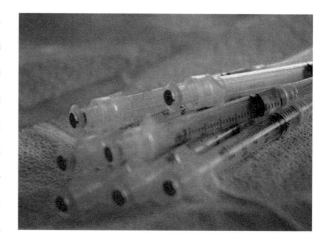

not doing the homework. She thought, "I (B) would / could rather not go to school tomorrow." However, she knew her parents would not allow her to miss school without a good reason. So she decided to pretend to be sick.

The following morning, Kelly's mother woke her up as usual. Kelly opened her eyes and said in a weak voice, "Mom, I don't feel well. I am afraid I can't go to school today. My stomach hurts." Then Kelly made a wry face as if she had stomach cramps.

"Oh dear, you must have a stomach virus! I'll get your father," said her mother with concern. When Kelly's father came in, he was not deceived by Kelly's expression at all. "Don't worry. I have some medicine for you," said her father. "It tastes so awful that you will lose your appetite for at least three days. But it is really (C) effecting / effective, so you don't have to miss school. But if you are still sick after taking the medicine, I will call the doctor and ask him to give you a couple of shots."

Hearing that, Kelly immediately jumped up from her bed and said, "Oh never mind, I feel better already!"

1 이 글의 분위기로 가장 적절한 것은?

① indifferent
② humorous
③ serious
④ exhausted
⑤ logical

2 **What is the moral of this passage?**

① Tricking others is troublesome.
② Attend school in any situation.
③ Always be honest.
④ Be more intelligent.
⑤ Don't watch television.

3 (A), (B), (C)의 각 네모 안에서 어법에 맞는 표현을 골라 짝지은 것으로 가장 적절한 것은?

	(A)		(B)		(C)
①	what	…	would	…	effective
②	what	…	could	…	effecting
③	that	…	could	…	effecting
④	that	…	would	…	effective
⑤	that	…	would	…	effecting

4 이 글의 내용과 일치하지 <u>않는</u> 것은?

① Kelly needed an acceptable reason to miss school.
② Kelly doesn't like injections.
③ Kelly's mom wasn't fooled by Kelly's expression.
④ Kelly's idea wasn't successful.
⑤ Kelly was scared of the test and punishment.

단어 조사해 오셔~ **Word**

screw up

be punished

miss

pretend

as usual

wry

stomach cramp

concern

deceive

expression

awful

appetite

a couple of shots

immediately

never mind

Review 😊

A **Translate into English.**

1   꼬리표 _____

2   광고하다, 선전하다 _____

3   세정제, 세제 _____

4   ~에서 회복하다 _____

5   가치관, 가치기준 _____

6   억지로 시키다 _____

7   금지, 금제 _____

8   구역질, 혐오 _____

9   차이점 _____

10 자음 _____

11 음료, 마실 것 _____

12 구토 _____

13 잘 알려진 _____

14 인정하다 _____

15 후회하다 _____

16 평판, 명성 _____

17 망치다 _____

18 걱정 _____

19 몹시 나쁜 _____

20 식욕 _____

B **Translate into Korean.**

1   awesome _____

2   content _____

3   stomachache _____

4   as a matter of fact _____

5   forbid _____

6   determine _____

7   delicacy _____

8   thrive _____

9   seem like _____

10 articulate _____

11 drop _____

12 tend to _____

13 pronunciation _____

14 overconfident _____

15 possibility _____

16 penniless _____

17 deceive _____

18 never mind _____

19 a couple of shots _____

20 stomach cramp _____

C Choose the correct answers to each question.

1 Stick the stamps on and then drop the letter into the _____ over there.
① mailbox   ② label
③ content   ④ awesome

2 The use of _____ to clean fruits and vegetables can also cause water pollution.
① determine   ② detergent
③ taboo   ④ appetite

3 One letter can have several _____.
① pronunciations   ② consonants
③ articulate   ④ vocabulary

D Translate into English or Korean.

1 The children were worried that there were no life guards on duty at the pool.

_____

_____

2 They want to know what they will get from their parents before Christmas day.

_____

_____

3 한국 연의 모양은 그 연들이 바람을 잘 이용하게 할 수 있도록 가능케 해 주는 과학적인 원리에 기초합니다. (make good use of, enable, which)
The shape of Korean kites are based on scientific principles _____
_____ the wind.

E Choose the correct words to fill in the blanks.

1 One of the things _____ they talked about was how to enforce laws against dumping waste into water sources.
① so   ② which   ③ what   ④ how

2 Nobody knows _____ will happen next. I know _____ you did last summer.
① so   ② that   ③ what   ④ which

3 When doing anything, just focus on _____ you are doing.
① so   ② that   ③ what   ④ which

4 다음 중 that이 생략되었을 곳을 고르시오.
Everyone knows (①) we need somebody to help (②) us to build (③) a tree house for (④) my younger brother.

F Match each word with its synonym and antonym (one synonym and one antonym for each word).

1 forbid   a. distinctness
                         b. prohibit
2 advertise   c. at once
                         d. publicize
3 difference   e. correspondence
                         f. later
4 fame   g. permit
                         h. celebrity
5 immediately   i. hide
                         j. obscurity

CHAPTER 5	DATE	SELF CHECK	TEACHER	PARENTS
Preview				
Unit 1				
Unit 2				
Unit 3				
Unit 4				
Unit 5				
Review				

Love from Valentine

서양에서는 2월 14일을 발렌타인데이라고 하여 아주 특별하게 보냅니다. 이날 사람들은 발렌타인데이 축하카드를 연인, 친구들, 가족들에게 보내죠. 상점들은 2월 14일이 되기 훨씬 전부터 발렌타인 용품과 장식을 팔고 어린 학생들은 교실을 하트와 레이스로 장식을 합니다. 그리고 사람들은 각자의 친구들에게 사탕, 꽃, 특별한 선물을 주곤 합니다. 이렇게 서양에서 시작된 발렌타인데이 행사는 이제 우리나라에서도 시끌벅적하게 지나가는 날 중에 하나가 되었습니다. 발렌타인데이엔 초콜릿이 빠질 수 없죠. 이날이 되면 길거리마다 초콜릿으로 꾸며져 있으며 사람들은 사랑하는 사람들을 위해서 그중 제일 예쁘고 맛있는 초콜릿을 구입합니다. 초콜릿처럼 달콤하고 풍만한 깊은 맛을 내는 특별하고 기분 좋은 하루를 보내기 위해서죠.

발렌타인데이의 기원에 관해 많은 이야기들이 있습니다. 어떤 전문가들은 로마의 성발렌타인(St. Valentine)에서 시작되었다고 합니다. 발렌타인은 당시 황제 클라디우스는 젊은 청년들을 군대로 끌어들이고자 결혼금지령을 내렸는데 이에 반대하고 서로 사랑하는 젊은이들을 결혼시켜준 죄로 A.D. 269년 2월 14일에 순교한 사제의 이름입니다. 그는 그 당시 간수의 딸에게 "Love from Valentine"이라는 편지를 남겼고, 발렌타인데이에 사랑의 메시지를 전하는 풍습의 기원이 되었죠. 발렌타인데이가 연인들의 날로 알려져 있는 것도 이런 까닭이라고 추측됩니다. 어떤이들은 발렌타인의 죽음을 추모하는 의식을 2월 중순에 가진 것이 유래라고 하기도 하고, 어떤이들은 이교도 축제인 Lupercalia를 기독교화하기 위해 발렌타인축제를 행사화 하였다고도 합니다. 당시 Lupercalia 축제에 도시의 젊은 여자들은 자기 이름을 큰 항아리에 적어 넣고 남자들이 항아리에서 이름표를 고르는 짝짓기 행사가 있었다고 합니다. 그 결과로 결혼까지 가는 경우가 많았다고 하네요. 이런 상황들을 교황이 보기에 이 축제행사가 매우 비기독교적이며 위법적이라고 생각하여 서기 498년에 2월 14일을 St. Valentine's Day로 선언하여 남녀간의 사랑을 표현하는 날로 삼았다고 전해집니다. 사실 영국과 프랑스에서 2월 14일을 이른바 새들의 짝짓기가 시작되는 날이라고 하며 그래서 이날을 그날로 정한 것이라고 하기도 합니다.

CHAPTER 06

Word 🏠 단어도 모르면서 영어 한다 하지 마!

- **poverty** *n.* 빈곤, 가난
- **dutiful** *a.* 의무를 다하는, 충성된
- **obedient** *a.* 순종하는, 충실한
- **thoughtful** *a.* 생각이 깊은, 친절한
- **inform** *v.* 알리다, 정보를 제공하다
- **intend** *v.* ~할 작정이다, 의도하다
- **relatively** *ad.* 상대적으로, 비교적으로
- **cost-effective** *a.* 비용 효율이 높은
- **standard** *n.* 표준, 기준 *a.* 표준의
- **excuse** *v.* 용서하다, 변명하다 *n.* 변명

- **disapprove** *v.* 안 된다고 하다, 찬성하지 않다
- **endanger** *v.* 위험에 빠뜨리다
- **release** *v.* 해방시키다 *n.* 석방, 해방
- **emission** *n.* 방사, 방출
- **atmosphere** *n.* 대기, 공기, 분위기, 환경
- **reduce** *v.* 줄이다, 진압하다, 줄다
- **rescue** *v.* 구출하다 *n.* 구출 *a.* 구제의
- **isolate** *v.* 고립시키다, 분리시키다 *n.* 분리
- **notify** *v.* 통지하다, 통보하다, 신고하다
- **risk** *n.* 위험, 모험 *v.* 위태롭게 하다

:: Mini Quiz

Draw a line from each word on the left to its definition on the right. Then, use the numbered words to fill in the blanks in the sentences below.

1   ruler   **a.** as a result

2   intend   **b.** someone who governs a state or nation

3   satisfaction   **c.** without delay

4   consequently   **d.** to have something in your mind as a plan or purpose

5   immediately   **e.** able to face danger, difficulty, uncertainty, or pain

6   courageous   **f.** a feeling of pleasure that comes when a need or desire is fulfilled

7   She got great _____ from helping people to learn.

8   The telephone rang, and he answered it _____.

9   We do have very good normal relations with China, and we _____ to keep on having those relations.

10   He was wrong, and _____ enough to admit it.

11   The _____ of the country was designated as king.

Grammar 👤 기본 문법도 모르면서 독해한다 하지 마!

★ 〈be used to + -ing〉 vs 〈be used to + 동사원형〉 vs 〈used to + 동사원형〉

I **am used to driving** on the left because I've lived in Japan for 3 years.

나는 일본에서 3년간 살았기 때문에 도로 왼편으로 운전하는 것이 익숙하다.

This book should **be used to develop** your English skills.

이 책은 너의 영어 실력을 발달시키는 데 사용되어야 한다.

They **used to skip** their English classes so they failed the test.

그들은 영어수업을 빼먹곤 해서 시험에 낙제했다.

★ 명사절 if vs 조건절 if

I am not sure **if** this question will be on the test. 나는 이 문제가 시험에 나올지 확신이 없다.

If this question is on the test, I will not be able to solve it.

만약 이 문제가 시험에 나온다면 나는 풀지 못할 것이다.

★ 〈원급 비교문: as + 원급 + as〉 vs 〈비교급: 비교급 ~ than〉 vs 〈최상급: the + 최상급 + of/in + 명사구〉

Be **as specific as** possible. 가능한 구체적으로 되어야 한다.

If the movie calls for rivers, mountains, or jungles, it may be **cheaper** to film in real places **than** to build imitation scenery.

만약 영화에 강, 산 혹은 정글이 필요하면 실제 장소에 가서 촬영하는 것이 가짜 풍경을 만들어 내는 것보다 더 싸다.

:: Mini Quiz

1   다음 괄호 안에서 알맞은 것을 고르시오.

I'm used to [speak / speaking] English since I came to Canada.

2   다음 괄호 안에서 알맞은 것을 고르시오.

The contract will not be signed if your boss [won't / doesn't] show up in ten minutes.

3   다음 문장에서 <u>틀린</u> 부분을 찾아 바르게 고치시오.

Time is the most precious than all things.

"Confucius" is a Latin form of the Chinese name "kung-fu-tse." [1] Confucius was a great Chinese thinker, who was born in 557 B.C. In his time, China had a lot of problems. The government was weak, and there were crimes everywhere. People suffered from poverty. Confucius's father died when he was only three years old. He was dutiful and obedient to his mother. [2] When Confucius grew up, he became a prudent, thoughtful and studious person. He liked to watch and study people and their behavior. [3] Confucius thought that he could help others live better lives, so he left his family. He taught people to be honest and considerate. He thought the most important thing in one's life was to obey his or her parents and rulers. In addition, he believed a mature person never gets angry. Most of his lessons are very similar to those of Jesus Christ. One goes, "Don't make others do what you don't want to do." [4] Later, a lot of people followed Confucius, and his ideas and beliefs became the school of Confucius, which is called "Confucianism." Confucius died in 479 B.C.

1 **What kind of writing is this paragraph?**

① report
② autobiography
③ biography
④ description
⑤ poem

2 **What would be Confucius's article of faith?**

① to think cautiously before making a decision
② to study people and their behavior
③ to obey one's parents and rulers
④ to help poor people
⑤ to be a prudent, thoughtful and studious person

단어 조사해 오셔~ **Word**

Confucius

thinker

in one's time

suffer from

poverty

dutiful

obedient

prudent

thoughtful

studious

obey

ruler

mature

be similar to

Confucianism

 **Drill 1** Grammar

부연 설명하는 관계사절

관계대명사나 관계부사 앞에 콤마(,)가 있으면 보충 설명하는 계속적 용법이다. 선행사에 대한 부연 설명을 나타내므로 앞에서부터 차례대로 해석한다. '그런데 앞 단어' 로 해석한다. 앞에 명사를 한번 다시 읽고 쭉 해석한다.

> 선행사, who (which) ..... ' 그런데 (그런데) 앞 그 선행사(사람, 그것)는'

• Teachers must maintain a good relationship with the parents, who are also an important part of the total community.
  교사들은 부모들과 좋은 관계를 유지해야 하는데, 이는 부모들 역시 모두 지역 공동체에서 중요한 역할을 하기 때문이다.

• The man, who looks scary, is in fact very shy. 그 남자, 그런데 그는 무섭게 보이는데, 사실은 매우 부끄러움을 탄다.

---

1 Vicky, who is wearing a heavy winter coat, is practicing on her high school stage for tomorrow's presentation of a play.

   해석 ◯ _____

2 Susan's smile is always big, showing off all her original teeth, which are still in good condition.

   해석 ◯ _____

3 그 소녀는 귀신을 좋아했다, 그런데 그 귀신은 그 애와 놀아줬다. (the ghost, played with)

   영작 ◯ _____

Drill 2 Translation

1 1번 문장 ◯ _____

2 2번 문장 ◯ _____

3 3번 문장 ◯ _____

4 4번 문장 ◯ _____

Television advertisements are not as effective as video advertisements. In the first place, it is very expensive to advertise on television. [1] In addition, even if a company spends a lot of money to advertise on television, they have no guarantee that enough customers will see the advertisements. [2] The problem is that they cannot make *people's eyes* fixed on the ads, because television has many channels. Moreover, there are some people who do not have a television set. So, actually, advertisers have no idea if anyone actually sees the television ads. [3] In addition, it is impossible to send the ads exclusively to the people who are likely to buy their products. Also, television ads are relatively shorter than video ads. It is hard to make *people* buy a product in less than a minute. In contrast, video advertisements can be as long as the advertiser wants them to be, but most of them are usually not longer than 7 minutes. As a result, customers can be more informed about the product when they see the advertisement on video rather than on television. [4] In addition, using a video tape to advertise is much more cost-effective, because manufacturers can send the video advertisement to people who really intend to buy their product.

1   **What is the best title of this paragraph?**

① Ads: Present and Future   ② Television: Present and Future

③ Ads: Video or television?   ④ Video: Problem and Solution

⑤ Products: Buy or Sell?

2   이 글의 내용과 일치하지 <u>않는</u> 것은?

① It is expensive to advertise on television.

② It is possible to gather enough customers through ads on TV.

③ Advertisers cannot send their ads selectively if they advertise on TV.

④ One minute is not enough to get information about a product.

⑤ Video ads make it possible to contact the potential buyers.

단어 조사해 오셔~ **Word**

advertise

advertiser

exclusively

be likely to

product

relatively

inform

cost-effective

manufacturer

intend to

 **Drill 1** Grammar

사역동사의 특징

대표적인 사역동사로는 make, have, let 이 있으며 기본적으로 '누구에게 ~를 시키다' 의 뜻이다. 목적어와 목적격보어의 관계가 '능동' 인 경우에는 목적격보어에 '동사원형' 을 취한다. 목적격보어 자리에 '-ed/en' 꼴이 왜~ 오는지도 생각해 보자!

> V(make, have, let) + X + Y(동사원형) : X에게 Y하라고 시키다

- A symphony orchestra can make *a whole building* ring with music.
  교향악단은 건물 전체를 음악으로 울리게 만들 수 있다.

- Don't let *your children* make too much noise or jump around in a restaurant.
  당신의 아이들이 식당에서 너무 떠들거나 뛰어다니도록 내버려 두지 마라.

---

1 Our teacher made us write it out five times again.

해석 ◎ _____

2 Still other chanteys let sailors complain about their hard lives.

해석 ◎ _____

chantey 뱃노래

3 나는 Mark에게 나의 자전거를 고치도록 시킬 것이다. (have, bicycle, fix)

영작 ◎ _____

🍴 **Drill 2** Translation

1 1번 문장 ◎ _____

2 2번 문장 ◎ _____

3 3번 문장 ◎ _____

4 4번 문장 ◎ _____

In every school there is a 'top' crowd that sets the pace, while the others follow their lead. Let's say the top crowd decided that it is cool to wear bright red sweaters. Pretty soon, everybody is wearing bright red sweaters. [1] There is nothing wrong with that, except the fact that on some people bright red is mightily unbecoming. [2] The situation can even become dangerous, if the top crowd decides that it is cool to drink alcohol or to drive cars at one hundred kilometers an hour. Then the people who follow the lead are endangering their very lives. They are like sheep being led to the slaughter. Now, chances are that you have come across situations like these more than once in your life. [3] In fact, chances are that, at one time or another, you probably did something you knew to be wrong. You may have excused yourself by saying, "Gee, the crowd does it." Well, let the crowd do it, but don't do it yourself. Learn to say "No." Develop your own standards and your own judgments. [4] If you know the crowd is planning something of which you disapprove, have the courage to bow out gracefully. You'll have the satisfaction of standing on your own feet.

1 이 글을 쓴 목적으로 가장 적절한 것은?

① 다수결의 원칙을 설명하려고
② 단체 생활에 있어서 협동심의 중요성을 강조하려고
③ 단체 생활에서 용기를 잃지 않게 하려고
④ 다수의 의견이더라도 자신만의 판단기준을 가지도록 하려고
⑤ 리더에게 다수를 이끌 판단기준을 가지게 하려고

2 이 글의 주제로 가장 적절한 것은?

① 타인의 생각과 내 생각 모두 존중되어야 한다.
② 상층부 생각에 절대적으로 따르는 게 성공하기에 좋다.
③ 다수의 의견에 휩쓸리지 말고 자신의 기준을 키워라.
④ '노'라고 말할 수 있는 자신감을 길러야 한다.
⑤ 어려운 상황에서도 침착성을 잃어서는 안 된다.

단어 조사해 오세요~ **Word**

set the pace
mightily
unbecoming
endanger
slaughter
excuse
standard
judgment
disapprove
have the courage to
bow out
gracefully
satisfaction
stand on one's feet

🍴 Drill 1 Grammar

may have + 과거분사

may have + p.p. ~했을지도 모른다	must have + p.p. ~였음에 틀림없다
cannot have + p.p. ~였을 리가 없다	

- The teenage girl may have been smoking for some time before her mother caught her doing it. 엄마가 자기 딸이 담배 피우는 것을 알기 전까지 그 10대 소녀는 한동안 담배를 피워 왔을지도 모른다.

- It must have been terrifying to see two ghosts in one night in the same house. I think I would move to a new house.
  같은 집에서 하룻밤 동안 두 유령을 보는 것은 무서운 일이었음에 틀림없다. 나는 새집으로 이사를 가야겠다고 생각한다.

---

1   The girl may have been spitting in the street. The police stopped her and told her that spitting in the street was against the law.

    해석 ◎ _____

    spit 침을 뱉다

2   She looked so happy that I thought something good must have happened to her.

    해석 ◎ _____

3   그녀의 창백한 얼굴을 봐. 뭔가 끔찍한 일이 그녀에게 일어났었음에 틀림없어.
    (pale face, to her, terrible, something)

    영작 ◎ _____

🍴 Drill 2 Translation

1   1번 문장 ◎ _____

2   2번 문장 ◎ _____

3   3번 문장 ◎ _____

4   4번 문장 ◎ _____

(A)

Scientists say that the temperature of the Earth is increasing because of the increasing amount of carbon dioxide in the atmosphere. Carbon dioxide is released when something is burned. Rising temperatures cause polar icebergs to melt, and consequently raises sea levels and floods coastal areas. In other words, we should

reduce carbon dioxide emissions. One solution for this problem is to develop alternative energy sources, such as solar power and wind energy, to replace fossil fuels, which produce a lot of carbon dioxide.

(B)

It is reported that 35.2 million acres of tropical forests, the size of New York state, are cut down every year. In Central America, rain forests are deforested for cattle ranching. Elsewhere, forests are used to provide people with furniture, housing materials, paper, etc. _____, expanding populations and growing needs for farmland are also

blamed for forest loss. At this point, half of the world's tropical forests are gone, and if the deforestation continues at the current rate, most of the world's rain forests will disappear by the end of this century. Thus, it is time to do something about it.

1 **Choose the appropriate subjects for (A) and (B).**

(A)		(B)
① Rise of Sea Levels	⋯	Use of Natural Resources
② Air Pollution	⋯	Lack of Farmland
③ New Energy Development	⋯	Change of Temperature
④ Global Warming	⋯	Decrease of Rainforests
⑤ Increase of CO₂	⋯	Cause of Environmental Destruction

2 **What are the style of the each topic?**

(A)		(B)
① informative	⋯	ceremonial
② persuasive	⋯	persuasive
③ informative	⋯	narrative
④ persuasive	⋯	ceremonial
⑤ ceremonial	⋯	informative

3 **What is a possible common title for (A) and (B)?**

① Let's Save the Earth!
② Stop Using Fossil Fuels!
③ Keep the Earth Clean!
④ Let's Live on a Clean Earth!
⑤ Develop the Earth Effectively!

4 **Choose the best answer to fill in the blank in (B).**

① On the contrary
② For example
③ Furthermore
④ To begin with
⑤ Nevertheless

단어 조사해 오세요~ **Word**

temperature

carbon dioxide

atmosphere

release

iceberg

consequently

reduce

emission

alternative energy

fossil fuel

acre

cut down

deforest

cattle ranching

provide A with B

be gone

deforestation

current rate

William Darling, the keeper of the Longstone Lighthouse in the early 19th century in England, (a) <u>had a daughter called Grace</u>. Their family lived on Farne Island off the coast of Northumberland. Often the sea was violent, and the island was isolated. But Grace (b) <u>loved playing with the baby sea animals and enjoying nature</u>.

On September 7, 1838, the steamship *Forfarshire*, sailing from Hull to Dundee in England, met a terrifying storm near Farne Island. Nine people on the ship cried for help and, finally, Grace heard them. She notified her father immediately. However, (c) <u>there was no other person to help him</u>, so he could not set out to rescue these people. Therefore, even though Mrs. Darling was against the idea, Grace decided to go with her father risking her life. Eventually, Grace and William rescued five passengers. Grace was worn out from

the first trip, (d) <u>so she could not make the second trip to rescue others</u>. Therefore, (e) <u>William and two men who rescued from the first trip</u> went out again to bring back the remaining people to safety. Along with her father, Grace became famous and received the Gold Medal of the Royal Humane Society for her courageous and humane act. Alas, Grace died of tuberculosis four years later. But Grace and her courage have not been forgotten.

1 Grace Darling에 관한 이 글의 내용과 일치하지 <u>않는</u> 것은?

① Grace enjoyed her environment.
② She received the Gold Medal of the Royal Humane Society.
③ She was afraid of the violent sea.
④ Grace and her father rescued five people.
⑤ Grace's father was the keeper of the lighthouse.

2 **Choose the best description of 'Grace.'**

① She is a charming daughter who only knows her family.
② She is an energetic girl who raised baby sea animals.
③ She is a courageous girl who knows the importance of life.
④ She is an insatiable girl trying to receive the Gold Medal.
⑤ She is an ordinary girl living by the sea.

3 (a)~(e) 중 어법상 <u>어색한</u> 것을 찾아 바르게 고치시오.

4 **Choose the best title for this passage.**

① The Brutal Nature of England.
② The Accommodation of Humans
③ Methods of Receiving a Gold Medal
④ The English Heroine of the Sea
⑤ Life of a Girl Called 'Grace'

단어 조사해 오세요~ **Word**

keeper

lighthouse

Northumberland

isolate

steamship

terrify

notify

immediately

set out

rescue

risk

worn out

receive

Royal Humane Society

courageous

humane act

tuberculosis

Review 😊

A Translate into English.

1 사상가, 사색가 _____

2 통치자, 지배자 _____

3 유교 _____

4 빈곤, 가난 _____

5 광고하다 _____

6 제조업자 _____

7 ~하려고 생각하다 _____

8 오로지, 독점적으로 _____

9 판단 _____

10 기준, 표준 _____

11 변명하다 _____

12 만족(감) _____

13 온도, 기온 _____

14 벌채하다 _____

15 현재 비율 _____

16 대체 에너지 _____

17 관리자 _____

18 고립시키다 _____

19 인도적 행위 _____

20 시작하다, 착수하다 _____

B Translate into Korean.

1 dutiful _____

2 prudent _____

3 thoughtful _____

4 mature _____

5 product _____

6 cost-effective _____

7 be likely to _____

8 inform _____

9 mightily _____

10 disapprove _____

11 slaughter _____

12 gracefully _____

13 iceberg _____

14 fossil fuel _____

15 cut down _____

16 be gone _____

17 lighthouse _____

18 terrify _____

19 worn out _____

20 tuberculosis _____

C **Choose the correct answers to each question.**

1 Confucius thought the most important thing in one's life was to _____ one's parents and rulers.
① suffer   ② mature
③ similar   ④ obey

2 One solution for carbon dioxide emissions is to develop _____ energy sources, such as solar power and wind energy, to replace fossil fuels.
① iceberg   ② fossil
③ deforestation   ④ alternative

3 The _____ team reported that they were approaching the site of the accident.
① receive   ② risk
③ notify   ④ rescue

D **Translate into English or Korean.**

1 These toys are from my relatives, who live with me.

_____

2 This is a new way to let people donate to charity while surfing and shopping online.

_____

_____

3 너는 학교 프로젝트를 끝내기 위해 지역 공공 도서관에 방문한 적이 있을지도 모른다. (visit, local public library, complete, school project)

_____

_____

E **Choose the correct words to fill in the blanks.**

1 Hope, _____ seems like the thinnest little thread, is an incredibly powerful force leading us from the most horrible problems into a bright new day.
① who   ② whose ③ that   ④ which

2 In a survey published earlier this year seven out of ten parents said they would never let their children _____ with toy guns.
① to play   ② playing
③ played   ④ play

3 They _____ the work by the end of last month because they are on vacation now.
① must have finished
② must finish
③ may finish
④ cannot finish

F **Match each word with its synonym and antonym (one synonym and one antonym for each word).**

1 mature   a. condemn
                    b. full-grown
2 standard   c. unusual
                    d. accept
3 disapprove   e. childish
                    f. reception
4 emission   g. regular
                    h. diffusion
5 isolate   i. cut off
                    j. integrate

CHAPTER 6	DATE	SELF CHECK	TEACHER	PARENTS
Preview				
Unit 1				
Unit 2				
Unit 3				
Unit 4				
Unit 5				
Review				

혈액형이 성격에 미치는 영향을 믿으세요?

대부분 사람들은 혈액형 점이나 혈액형으로 사람의 성격을 믿습니다. 하지만 이러한 얘기들은 근거가 있는 사실들일까요? 유독 우리나라와 일본에만 있는 특이한 경우인데 외국에선 이런 현상을 이상하게 생각하고 있습니다. 단도직입적으로 말해서 혈액형과 성격과는 아무런 관계가 없습니다. 사람의 성격을 좌우하는 것은 혈액형이 아니라 그 사람이 살았던 환경적 여건에 영향을 많이 받는다고 합니다. 사람의 혈액형이 A형, B형, O형, AB형이다 해서 그 사람의 성격이 정해져 있진 않죠. 혈액형으로 다룬 점이나 또는 성격분류 같은 것에 얽매이지 않아도 됩니다.

그럼 혈액형 점이 형성된 기원을 알아보죠. 혈액형 점은 1971년 일본의 삼류작가인 노오미라는 사람이 단지 자기 생각대로 쓴 아무 근거 없는 하나의 이야기일 뿐입니다. 1971년 일본에 출판되기 시작하여 1980년 당시 일본에선 뜨거운 반응을 얻었고 그게 우리나라로 넘어와 많은 사람들에게 전달이 된 것이죠. 요즘에도 서점에서 찾아볼 수 있는 이 책은 마치 노오미가 대단한 과학자인 양 소개가 되어 있습니다.

노오미가 죽은 후에도 그의 자식이 이어서 그 이론을 부풀려나가서 오늘날까지 그 책이 존재한다고 추측됩니다. 그 책은 우리나라에 들어오면서는 마치 전 세계 과학자들이 열심히 연구한 결과 얻어진 무슨 과학이론이나 엄밀한 통계이론인 것처럼 포장되어 퍼지고 열렬한 신자들도 생겼습니다.

하지만 혈액형 점의 처음 시작과 어떻게 발견되었는지를 발견한 사람은 없죠. 혈액형 점의 실체가 없기 때문입니다. 엄밀한 통계학 조사로도 의학 조사로도 증명할 수 있는 단서는 아직 하나도 얻어지질 못 했습니다. 즉 과학적 증명이 수십 년에 걸쳐 시도되어 왔지만 확실한 정답은 아직 찾지 못했죠. 그런데도 혈액형 점은 내용이 점점 더 방대해지고 더 세밀해졌습니다. 그러므로, 혈액형 점이나 혈액형으로 성격을 나타내는 자료는 아직은 근거 없는 자료인 것입니다.

CHAPTER 07

Word 🏠 단어도 모르면서 영어 한다 하지 마!

- □ **harsh** *a.* 거친, 가혹한
- □ **practice** *n.* 습관, 실행, 연습 *v.* 연습하다
- □ **teammate** *n.* 같은 팀의 사람
- □ **skill** *n.* 솜씨, 노련, 기능, 기술
- □ **addiction** *n.* 탐닉, 중독, 열중, 몰두
- □ **compulsive** *a.* 강제적인, 강요하는
- □ **reality** *n.* 진실, 현실, 실재, 본체
- □ **futile** *a.* 헛된, 효과 없는, 무익한
- □ **devote** *v.* 바치다, 쏟다, 기울이다
- □ **ordinary** *a.* 평상의, 보통의, 정규의

- □ **means** *n.* 방법, 매체, 자력, 수입
- □ **goal** *n.* 목적, 목표, 결승선, 골
- □ **excel** *v.* 능가하다, 빼어나다, 탁월하다
- □ **aptitude** *n.* 경향, 습성, 소질, 적성, 능력
- □ **unfair** *a.* 불공평한, 교활한, 부당한
- □ **expand** *v.* 넓히다, 확장하다, 퍼지다
- □ **claim** *v.* 요구하다, 주장하다 *n.* 요구, 주장
- □ **linguistic** *a.* 말의, 언어의, 어학(상)의
- □ **prehistory** *n.* 유사 이전, 선사 시대
- □ **assume** *v.* 사실이라고 보다, 가정하다

∷ Mini Quiz

Draw a line from each word on the left to its definition on the right. Then, use the numbered words to fill in the blanks in the sentences below.

1   gym   **a.** to travel around an area in order to find out about it

2   agree   **b.** a planned way of doing something, especially one that a lot of people know about

3   explore

4   qualified   **c.** a sudden event such as a flood, storm, or accident which causes great damage

5   method   **d.** to have or express the same opinion about something as someone else

6   disaster   **e.** a special building or room that has equipment for doing physical exercise

     f. having suitable knowledge, experience, or skills, especially for a particular job

7   I think we should try again using a different _____ to solve the problem.

8   One hundred and twenty people died in China's worst air _____.

9   If she felt he was right, she would _____ with him.

10   If you don't speak German, you're not _____ to comment.

11   I try and work out at the local _____ once a week.

12   Venice is a wonderful city to _____.

Grammar

기본 문법도 모르면서 독해한다 하지 마!

★ 〈관계대명사 + 불완전한 문장〉 vs 〈관계부사 + 완전한 문장〉

The true mark of heroes lies not necessarily in the result of their actions, but in **what** they are willing to do for others and for their chosen causes.

영웅의 진정한 특징은 반드시 그들의 행동의 결과에 있는 것이 아니고, 그들이 타인들과 그들이 선택한 대의명분을 위해 기꺼이 일을 한다는 것에 있다.

According to the study, violence and property crimes were nearly twice as high in sections of the buildings **where** vegetation was low, compared with the sections **where** vegetation was high.

연구에 따르면 초목이 없는 곳에서 초목이 많은 곳에 비교하여 폭력과 절도가 거의 두 배 이상 높았다.

★ try, stop, remember, forget 등의 뒤에 오는 to부정사 vs 동명사

Disharmony enters our relationships when we **try to impose** our values on others by wanting them to live by what we feel is "right," "fair," "good," "bad," and so on. 부조화는 우리가 다른 사람들에게 우리가 "옳다", "공정하다", "좋다", "나쁘다"라고 느끼는 것대로 살기를 원함으로써 그들에게 우리의 가치를 강요하려고 할 때 우리의 관계에 들어온다.

Finally, Simba **stopped breathing**. 결국, Simba는 호흡을 멈추었습니다.

★ 비교급 강조: much, a lot, far, by far, still, even

However, it can also happen that one's memories grow **much sharper** even after a long passage of time.

그러나 사람의 기억력은 오랜 시간이 경과한 후에 훨씬 더 날카로워지는 일이 또한 일어날 수도 있다

:: Mini Quiz

1 다음 괄호 안에서 알맞은 것을 고르시오.

I was on the plane heading to Germany, the place [which / where] I was born.

2 다음 괄호 안에서 알맞은 것을 고르시오.

I forgot [to lock / locking] the door of the car and someone had attempted to steal it.

3 다음 괄호 안에서 알맞은 것을 고르시오.

It is [very / much] easier to read than the first one and it is by far easier to maintain.

(A) I saw a boy in the gym playing basketball. [1] He dribbled the ball between his legs, around his back, and took the ball to the basket. I really wanted to do that. So I went out for the basketball team. I was sixteen. This was very late, because most people start playing before they are ten. [2] People told me I couldn't make it, but I didn't care. I practiced even on Sundays when my teammates were at home. I kept practicing, and finally made it on a professional team. Playing basketball also gave me a way to work out my feelings.

(B) (a) [3] I didn't start playing volleyball until I was fifteen, and sometimes the other girls made fun of me because my skills weren't like theirs. (b) I tried not to let their harsh words break me. (c) I practiced and practiced, trying to catch up with the other girls. (d) Poor, I couldn't buy good shoes or clothes for volleyball, and sometimes felt sad. (e) [4] But hard work and determination helped me make it on a professional volleyball team. 기출

---

1 이 글 (A)와 (B)를 통해 얻을 수 있는 교훈으로 가장 적절한 것은?

① Practice makes perfect.
② Easier said than done.
③ Out of sight, out of mind.
④ A friend in need is a friend indeed.
⑤ A picture is worth a thousand words.

2 글 (A)의 밑줄 친 I didn't care.에 상응하는 문장을 (B)에서 고른다면, 가장 적절한 것은?

① (a)　　② (b)　　③ (c)　　④ (d)　　⑤ (e)

단어 조사해 오세요~ **Word**

gym

dribble

practice

teammate

keep practicing

work out

make fun of

skill

harsh

catch up with

Drill 1 Grammar

명사 + -ing

-ing의 형태는 영어에서 다양하게 쓰이는데 명사 뒤에 위치할 경우 앞에 있는 명사를 꾸며 주는 역할을 하여 '~하는, 하고 있는' 정도로 해석한다. 이를 현재분사라고 하는데, 분사가 단독으로 쓰일 때는 명사 앞에 위치하나, 분사가 다른 딸린 어구(보통 전명구)를 데리고 올 경우 명사 뒤에서 수식을 한다. 이때 명사와 분사 사이에는 〈주격 관계사 + be동사〉가 생략되어 있다. 현대 영어에서는 거의 생략한다.

- When I saw the ghost coming down the street, I went running home as fast as I could.
  내가 그 거리를 내려오는 귀신을 보았을 때 나는 할 수 있는 한 빨리 집으로 달려갔다.

- The girl picking up seashells on the shore will use them to make necklaces which she will sell to tourists. 바닷가에서 조개를 줍고 있는 그 소녀는 그것으로 관광객들에게 팔 목걸이를 만들 것이다.

---

1 The man running down the street was followed by three police officers. After a while, the man finally turned down a blind alley and had nowhere to go.

해석 ◯ _____

2 A boy swimming in the river started to drown. He called out to a woman that was passing by for help, but could not make himself heard.

해석 ◯ _____

3 휴대폰으로 전화하고 있는 그 남자분이 나의 아빠이다. (talk, the man, cell phone)

영작 ◯ _____

Drill 2 Translation

1 1번 문장 ◯ _____

2 2번 문장 ◯ _____

3 3번 문장 ◯ _____

4 4번 문장 ◯ _____

[1] Life as a smoker is a life of addiction. You can't quit. You may think you can quit. You may live your whole life, thinking you can quit. But the reality is, you can't. Sure, some people do quit, but only through extreme effort. [2] Even those who do quit fight to remain non-smokers for the rest of their lives.

Once you are addicted, you have to smoke. There isn't any choice because smoking is compulsive. You will smoke. Resistance is futile. You wish you could quit. [3] You intend to quit someday, but not today. Today you will smoke. And every time you smoke you'll think back and wish _____. Am I right? Talk to anyone who smokes. [4] They will tell you themselves. Both smokers and non-smokers alike agree that a person who doesn't smoke shouldn't start.

1 **Choose the best answer to fill in the blank.**

① you never drank alcohol

② you were never a smoker

③ you could quit

④ you never spent your life addicted

⑤ you never started

2 이 글의 요지로 가장 적절한 것을 고르시오.

① 흡연자의 강한 의지에 따라 금연에 성공할 수 있다.

② 많은 사람들이 자신의 건강을 위해 금연을 하고 있다.

③ 청소년은 담배를 처음부터 시작하지 않는 것이 좋다.

④ 한번 흡연을 시작하게 되면 중독이 되어 끊기가 어렵다.

⑤ 금연에 성공한 사람일지라도 담배의 중독을 이겨내기 위해 계속 노력해야 한다.

단어 조사해 오셔~ **Word**

addiction

reality

extreme

effort

compulsive

resistance

futile

intend to

think back

agree

Drill 1 Grammar

......, -ing ......

문장 중간에 '-ing' 형태가 있는데 앞에 있는 명사를 꾸며 주는 분사의 후위수식이 아닌 경우가 있다. 콤마(,)를 찍어주는 게 보통이지만, 소설이나 수필, 영자신문 같은 곳에 서는 콤마(,)를 찍지 않는 경우가 더 많다. '~하면서'로 해석하며 실제 많은 영문을 통해 문장을 정확히 이해해야 한다. 보통은 주절의 동작과 같이 행해지는 동시동작을 나타낸다고 설명한다.

• I handed in my paper, leaving the question blank.   나는 그 문제를 공백으로 남긴 채 시험지를 제출했다.

• The boy sat watching television, playing computer games, and listening to the radio instead of studying.   그 소년은 공부하는 것 대신 앉아서 텔레비전을 보고 컴퓨터 게임을 하고 라디오를 듣고 있었다.

1   The ash continued to fall for two days, covering Pompeii completely. And so the town slept for 1,700 years, under a 30-foot blanket of volcanic ash.

해석 ◐ _____

2   The earthquake came and went quickly, causing great human and financial casualties. After three days, the city still had not been able to function normally.

해석 ◐ _____

3   그는 집에 돌아오는 아들을 기다리면서 책을 읽었다. (wait for, come home, read, a book)

영작 ◐ _____

Drill 2 Translation

1   1번 문장 ◐ _____

2   2번 문장 ◐ _____

3   3번 문장 ◐ _____

4   4번 문장 ◐ _____

[1]There are so many reasons why people need to work. There are some people who work, not necessarily for money or any other material values, but for their own joy or self-satisfaction. [2]A good example of those who could not live without working might be Wolfgang Amadeus Mozart, one of the greatest composers in history. He could care less about money as long as he could buy a piece of paper and some ink to write music. Another good example is Jack

London. [3]Jack London, an American writer, devoted his whole life to writing stories about ordinary people who tried their best to achieve their goals in life. In addition, Roald Amundsen, the great Norwegian explorer, spent his whole life exploring the world. He was the first person who reached both the North and the South Pole. The people mentioned here tried to get excitement through their work. [4]They considered work as a means of amusement. It made their life enjoyable; it gave them reasons to live. In other words, _____ were the same for them.

---

1 **Choose the best phrase to fill in the blank.**

① work and play
② life and work
③ truth and life
④ work and honor
⑤ joy and effort

2 **From this paragraph, what can we know about the three people?**

① They were the best in their fields.
② They all sought the truth of life.
③ They all worked for money.
④ They sacrificed their personal lives.
⑤ They worked for their own joy.

단어 조사해 오세요~ **Word**

necessarily

material value

self-satisfaction

composer

devote

ordinary

achieve

goal

explore

mention

means

amusement

 **Drill 1** Grammar

those who

> those who ~ (= people who ~)   ~하는 사람들
> he who ~ (= a man who ~)   ~하는 사람

- Heaven helps those who help themselves. 하늘은 스스로 돕는 자를 돕는다.
- Those who wish to travel in Asia must learn how to use chopsticks. If they do not, they may starve to death.
  아시아를 여행하고 싶어하는 사람들은 젓가락을 어떻게 사용하는지 배워야 한다. 만약 배우지 않으면 굶어 죽을지도 모른다.

---

1   Those who understand their own history and the history of the world, will have an easier time anticipating what will happen in the future.

   해석 ◯ _____

2   In regions where water is abundant, people fail to realize what a real luxury it is to those who live where it is scarce.

   해석 ◯ _____

3   다른 사람들을 도와주지 않는 사람들은 다른 이들의 도움을 받지 못할 것이다. (help, others, won't be helped)

   영작 ◯ _____

Drill 2 Translation

1   1번 문장 ◯ _____

2   2번 문장 ◯ _____

3   3번 문장 ◯ _____

4   4번 문장 ◯ _____

Person A: Since people generally like what they are good at, I propose that our children focus on areas in which they excel. (a) To this end, we should test our children's aptitudes in various subject areas during their last year of elementary school. For example, if a child

scores well in science, he or she would then attend middle and high schools which specialize in science. (b) Such a system would prepare students for employment after high school as well as further specialized study at university. There is plenty of time in life for people to follow other interests. School should be a time for students to develop their strengths because _____.

Person B: I think it is rather unfair to decide our children's career paths based on the results of an aptitude test taken when they are 11 or 12 years old. (c) Areas which children are considered good at in sixth grade may not be the same ones in which they excel by the end of their senior year. (d) Secondary school should be a time for expanding horizons – not limiting them. (e) Since educational expenses are rising, students should graduate from school as soon as possible. The only thing students should be required to do is to study a broad range of subjects throughout middle and high school. By the end of high school they would have a much better idea of what they would like to study at university. The time for specialized study is in university and graduate school, not earlier.

기출

1 이 두 글의 핵심 쟁점으로 가장 적절한 것은?

① the time to decide the students' field of study
② types of special education for children
③ teacher's role in secondary education
④ the number of majors at university
⑤ ways of improving aptitude tests

2 Person A의 빈칸에 들어갈 말로 가장 적절한 것은?

① today's world requires specialists, not generalists
② higher salaries attract highly qualified teachers
③ students need to excel on their aptitude tests
④ science majors need a strong background in humanities
⑤ after-school programs require active student participation

3 이 두 글의 내용과 일치하는 것은?

① A는 언어 능력보다 수리 능력의 중요성을 강조한다.
② A는 어릴 때의 적성과 능력은 중요하지 않다고 믿는다.
③ B는 국가의 미래를 위해 조기 영재교육을 지지한다.
④ B는 초등학교 적성 검사 결과에 따른 전공 선택을 지지한다.
⑤ B는 중·고교에서 다양한 교과를 배워야 한다고 주장한다.

4 (a)~(e) 중, 이 글의 전체 흐름과 관계 <u>없는</u> 문장은?

① (a)　　② (b)　　③ (c)　　④ (d)　　⑤ (e)

Word 단어 조사해 오셔~

generally

be good at

excel

end

aptitude

specialize in

plenty of

unfair

expand

secondary school

horizon

range

graduate school

generalist

qualified

humanity

It has been claimed that without language, our society could not have developed as much as it has. It would be impossible for people to live together.

Let's imagine that we did not have any linguistic ability. If we didn't have written or spoken languages, our society would be in big trouble. Because our modern methods of (A) _____ heavily rely upon the use of language, these methods would not be available. There would be no letters, e-mails, websites, newspapers, telephones, radios, or televisions. In addition, there wouldn't be any public services, such as schools, libraries, courts, or hospitals, since communication is also necessary for all of these services.

Second, we would have no modern means of (B) _____. The operators of trains, ships, automobiles, or airplanes must strictly follow written directions and oral communication to avoid any possible disasters. If there was no language, no transportation would be safe.

Third, our complex exchange of goods would also not exist. Without the help of language, merchants cannot sell their goods, and without transportation, they cannot ship their merchandise. We suspect that people in prehistory did not have written or spoken language. Can you tell how different their world was from our world? Maybe, you can't. Because no written or spoken language existed, there was no means of keeping (C) _____ which would have described the lifestyle of prehistoric people. We can only guess how these people lived without words from the few things they left behind.

1 Choose the best words to fill in the blank in (A), (B), (C).

	(A)		(B)		(C)
①	records	⋯	transportation	⋯	communication
②	records	⋯	communication	⋯	transportation
③	communication	⋯	transportation	⋯	records
④	communication	⋯	records	⋯	transportation
⑤	transportation	⋯	records	⋯	communication

2 Choose the best title for this paragraph.

① The Importance of Technology
② The Importance of Language
③ The Importance of Transportation
④ The Necessity of International Trade
⑤ The Change of Spoken and Written Language

3 Which sentence best summarizes this passage?

① Language occupies a great position in our society.
② People should learn as many languages as they can.
③ Knowing many languages leads to successful career.
④ Language is the most important task for our study.
⑤ Prehistoric people must have had inconvenient lives without languages.

4 이 글의 내용과 일치하지 <u>않는</u> 것은?

① Linguistic ability helps avoid disasters.
② It is certain that there were no languages in prehistory.
③ The operators must follow directions and communication precisely.
④ Without modern methods, there would be no public services.
⑤ International business wouldn't be possible without languages.

Review 😊

A **Translate into English.**

1 체육관 _____

2 기술 _____

3 거친, 불쾌한 _____

4 따라잡다 _____

5 노력 _____

6 강압적인 _____

7 무익한, 헛된 _____

8 동의하다 _____

9 부득이, 할 수 없이 _____

10 성취하다, 획득하다 _____

11 목표 _____

12 수단 _____

13 일반적으로 _____

14 확대하다 _____

15 부당한, 불공정한 _____

16 범위, 영역 _____

17 주장하다 _____

18 상상하다 _____

19 교환 _____

20 재난, 참사 _____

B **Translate into Korean.**

1 dribble _____

2 make fun _____

3 keep practicing _____

4 teammate _____

5 extreme _____

6 resistance _____

7 intend to _____

8 think about _____

9 explore _____

10 amusement _____

11 mention _____

12 devote _____

13 excel _____

14 end _____

15 graduate school _____

16 qualified _____

17 operator _____

18 transportation _____

19 merchant _____

20 rely upon _____

C **Choose the correct answers to each question.**

1 Some people quit smoking through _____ effort.
① futile   ② addiction
③ extreme   ④ reality

2 Jack London, an American writer, _____ his whole life to writing stories about ordinary people.
① means   ② devoted
③ mentioned ④ amused

3 Many employers have recognized that age discrimination is _____.
① qualified ② generally
③ unfair   ④ aptitude

D **Translate into English or Korean.**

1 The next day, he saw the girl playing with someone else so he stayed far away from her.

_____

_____

2 Recently, a severe disease hit Asian nations hard, causing several hundred deaths.

_____

_____

3 결코 성공하지 못하는 사람들은 너무 빨리 그만두는 사람들이다. (those, never, make it)

_____

are the ones who quit too soon.

E **Choose the correct words to fill in the blanks.**

1 I took my seat which was directly in front of the man _____ by the window.
① sitting   ② sit
③ sat   ④ being sat

2 If schools only provide knowledge, however, they may destroy creativity, _____ ordinary people.
① produced   ② being produced
③ produce   ④ producing

3 Among _____ go to sea there are the explorers who discover new worlds, adding continents to the Earth and stars to the heavens.
① those   ② who those
③ those who   ④ who

4 Ask _____ know if you do not know.
① people   ② them
③ those who   ④ me

F **Choose the proper word for each sentence.**

1 He was trying to [expend / expand] his business.

2 We [expended / expanded] a great deal of time in this project.

3 These robots will [explode / explore] the lunar surface, mapping out landing sites and places for human exploration.

4 Everybody is trying to establish a new brand and [exploit / explode] it.

CHAPTER 7	DATE	SELF CHECK	TEACHER	PARENTS
Preview				
Unit 1				
Unit 2				
Unit 3				
Unit 4				
Unit 5				
Review				

SURVIVOR에서 우승하면 100만 달러! 어때요?

SURVIVOR에서 우승하면 100만 달러! 어때요?1999년 미국 최고의 시청률(audience rating) 기록을 세운 TV 프로그램은 서바이버(SURVIVOR)였습니다. 이 프로그램에 대해 얘기하자면 한 섬 안에서 생존 게임을 펼쳐 수천만 미국인들을 TV 앞에 고정시켰던 엿보기(voyeurism) 프로그램의 일종이었습니다. 서바이버는 100만 불이라는 거액의 상금을 걸어놓고 미국 전역에서 모집한 남녀노소 16~20명을 세계 곳곳의 오지에 가둬두고 매 주 한 명씩 탈락시키며 최후의 1인을 가리는 리얼리티 쇼입니다. 게임의 초반에는 보통 2개의 그룹으로 나누어 그룹간 경쟁을 통해 진 그룹에서 1명을 탈락시키며, 10명 정도가 남은 상황에서 두 그룹을 통합시킨 후 개인 대결을 벌입니다. 많은 게임들이 기본적으로 체력적인 대결이기 때문에 강인한 체력은 가장 중요한 요소의 하나이지만, 종종 등장하는 퀴즈게임 등에서는 지능과 기억력 또한 필요합니다. 또한 팀 대결이니 만큼 팀원들의 팀워크 또한 중요하며, 게임이 이뤄지는 짧은 순간을 제외하고는 오지에서 스스로의 힘에 의해 기본적인 생활을 영위해야 하는 만큼, 근면함, 야외에서의 생활능력 등 다양한 능력이 요구됩니다. 하지만 이 모든 것보다 중요한 것이 사교성으로 대표되는 사회적 능력인데, 결국 최종 우승을 이뤄내기 위해서는 다른 사람들의 투표에 의해 추방당하지 않아야 되기 때문입니다. 이 프로그램의 참가자들은 끝까지 살아남아야겠다는 일념 하에 어떠한 원시적 행동도 서슴지 않을 정도였습니다. 서바이버 '호주의 오지(the Australian Outback)' 편을 방영했을 때도 이 프로그램은 최고의 시청률을 자랑하며 인정받았습니다. 이 프로그램은 사생활에 대해 굉장히 예민한 미국인들에게 남의 사생활을 엿보게 해주는 프로그램이므로 시청률의 성공적인 성과를 올릴 수밖에 없었습니다. 서바이버가 재미있는 이유는 사람들과의 인간관계속에서 벌어지는 이기심이나 역경을 같이 이겨내는 인간들의 아름다운 모습을 설정 없는 모습 그대로 담아내기 때문입니다.

CHAPTER
08

Word 🏠 단어도 모르면서 영어 한다 하지 마!

- **party** *n.* 파티, 일행, 정당, 상대방
- **supreme** *a.* 최고의, 최상의 *n.* 최고의 것
- **crack** *n.* 틈, 날카로운 소리, 시도
- **steep** *a.* 가파른, 엄청난 *n.* 낭떠러지
- **official** *n.* 공무원 *a.* 공식의, 공무의
- **vegan** *n.* 완전 채식주의자
- **bank** *n.* 은행, 둑, 제방
- **reluctant** *a.* 마음이 내키지 않는
- **mirage** *n.* 신기루, 망상
- **foresee** *v.* 예견하다, 선경지명이 있다

- **mythical** *a.* 신화의, 상상의, 근거 없는
- **exhaust** *v.* 소진(피폐)시키다 *n.* 배기가스
- **ridiculous** *a.* 웃기는, 터무니없는
- **appeal** *v.* 간청하다, 항소하다 *n.* 애원
- **modify** *v.* 변경하다, 조절하다, 수식하다
- **dominate** *v.* 지배하다, 억누르다
- **excavate** *v.* 굴을 파다, 발굴하다
- **slope** *v.* 경사지다 *n.* 비탈, 경사도
- **enormous** *a.* 거대한, 엄청난
- **vent** *n.* 배출구, 분출구 *v.* 발산하다

⁚⁚ Mini Quiz

Draw a line from each word on the left to its definition on the right. Then, use the numbered words to fill in the blanks in the sentences below.

1 oxygen   **a.** to save someone or something from a situation of danger or harm

2 sacred   **b.** to burst out suddenly or violently

3 rescue   **c.** very important or greatly respected

4 tournament   **d.** to happen or exist in a particular place or situation

5 occur   **e.** a competition in which players compete against each other in a series of games until there is one winner

6 erupt   **f.** a gas that is present in air and is necessary for most animals and plants to live

7 The soccer player surpassed himself at the _____.

8 My nettle rash has _____ again.

9 We yawn to gulp in extra _____.

10 Survivors of the crash were _____ by helicopter.

11 The explosion _____ at 5:30 a.m.

12 Certain animals were considered _____.

Grammar 🙎 기본 문법도 모르면서 독해 한다 하지 마!

★ 〈It is ~ to부정사 / that절〉은 부정사나 that절을 주어로 해석한다.

The more contact a group has with another group, the more likely **it is that** objects or idea will be exchanged.
한 그룹이 다른 그룹과 더 많이 접촉할수록, 사물이나 생각은 더 활발히 교류될 수 있다.

Why is **it that** if you tickle yourself, it doesn't tickle, but if someone else tickles you, you cannot stand it?   자기가 자신을 간질이면 안 간지럽고, 다른 사람이 간질이면 참을 수 없는 것은 왜 그럴까요?

★ 〈to be p.p.〉 vs 〈to 동사원형〉 준동사에서도 수동의 의미인지 능동의 의미인지 구별해야 한다.

Some of us have faith that we shall solve our food problems with genetically modified crops newly or soon **to be developed**.
우리들 몇 명은 새롭게 개발된 또는 머지않아 개발될 유전자 변형 곡물로 식량문제를 해결할 것이라는 믿음을 가지고 있다.

★ 〈It is(was) + 강조어구 + that / which / who / whom / when / where〉

It is those explorers, through their unceasing trial and error, **who** have paved the way for us to follow.   끊임없는 시행착오에도 불구하고 우리가 따라 나아갈 길을 마련해온 것은 바로 그런 탐험가들이다.

:: Mini Quiz

1   다음 괄호 안에서 알맞은 것을 고르시오.

[This / It] is expensive for me to study abroad.

2   다음 괄호 안에서 알맞은 것을 고르시오.

The team may be familiar or unfamiliar with the tools [to use / to be used] on the project.

3   다음 괄호 안에서 알맞은 것을 고르시오.

It was yesterday [when / where] the most unpopular boy came to me and said he had a girlfriend.

The two men started at 4 a.m. The way led from Camp V, at 28,720 feet, to the top. [1] The last 300 feet led up a steep, narrow ridge. For eight hours they clawed their way up the ice. Winds of 110 miles an hour tore at them. First roaring gusts; then eerie silence. They were on oxygen, but each step was a supreme effort. Shortly after 12 noon on June 2, 1953, [2] Edmund Hillary and Tenzing Norkay, his Sherpa guide, pulled themselves to the top of the world, Mount Everest. A newsman had climbed part of the way up with Hillary's party. [3] When Hillary came down the newsman asked him, "Why did you do it?" "Because it was there," said the tall New Zealander. Twelve years later, Edmund Hillary took another crack at what made him try the risky climb. He wrote a book about his life. In it, he said: "You don't have to be a far-out hero to do great things. You can be an ordinary chap. The main thing is _____ _____. I never liked the danger of climbing. [4] But danger makes you give everything you've got. And that, strangely enough, is a very pleasant thing."

1 **Choose the most suitable answer to fill in the blank.**

① that your challenge provides an opportunity to develop your talent
② how much you like Mount Everest
③ how much you want to do it
④ how many people you meet on the mountain
⑤ how much you want to be a professional climber

2 이 글의 주제로 가장 적절한 것은?

① 최초로 에베레스트 산을 올라가는 것은 쉽지 않은 일이다.
② 도전적인 사람만이 꿈을 이룰 수 있다.
③ 험난한 산일수록 등반의 어려움이 더 많다.
④ 모든 것을 걸고 도전해 볼 때 성공할 수 있다.
⑤ 여러 사람이 함께 힘을 모으면 이루지 못할 것이 없다.

단어 조사해 오세요~ **Word**

lead up

steep

ridge

claw one's way up

eerie

on oxygen

supreme effort

pull themselves to the top

party

crack

far-out

chap

danger

Drill 1 Grammar

had + p.p.

과거완료〈had + p.p.〉는 기준 시점이 과거이다. 따라서 문맥이나 문장 안의 시간을 나타내는 부사를 통해서 기준시점인 과거를 나타내는 표현이 있어야 하며, 현재를 나타내는 표현과는 함께 사용되지 못한다. 한편, 특정 과거시점보다 먼저 일어난 일은 '대과거'로〈had + p.p.〉를 써서 표현한다. 우리말에는 없는 표현이기 때문에 문법적으로 끼워 맞춰서 해석하기보다는 '과거'로 해석해 주는 게 더 매끄럽다.

- Arthur was running out of money, because he had bought an expensive birthday gift for Jack. Arthur는 돈을 다 써가고 있었다. 왜냐하면 그는 Jack을 위해 비싼 생일 선물을 사버렸기 때문이다.

- Robert was going steady with Susan and was thinking of marrying her. He wanted to know what kinds of girls her sisters were, what her father was like, and how long her mother had been dead. Robert는 Susan과 사귀어 왔고 그녀와 결혼할 생각이었다. 그는 그녀의 여동생들이 어떤 사람인지, 아버지는 어떤 분인지, 그녀의 어머니는 돌아가신지 얼마나 되었는지 알고 싶어 했다.

---

1   All the ghost stories that he had heard in the evening now returned to his memory.

   해석 ◯ _____

2   We found that we had hit a car coming from the other direction.

   해석 ◯ _____

3   내가 전에 그녀의 끔찍한 얼굴을 봤기 때문에, 나는 그녀를 한번에 알아봤다.
   (her terrible face, recognized, at once, had seen, before)

   영작 ◯ _____

Drill 2 Translation

1   1번 문장 ◯ _____

2   2번 문장 ◯ _____

3   3번 문장 ◯ _____

4   4번 문장 ◯ _____

There are many religions, such as Buddhism, Christianity, Hinduism, Judaism, or Islam, in the world. [1] In India, there are some people who follow Islam, Christianity, Sikhism, Buddhism, and many other religions, but the official religion of India is Hinduism. Most Hindus believe that all living things have souls.

Therefore, many Indian people feel reluctant to kill and eat animals. [2] Some Hindus are vegans, so they eat neither meat nor any dairy products like cheese, eggs or milk. However, most Hindus eat poultry and fish, but not other kinds of meat. [3] It is illegal to eat beef in India, for cows are considered as sacred animals among Hindus. It is not unusual to see a cow wandering the streets of an Indian city. The Ganges River is considered sacred and worshiped by Hindus. Hindus believe the water from the Himalayas, which is the source of the Ganges, purifies one's soul. So the followers of Hinduism make a pilgrimage to the Ganges to drink the water and, sometimes, bathe. [4] Often, people who expect to die soon come to the river in order to purify their souls before "rebirth." As a result, there are many people who die near the banks of the Ganges River.

1 **Choose a word to replace the underlined word rebirth.**

① birthday   ② revival   ③ Hinduism
④ eternity   ⑤ worship

2 **Choose an answer that is a part of the characteristics of Hindus.**

① They despise other religions such as Buddhism, Christianity, Hinduism, Judaism, or Islam.
② They do not visit the Ganges River until they get old.
③ They feel disinclined to kill and eat animals.
④ Hinduism is an official religion of India.
⑤ They do not drink the water of the Ganges River.

단어 조사해 오셔~ **Word**

religion
official
soul
reluctant
vegan
dairy product
poultry
sacred
wander
purify
pilgrimage
bank

 **Drill 1** Grammar

접속사 for

for는 보통 전치사로 사용되는 경우가 보통이지만, 접속사로 사용될 때 '~때문에' 라는 뜻의 'because' 의 뜻이 있다. 물론 구문 상 드러나는 특징은 문장 중간에 콤마(,)로 분리되어 나오는 for이며, 그리고 콤마(,)가 없을 때는 for 뒤에 주어, 동사가 연이어 나오는 것을 보면 알 수 있다.

- I decided to stop and have lunch, for I was feeling quite hungry.
  나는 멈추어 점심을 먹기로 결정했는데, 왜냐하면 나는 아주 허기를 느끼고 있었기 때문이다.

- The little children always slept with the light on, for they were afraid of ghosts and witches. 귀신과 마녀를 무서워했기 때문에, 어린아이들은 항상 불을 켠 채로 잤다.

---

1   The old man loved to talk about France with anyone who would listen, for he had been there as a young soldier during World War II.

  해석 ◯ _____

2   Because he lived through the Great Depression, the man did not trust banks. He considered himself a lucky man, for he kept all his money at home and never paid for anything with credit.

  해석 ◯ _____

3   온도가 매우 낮아서 겨울처럼 느껴진다. (the temperature, low, so, feel like, it)

  영작 ◯ _____

 Drill 2 Translation

1   1번 문장 ◯ _____

2   2번 문장 ◯ _____

3   3번 문장 ◯ _____

4   4번 문장 ◯ _____

In the sea, there live beautiful creatures named mermaids. [1] A mermaid has an upper body which resembles that of a human female, but she has the tail of a fish instead of two legs. Mermaids live in a beautiful castle deep under the sea. [2] Their beautiful faces and voices often seduce sailors who jump into the sea and eventually drown. _____, sometimes, they are kind enough to rescue sailors who fall into the water during storms. They also have supernatural powers to foresee the future.

Do mermaids actually exist? Are those fascinating stories about the mermaids real? [3] Actually, mermaids are mythical creatures, just like unicorns and fairies which only exist in folklore and myths. Almost every culture has interesting stories about the origins of mermaids. [4] In many cultures, it is believed that exhausted sailors saw a mirage or a sea creature in the distance and thought it had a human face. Since no human can survive in the sea, they assumed that it might have fins instead of legs.

1 **Choose the best answer to fill in the blank.**

① As a result   ② Similarly   ③ However
④ That is   ⑤ To begin with

2 이 글에서 밑줄 친 in the distance의 의미로 알맞은 것은?

① within approach
② far away
③ to a great extent
④ in a big space
⑤ very close

단어 조사해 오셔~ **Word**

creature

mermaid

upper body

seduce

rescue

sailor

supernatural

foresee

mythical

exhaust

mirage

assume

fin

🍴 Drill 1 Grammar

enough to do

보통 enough 하면 모든 학생들이 '충분히'의 뜻만을 알고 있다. 물론 enough가 명사를 단독으로 수식할 경우 '충분히'의 뜻이지만, to부정사와 함께 쓰일 때는 '~할 정도로'의 뜻으로 해석하는게 좋다.

• The pungsan dog of North Korea is brave enough to fight with a tiger.

북한의 풍산개는 호랑이와 싸울 정도로 용감하다.

• This book is easy enough for a ten-year-old child to read. 이 책은 열 살 먹은 아이가 읽을 정도로 쉽다.

---

1 He was adventurous enough to cross the Pacific in a small yacht by himself.

해석 ⊙ _____

2 After refining and improving the program, the computer engineers were confident enough to present it to Microsoft Corporation.

해석 ⊙ _____

3 Karen은 겨울 방학 동안 그녀가 원한 모든 나라를 여행할 정도로 부자였다.
(rich, any country, wish, form winter vacation, tour)

영작 ⊙ _____

🍴 Drill 2 Translation

1 1번 문장 ⊙ _____

2 2번 문장 ⊙ _____

3 3번 문장 ⊙ _____

4 4번 문장 ⊙ _____

(A)

Not everyone is in favor of using (a) the big ball, however. Some players, such as hard hitting, six-time Wimbledon champ Pete Sampras, call the change "simply ridiculous." Also, aside from modifying the current game, there is some concern that players may _____ as they swing harder tying to draw more speed out of the ball.

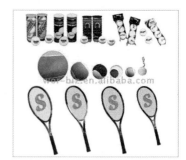

(B)

In short, the game has (b) little action. Top male players play for an average of only four minutes per hour on grass, according to recent studies. The hope is that the introduction of the new, bigger ball will cause first-class games to be dominated again by play involving (c) skill and artistry remindful of players like Bjorn Borg, Jimmy Connors and John McEnroe.

(C)

Tennis is in some trouble. People seem to be losing interest in the game. One major reason for this is that the men's professional game has lost some of its appeal. The pro game has become a contest of (d) strength, where powerful hitters with their high-tech rackets dominate. At Wimbledon, for example, Britain's Greg Rusedski hit the ball at 138 mph, the fastest recorded serve for the tournament. As a result of (e) this speed, very few points last more than three shots – serve, return and winning point.

(기출)

1 (A), (B), (C)를 이어 하나의 글로 구성할 때 가장 적절한 순서는?

① (A) - (B) - (C)
② (A) - (C) - (B)
③ (B) - (A) - (C)
④ (C) - (A) - (B)
⑤ (C) - (B) - (A)

2 (a)~(e) 중, 밑줄 친 <u>some of its appeal</u> 에 해당하는 것으로 가장 적절한 것은?

① (a)　　　② (b)　　　③ (c)　　　④ (d)　　　⑤ (e)

3 **What is the passage mainly about?**

① The decreasing popularity of tennis and a possible solution
② Arguments about changing the size of the ball
③ Comments from world famous tennis players
④ Shortage of average time played on grass
⑤ Advantages of the powerful hitters

4 **Choose the best answer to fill in the blank.**

① suffer headache and stomachache
② experience an unexpected power
③ suffer from an impediment in player's speech
④ suffer arm and ligament injuries
⑤ suffer from mental sickness

impediment 장애 | ligament 인대

(A)

It was Mount Vesuvius which destroyed Pompeii, the famous ancient Roman city. On August 24, 79 AD, Pompeii was covered with volcanic ash and dust. The city was rediscovered in 1748 and has since been excavated. However, not all volcanoes are as explosive as Mount Vesuvius or Mount Pelee. Some  volcanoes, like Stromboli in the Mediterranean Lipari Islands or Mount Etna, erupt regularly. Some volcanoes do not show any sign of volcanic activity for many years. These are called dormant volcanoes. Still other volcanoes are thought to be dead. They are called 'extinct.' Most volcanoes are found where two tectonic plates are pulled apart or come together.

(B)

Mostly, the flowing speed of lava determines _____ of a volcanic mountain. This speed is determined by the temperature of lava. Hot temperatures make the lava more liquid so it flows faster, forming gentle mountain slopes. Colder and more solid lava makes steeper slopes. Highly explosive volcanoes, such as Krakatoa, shoot largely gas, ash and pumice, but little lava.

(C)

Apparently, a volcano is a mountain which has a large opening on the top. Through the opening, molten rocks and gases come out with enormous force. Hot gases and molten rocks escape from below the Earth's crust through the opening of a volcano. Lava, the molten rock, comes from 30 to 60 kilometers below the ground.

(D)

Mount Pelee on the Caribbean Island of Martinique is one of the world's biggest explosive volcanoes. Until 1902, the town of St. Pierre sat peacefully at the mountain's base. However, on one morning of 1902, a volcanic eruption occurred. A fiery blast of steam and ash was shot out of the vent with a crashing roar and in less than a minute, the peaceful town turned into ash.

1 (A), (B), (C), (D)의 글을 하나의 글로 구성할 때 가장 적절한 순서는?

① (A) - (C) - (D) - (B)

② (D) - (C) - (A) - (B)

③ (B) - (A) - (D) - (C)

④ (C) - (B) - (D) - (A)

⑤ (A) - (B) - (C) - (D)

2 Choose the best answer to fill in the blank (B).

① the size

② the eruption

③ the height

④ the characteristic

⑤ the steepness

3 Choose the best description of a volcano.

① Volcano flows down the mountain and it is always fatal.

② Volcanoes exist in many mountains of the world.

③ Volcano is an opening in the Earth's crust through which hot gases and molten rock are erupted or blown out.

④ Every volcano shows several signs of volcanic activity.

⑤ The enormous force of the gas make volcanoes erupt.

4 Which of the following is true from the passage?

① Molten rocks come from below the earth's crust.

② Most of the volcanoes erupt regularly.

③ The flowing speed is determined by gas.

④ Volcanoes that have shown no sign of activity for many years are called 'explosive.'

⑤ Krakatoa is not a highly explosive volcano.

단어 조사해 오세요~ **Word**

destroy

be covered with

volcanic ash

excavate

erupt

volcanic activity

dormant volcano

extinct

tectonic plate

flowing speed

lava

steepness

temperature

gentle

slope

molten rock

enormous

earth's crust

occur

fiery blast

shot out

vent

crashing roar

Review ☺

A **Translate into English.**

1 가파른 언덕 _____
2 섬뜩한 _____
3 일행 _____
4 위험 _____
5 종교 _____
6 어슬렁거리다 _____
7 신성한 _____
8 영혼 _____
9 생물체 _____
10 기진맥진하다 _____
11 지느러미 _____
12 인어 _____
13 우스운, 어처구니없는 _____
14 매력, 호소력 _____
15 대회, 승자 진출전 _____
16 최근에 _____
17 분화하다 _____
18 활동을 멈춘 _____
19 용암 _____
20 거대한 _____

B **Translate into Korean.**

1 lead up _____
2 ridge _____
3 on oxygen _____
4 dominate _____
5 Judaism _____
6 Buddhism _____
7 reluctant _____
8 purify _____
9 seduce _____
10 supernatural _____
11 mythical _____
12 mirage _____
13 in favor of _____
14 aside from _____
15 modify _____
16 artistry _____
17 dormant volcano _____
18 excavate _____
19 volcanic ash _____
20 molten rock _____

C **Choose the correct answers to each question.**

1 She seemed _____ to go with him because she was very tired.
   ① sacred   ② reluctant
   ③ pilgrimage   ④ official

2 Few analysts _____ that oil prices would rise so steeply.
   ① seduced   ② dominated
   ③ foresaw   ④ excavated

3 Water boils at a(n) _____ of 100˚C.
   ① temperature   ② steep
   ③ erupt   ④ slope

D **Translate into English or Korean.**

1 The secretary reported that the following projects had been approved.

   _____

2 She must be very happy with the news, for she is singing.

   _____

   _____

3 일본의 고령인구가 늘어나는 현상은 그들이 여전히 일을 계속하기에 충분히 젊다는 결정을 내리게 했다. (keep -ing, still, young)
   An increasing number of elderly people in Japan are deciding that _____

   _____ .

E **Choose the correct words to fill in the blanks.**

1 The authorities found documents in the car which _____ to the terrorist.
   ① have belonged   ② belong
   ③ belonging   ④ had belonged

2 Let me stay here for a while, _____ I am so exhausted.
   ① that   ② for
   ③ therefore   ④ but

3 They were rich _____ afford high-cost private tuition or send their children overseas to study.
   ① so   ② to enough
   ③ enough to   ④ too to

4 Engineers make skyscrapers _____ to withstand earthquakes, high wind, and severe changes in temperature.
   ① strong enough   ② enough strong
   ③ too strong   ④ so strong

F **Choose the proper word for each sentence.**

1 [Dairy / Daily] products are generally defined as foodstuffs produced from milk.

2 Please contact us to get more information of our [dairy / daily] products for kitchens, bathrooms, restaurants and so on.

3 He was found [wandering / wondering] the streets of New York.

4 I was [wandering / wondering] if you'd like to come to dinner.

CHAPTER 8	DATE	SELF CHECK	TEACHER	PARENTS
Preview				
Unit 1				
Unit 2				
Unit 3				
Unit 4				
Unit 5				
Review				

물고기는 왜 죽으면 배를 내밀까요?

 국제 야생 조수 및 어류 협회의 특별 기획팀 조사 결과 물고기는 죽으면 빨리 부패하는 현상을 보이는데, 속부터 썩어 점점 바깥으로 진행된다고 합니다. 물고기나 익사한 사람이 물위에 뜰 때 배가 위로 향하는 이유는 물고기의 경우 뱃속의 부레(공기 주머니)가 고기의 횡선 중심에서 아래쪽에 있으므로 등보다 가벼운 배가 위로 가는 것은 물리법칙 때문입니다. 부레는 저장된 공기의 양을 조절하여 뜨고 가라앉는 것을 조절합니다. 이 부레는 앞뒤로 긴 구조로 중간이 나뉘어져 잠수할 때는 앞쪽 주머니를 수축시켜 꼬리쪽이 올라가게 하고 수면으로 올라올 때는 뒷쪽 주머니를 수축시켜 머리 부분이 올라가게 합니다. 물고기들이 깊은 바다에서도 자유롭게 생활할 수 있는 이유도 부레가 있고 또 큰 역할을 하기 때문입니다. 부레에는 가는 혈관이 많이 모여 있는데, 이 혈관이 모여 만들어진 적샘이라는 구조에서 혈액 속의 산소나 이산화탄소를 부레 속으로 내보냅니다. 이 적샘에서 이산화탄소가 많이 나오면, 부레는 부풀어 오릅니다. 또, 부레 윗부분에 난원샘이라는 기관이 있어서 이산화탄소를 빨아들일 수 있습니다. 물고기들은 이 기관들을 조절하여 몸의 균형을 조절합니다. 그러나 물고기가 죽고 나면 부레나 지느러미도 제기능을 다할 수 없게 됩니다. 또 죽은 물고기가 머리를 물에 담근 채 떠있는 것도 자주 보는 일입니다. 이 이유는 물고기의 머리는 매우 무겁고 그에 비해 꼬리는 훨씬 가벼워서입니다. 때로는 어떤 종류의 물고기들은 부레가 없어서 그냥 바다에 가라앉기도 합니다.

CHAPTER

09

Word 🏠 단어도 모르면서 영어 한다 하지 마!

- **glow** *n.* 백열,홍조 *v.* 빛을 내다, 빛나다
- **vessel** *n.* 배, 용기, 관
- **whereas** *conj.* ~에 반하여, 그러나
- **reflect** *v.* 반사하다, 반영하다
- **controversy** *n.* 논쟁, 언쟁, 논의
- **acknowledge** *v.* 인정하다, 감사하다
- **trigger** *n.* 방아쇠, 계기 *v.* 유발하다
- **intense** *a.* 강렬한, 격렬한, 긴장된
- **placate** *v.* 달래다, 진정시키다
- **devote** *v.* 바치다, 쏟다, 봉납하다

- **treat** *v.* 간주하다, 치료하다 *n.* 대접
- **combination** *n.* 결합, 배합, 단체
- **vital** *a.* 생명의, 치명적인 *n.* 핵심
- **reanimate** *v.* 소생시키다, 부활시키다
- **spontaneous** *a.* 자발적인, 임의의, 무의식적인
- **metabolism** *n.* 물질대사, 신진대사
- **occupation** *n.* 직업, 종사, 점령, 주거
- **consume** *v.* 소비하다, 소멸하다, 먹다
- **circulate** *v.* 순환하다, 돌리다, 퍼지다
- **synthesize** *v.* 종합하다, 합성하다

⁞⁞ Mini Quiz

Draw a line from each word on the left to its definition on the right. Then, use the numbered words to fill in the blanks in the sentences below.

1   layer

2   extinct

3   shorten

4   injection

5   nutrient

6   significance

a. an animal or plant that does not exist any more

b. an amount or piece of a material or substance that covers a surface or that is between two other things

c. a chemical or food that provides what is needed for plants or animals to live and grow

d. the quality of having importance

e. to become shorter or make something shorter

f. an act of putting a drug into someone's body using a special needle

7   His name is often _____ to Pat.

8   A thick _____ of dust lay on the furniture.

9   They did not comprehend the _____ of his remark.

10   Dinosaurs have been _____ for millions of years.

11   The nurse gave me a flu _____ .

Grammar 🎯 기본 문법도 모르면서 독해한다 하지 마!

★ this와 that이 부사로 사용되어 형용사를 꾸며 주는 경우

I've never been able to fall asleep **that** *fast* even when quite tired.

나는 매우 피곤할 때조차 그렇게 빨리 잠든 적이 없다.

It isn't like him to come home **this** *late*.　이렇게 늦게 집에 오는 것은 그 사람답지 않다.

★ ⟨a number of + 복수명사⟩는 복수 취급, ⟨the number of + 복수명사⟩는 단수 취급

There are **a number of** people who identify themselves specifically as "Taoist."

그들 자신을 특별히 도교 신자라고 말하는 많은 사람들이 있다.

I don't think **the number of** features is what makes software better or worse.

나는 기능의 수가 소프트웨어를 더 좋게 혹은 더 나쁘게 만드는 것이라고 생각하지 않는다.

★ ⟨that + 전치사⟩ vs ⟨those + 전치사⟩ 병렬구문에서 앞의 명사를 가리키는 지시대명사의 단/복수형

It is interesting to note that the author believes that **the conquest of** the South Pole was easier than **that of** the North Pole.

남극 정복이 북극의 그것보다 더 쉽다고 그 작가가 믿는다는 것을 주목하는 것은 흥미로운 일이다.

∷ Mini Quiz

1　다음 문장에서 <u>틀린</u> 부분을 찾아 바르게 고치시오.

Japan is not those expensive compared to other countries that tourists might visit.

2　다음 문장에서 <u>틀린</u> 부분을 찾아 바르게 고치시오.

Tell me a number of guests and I will calculate how many plates and cups we need.

3　다음 문장에서 <u>틀린</u> 부분을 찾아 바르게 고치시오.

Researchers at the University of Chicago compared the global warming impact of meat eaters with those of vegetarians.

[1] When it is dark, you may have seen *the eyes of dogs or cats* glowing. (a) Sometimes it scares people, because human eyes do not glow or shine in most cases. (b) [2] However, it is not that scary if you know the reason why their eyes seem to glow: their eyes can reflect light in the distance even when the light is not directly shining toward them. The light can be from car headlights, flashlights, light bulbs or anything else. Most animal eyes have a layer of crystalline substance which gives them the ability to reflect light. (c) Sometimes we see different colors in their eyes like red, blue or white. (d) [3] This color depends on the number of blood vessels in their eyes. (e) The eyes of an animal that has many blood vessels in them will glow red; whereas the eyes of an animal which has fewer vessels in them will glow white.

1 글의 흐름으로 보아, 주어진 문장이 들어가기에 가장 적절한 곳은?

> This ability is quite useful since it helps the animals see in the dark.

① (a)   ② (b)   ③ (c)   ④ (d)   ⑤ (e)

2 What makes the eyes of animals glow at night?

① Car headlights, flashlights, light bulb or anything else
② Blood vessels in their eyes
③ The crystalline substance in their eyes
④ Red and blue lights
⑤ All of the above

단어 조사해 오셔~ **Word**

glow

scare

scary

reflect

in the distance

directly

light bulb

layer

crystalline substance

the number of

blood vessel

whereas

 **Drill 1** Grammar

목적격보어 자리에 오는 -ing(현재분사)

사람의 감각을 나타내는 see, watch, hear, feel, notice, smell, taste 등의 동사는 목적격보어 자리에 동사원형이나 현재분사를 사용한다. 현재분사를 사용할 경우 목적어가 '동작, 행동'이 필요한 경우이기도 하지만, 그 행동의 '진행 중인 순간에 초점'을 맞추고 있거나, 그 동작의 '일부'를 표현할 때 사용한다.

- Through the train window, I could see *crops* ripening in the fields and *trees* turning red and yellow. 열차의 창문을 통해서, 나는 곡식이 들판에서 익어가고 나무들이 빨갛고 노랗게 물이 들어가는 것을 볼 수 있었다.

- Since we moved into this house, Jack and I have watched *you* grow from the little girl next door into a confident young woman.
  우리가 이 집으로 이사 온 이래로, Jack과 나는 네가 옆집의 어린 소녀에서 자신감 있는 젊은 여성으로 성장하는 것을 지켜보아 왔다.

1 The children saw the big spider swing on his web and heard the little bird singing.

해석 ◯ _____

2 No one on the ship saw the boy falling into the water a little after seven o'clock in the morning. I saw the whole accident with my own eyes.

해석 ◯ _____

3 나는 그녀가 이상하게 보이는 여자와 함께 거울 앞에서 춤을 추고 있는 것을 보았다.
   (watch, in front of, a strange-looking, mirror, dancing)

영작 ◯ _____

Drill 2 Translation

1 1번 문장 ◯ _____

2 2번 문장 ◯ _____

3 3번 문장 ◯ _____

[1] Dinosaurs (a) have been extinct for 65 million years, but the controversy over what killed them goes on, having apparently developed a life of its own. [2] Last week the Great Dinosaur Debate was in the news again, as scientists (b) sparred over two of the newer theories about the prehistoric doomsday. Scientists acknowledge that (c) the death of the fabled beasts triggered by the impact of a huge asteroid. With all these bright ideas, scientists are still a long way from knowing exactly how dinosaurs died. However, they present different views of the blast's disastrous aftermath. [3] One holds that clouds of sulfuric acid, resulting from the impact, (d) destroyed much of life on earth. [4] The other suggests that the collision also caused intense volcanic activity on the opposite side of the earth, (e) creating a double blow that made the extinctions inevitable.

---

1 이 글의 요지로 가장 적절한 것은?

① 공룡 멸종에 대한 과학적 이론
② 혜성 충돌 후에 공룡이 멸종 되었다는 이론
③ 혜성 충돌 여파로 인한 화산 활동이 멸종에 이르게 되었다는 견해
④ 공룡 멸종 원인에 관한 끊이지 않는 논쟁
⑤ 공룡 멸종 원인이 미래역사에 미치는 영향

2 (a)~(e) 중 어법상 어색한 것은?

① (a) ② (b) ③ (c) ④ (d) ⑤ (e)

단어 조사해 오셔~ **Word**

extinct

controversy

apparently

spar

prehistoric

doomsday

acknowledge

fabled

beast

trigger

asteroid

present

blast

disastrous

aftermath

sulfuric acid

collision

inevitable

 **Drill 1** Grammar

with all = for all

문장 맨 앞에 with all 의 구문이 나와서 양보의 부사구 역할을 할 때가 있다. '~임에도 불구하고' 라는 뜻으로 해석하며 in spite of와 같은 역할을 하게 된다.

- **With all** her faults, I still love her. 그녀의 결점에도 불구하고, 나는 그녀를 아직 사랑한다.

- It is not because he was lacking in ability but because he was lacking in sincerity, that **with all** his leaning he could not become respected by people.
  지식이 있음에도 불구하고 그가 사람들에게 존경을 받지 못하는 것은 그가 능력이 부족한 것이 아니라 성실성이 부족하기 때문이다.

---

1   With all his health problems, he lived to an old age. Everyday, he exercised, ate good food, and went to bed early.

     해석 ◎ _____

2   For all her poverty, she was not ashamed of herself.

     해석 ◎ _____

3   그의 높은 점수에도 불구하고 그는 대학에 갈 수 없었다. (his high test scores, university)

     영작 ◎ _____

Drill 2 Translation

1   1번 문장 ◎ _____

2   2번 문장 ◎ _____

3   3번 문장 ◎ _____

4   4번 문장 ◎ _____

The name Halloween is shortened from "All-hallow-eve," since it is the day before All Hallow's Day. [1] This is a festival held on October 31st to celebrate the end of the harvest season. Halloween has its origin in ancient Celtic culture. [2] The Celts believed that the gap between the world of the living and that of

the dead disappeared on October 31, and the dead would come back to life. They also believed that the deceased would bring them sickness. [3] Therefore, they held a huge festival at night in order to placate the ghosts and evil spirits which might look for living victims. They also wore masks so that the evil spirits could not find them. [4] The Romans also had a holiday in late October to celebrate their goddess Pomona, the goddess of fruits. Since the symbol of Pomona was an apple, candy apples became a common Halloween treat. Halloween seems to _____. In Western culture, people tell spooky tales and scare each other on Halloween night. Halloween has become a holiday devoted to witches and ghosts.

1 Which of the following is <u>NOT</u> true about Halloween?

① Halloween is a combination of the Roman and Celtic festivals.
② People placated the ghosts and evil spirits for their harvest.
③ The origin of the Halloween is from ancient Celtic culture.
④ Celts thought that there was a gap between the world of the living and the dead.
⑤ People wore masks so that the evil spirits could not recognize them.

2 Choose the best answer to fill in the blank.

① be proceeded by the tradition of Celtic
② terrify people on the day because something harmful always happened
③ be a combination of the Roman and Celtic festivals
④ be opening a gap between death and living theoretically
⑤ be affected a lot by the Roman customs

단어 조사해 오세요~ **Word**

shorten

celebrate

harvest season

Celtic

deceased

hold

placate

evil spirit

treat

combination

spooky

devoted to

 Drill 1 Grammar

... so that ~ 조동사

⟨so that ~ 조동사⟩는 ⟨in order to = so as to = 이동 동사 + to부정사⟩와 비슷한 역할을 한다. 문장 중간에 so that이 나와서 조동사 may, can, will 등과 함께 쓰이면 '~하기 위하여'로 해석한다.

• I got up early so that I might catch the first train. 나는 첫 기차를 타기 위해 일찍 일어났다.

• I make it a rule to read the newspaper every morning in order not to fall behind the times.
나는 시대에 뒤떨어지지 않기 위해 매일 아침 신문 읽는 것을 규칙으로 하고 있다.

1   Language exists in order that people may communicate with each other. Often, however, language can be a source of misunderstanding, both between individuals and between peoples.

해석 ◯ _____

2   The teacher spoke slowly so that the children could understand what he said.

해석 ◯ _____

3   그 도둑은 사람들이 그를 알아보지 못하게 하려고 검은 옷을 입었다. (the thief, recognize, so that, black)

영작 ◯ _____

 Drill 2 Translation

1   1번 문장 ◯ _____

2   2번 문장 ◯ _____

3   3번 문장 ◯ _____

4   4번 문장 ◯ _____

Modern scientists divide the process of dying into two phases, clinical or temporary death and biological death. Clinical death occurs when the vital organs, such as the heart, or lungs, have ceased to function, but have not suffered permanent damage. The organism (A) can still be revived / can still revive . Biological death occurs when changes in the organism lead to the disintegration of vital cells and tissues. Death is then irreversible and final.

Scientists have been seeking a way to prolong the period of clinical death so that the organism can be reanimated before biological death occurs. The best method developed so far involves cooling of the organism, combined with narcotic sleep. By (B) slow / slowing down the body's metabolism, cooling delays the processes leading to biological death.

To illustrate how this works, scientists performed an experiment on a six-year-old female baboon called Keta. The scientists put Keta to sleep with a narcotic. Then they surrounded her body with ice-bags and began checking her body temperature. When it had dropped to 28 degrees the scientists began draining blood from an artery. The monkey's blood pressure decreased and an hour later both the heart and respiration stopped; _____ _____ set in. For twenty minutes Keta remained in this state. Her temperature dropped to 22 degrees. At this point the scientists pumped blood into an artery in the direction of the heart and started artificial respiration. After two minutes the baboon's heart became active once more, after fifteen minutes, spontaneous respiration began, and after four hours Keta opened her eyes and lifted her head. After six hours, when the scientists tried to give her a penicillin injection, Keta seized the syringe and ran with it around the room. Her behavior differed little from (C) those / that of a healthy animal.

1 빈칸에 들어갈 내용으로 가장 적절한 것을 고르시오.

① biological death   ② clinical death

③ spontaneous respiration   ④ organ demage

⑤ changes in organism

2 (A), (B), (C)중에서, 어법에 맞는 표현을 골라 짝지은 것은?

	(A)		(B)		(C)
①	can still revive	…	slow	…	that
②	can still be revived	…	slow	…	those
③	can still be revived	…	slowing	…	that
④	can still revive	…	slowing	…	those
⑤	can still be revived	…	slowing	…	those

3 이 글을 통해 추론할 수 있는 결론으로 알맞은 것은?

① 무분별한 연구를 위해 동물을 죽여서는 안 된다.

② 생물학적 죽음과 임상적 죽음 두 가지에 아무런 상관관계가 없다.

③ 급속 냉각은 임상적 죽음에 이르는 과정을 지연시킨다.

④ 원숭이 행동은 다른 동물들의 행동과 별반 차이가 없다.

⑤ 원숭이 실험을 통해 임상적 죽음의 연장이 가능해졌다.

4 이 글의 내용과 일치하지 <u>않는</u> 것은?

① The monkey's blood pressure dropped as its blood was drained.

② The monkey's heart became active after fifteen minutes of artificial respiration.

③ Clinical death doesn't include permanent damage of the organs.

④ The scientists are still researching to make improvements.

⑤ The baboon and the monkey are the same character in the passage.

단어 조사해 오셔~ Word

divide

clinical

temporary

biological death

vital

cease

permanent

organism

disintegration

tissue

irreversible

prolong

reanimate

narcotic sleep

metabolism

illustrate

drain

artery

blood pressure

respiration

set in

artificial respiration

spontaneous

specific

injection

seize

syringe

People say that what you are is determined by what you eat. These days, many people seem to be concerned about their health and eating healthy food, _____. This may be because of personal habit, taste, advertising, peer pressure, economic resources, traditions, household structures, health beliefs, occupation or health status.

(a) Generally, the food which contains all six nutrients – carbohydrates, lipids, proteins, vitamins, minerals and water – is considered as healthy food or a balanced diet. Carbohydrates, which are mostly found in crops, give <u>fuel</u> for the body. (b) Lipids help control blood pressure, yield high energy, synthesize and repair vital cell parts. Proteins, which we can consume from milk, eggs, fish, peas or beans, constitute the building blocks of the major parts of our bones, muscles, blood, cell membranes and immune system. Vitamins help in many chemical reactions in the human body and are found in fruits and vegetables. (c) For instance, lemon, broccoli, tomatoes and raw cabbage contain vitamin C; papaya contains vitamin A; and milk is rich in vitamin D. (d) Therefore, the price of cows has risen dramatically due to the significance of milk. Minerals by themselves do not yield any energy but help in carrying out various important human functions and in maintaining water balance. Water helps our body clean blood and acts as a solvent and lubricant. A normal human being must consume at least eight glasses of water everyday to circulate blood. (e) However, one must keep in mind that eating good food is not the ultimate solution to maintain good health. The solution lies in consuming a healthy diet and exercising on a regular basis.

1 **Choose the best answer to fill in the blank.**

① but they may not eat as smart as they talk

② so that most of them only eat nutritional products

③ and it is not so difficult to do so

④ so they try hard to memorize the nutritional standards

⑤ so there exists many vegetarians these days

2 (a)~(e) 중 글에서 전체 흐름과 관계 없는 문장은?

① (a) ② (b) ③ (c) ④ (d) ⑤ (e)

3 **What does this article explain?**

① How to lose weight quickly and keep it off

② Explanation of the vitamins and human body parts

③ Description of bad nutrients and good nutrients

④ Giving examples of the healthy foods

⑤ Tips for ingesting the right nutrients and how this affects our body

4 밑줄 친 fuel과 같은 의미로 사용된 것은?

① The price of fuel is rising every year.

② Fuel is one of the most important items in our society.

③ Our pets needed some fuel in order to run around.

④ He was waiting until the fuel tank was fully filled.

⑤ His house was freezing because the fuel ran out.

단어 조사해 오세요~ **Word**

peer pressure

occupation

health status

contain

nutrient

carbohydrate

lipid

balanced diet

blood pressure

yield

synthesize

repair

vital cell

consume

constitute

membrane

immune system

vast

significance

solvent

lubricant

circulate

ultimate solution

maintain

on a regular basis

A **Translate into English.**

1 빛나다, 빛을 내다 _____

2 전구 _____

3 똑바로, 정확히 _____

4 혈관 _____

5 논쟁 _____

6 여파, 결과, 후유증 _____

7 충돌 _____

8 인정하다 _____

9 음식, 먹을거리 _____

10 바치다, 쏟다 _____

11 고인, 죽은 자 _____

12 달래다, 위로하다 _____

13 나누다, 분류하다 _____

14 유기체 _____

15 연장하다 _____

16 빼내다 _____

17 중요성 _____

18 막, 세포막 _____

19 순환시키다 _____

20 유지하다 _____

B **Translate into Korean.**

1 crystalline substance _____

2 in the distance _____

3 the number of _____

4 reflect _____

5 trigger _____

6 spar _____

7 inevitable _____

8 present _____

9 spooky _____

10 hold _____

11 immune system _____

12 shorten _____

13 respiration _____

14 set in _____

15 blood pressure _____

16 syringe _____

17 solvent _____

18 consume _____

19 balanced diet _____

20 health status _____

C Choose the correct answers to each question.

1 Disease was an _____ consequence of poor living conditions.
① inevitable ② intense
③ prehistoric ④ extinct

2 For security reasons, management has been reluctant to hire _____ employees.
① temporary ② organism
③ clinical ④ irreversible

3 A normal human being must _____ at least eight glasses of water everyday to circulate blood.
① significance ② consume
③ vast ④ yield

D Translate into English or Korean.

1 I heard my sister playing the flute in the kitchen while cooking.

_____

2 For all his success and accomplishment, he still sees himself as a failure.

_____

3 그룹의 지도자는 생산적이고 긍정적인 결과를 얻기 위해서 이 교훈을 배워야 하며 이것을 실행으로 옮겨야 한다. (achieve, productive, positive, result)
Group leaders must learn this lesson and put it into practice _____
_____.

E Choose the correct words to fill in the blanks.

1 I saw my dog _____ across the street while I was eating in Burger King.
① be run ② to run
③ running ④ ran

2 _____ her effort, her son still began to say things like "School is boring," and "I hate math."
① In spite all ② With all
③ All for ④ For

3 King Sejong presided over the introduction of the 28 letters of the Korean alphabet _____ Koreans from all classes could read and write.
① so as to ② in order not to
③ in order to ④ so that

4 This report is submitted _____ the Council can make the necessary resolutions.
① so as ② in order that
③ in order to ④ so as to

F Choose the proper word for each sentence.

1 Pandas could become [distinct / extinct / instinct] in the wild.

2 The learning needs of the two groups are quite [distinct / extinct / instinct] from each other.

3 She doesn't think her co-workers [treat / threat / tread] her as an equal.

4 The government will not give in to terrorist [treats / threats / treads].

CHECK
BOX

CHAPTER 9	DATE	SELF CHECK	TEACHER	PARENTS
Preview				
Unit 1				
Unit 2				
Unit 3				
Unit 4				
Unit 5				
Review				

암모기만 피를 고집한다는 거 아셨나요?

 잘 알려진 것처럼, 숫모기는 넥타만 먹고도 잘 살아갈 수 있습니다. 숫모기는 알을 낳거나 할 필요가 없어서 혈액 같은 여분의 영양 에너지원이 필요 없습니다. 반면 암모기들은 살을 잘 찌르려면 특수한 침과 톱을 장착한 입의 구조가 필요합니다. 숫모기는 입의 구조상 사람이나 짐승의 피부를 뚫을 수 없습니다. 모기는 체중이 대개 2mg 정도인데 한꺼번에 3mg 정도의 피를 빨아 먹을 수 있다고 합니다. 암모기는 땀이나 발냄새, 화장품 등 각종 냄새와 젖산, 이산화탄소 등의 예민한 감지능력이 있습니다. 따라서 모기한테 잘 물리는 사람들은 이런 여건 중에 하나를 갖췄다고 보면 될 것입니다. 모기가 체온과 땀 냄새를 감지할 수 있는 거리는 1m밖에 안되지만, 사람들이 숨쉴 때 내쉬는 이산화탄소가 바람에 실려서 멀리 퍼지기 때문입니다. 알을 낳는 데 혈액의 단백질이 필수적이지만 암수모기 둘 다 넥타를 주로 먹습니다. 또한 피를 먹는 모기들의 경우도 사람이 첫 번째나 두 번째의 상대가 아닙니다. 주로 말, 소, 돼지 기타 포유류나 조류가 우선적인 대상입니다. 그러므로 가축이 없는 도시에서는 사람이 어쩔 수 없는 표적이 되는 것입니다.

모기에게 물리면 간지러운 이유는 피는 공기 중에서 금방 굳어져 버리고 그렇게 되면 모기가 못 먹게 됩니다. 그래서 모기는 피를 빨 때, 혈액이 응고되는 걸 방지하기 위해서 침으로 히스타민을 주입시키는데, 바로 이 때문에 모기에 물리면 가려운 것입니다. 모기가 안심하고 피를 충분히 빨아먹을 때는 자신의 침도 함께 빨려 나가서 가렵지 않게 됩니다. 암모기들이 피는 빠는 원인은 알을 낳기 위한 영양보충 때문입니다. 영양보충으로 인해 암모기가 낳을 수 있는 알의 개수는 엄청난 차이를 보입니다. 피를 빨지 않은 모기는 5개 내지 10개 정도를 낳을 수 있지만 피를 빨면 약 200개까지도 낳을 수 있다고 합니다.

CHAPTER 10

Word 🏠 단어도 모르면서 영어 한다 하지 마!

- **matter** *n.* 물질, 소재, 사건 *v.* 중요하다
- **examine** *v.* 검사(시험)하다, 진찰하다
- **desperately** *ad.* 절망적으로, 필사적으로
- **scent** *n.* 냄새, 향기 *v.* 냄새를 풍기다
- **passion** *n.* 열정, 열애, 수난
- **drastic** *a.* 격렬한, 맹렬한, 철저한
- **attainment** *n.* 달성, 도달, 학식
- **reinforce** *v.* 강화하다, 증강하다
- **comprise** *v.* 포함하다, 의미하다
- **inhabit** *v.* ~에 살다, 거주하다

- **capable** *a.* 유능한, 능력이 있는
- **orientation** *n.* 적응, 귀소 본능, 예비 교육
- **misleading** *a.* 오도하는, 혼동케 하는
- **innocent** *a.* 순진한, 결백한, 흠 없는
- **density** *n.* 밀도, 농도, 짙음
- **transmit** *v.* 부치다, 전하다, 송신하다
- **measure** *v.* 재다, 측정하다 *n.* 측정, 계량법
- **represent** *v.* 묘사하다, 나타내다, 표현하다
- **perpendicular** *a.* 수직의, 직립한 *n.* 수직
- **stick** *v.* 찌르다, 찔리다, 고집하다

✸ Mini Quiz

Draw a line from each word on the left to its definition on the right. Then, use the numbered words to fill in the blanks in the sentences below.

1 yell

2 transform

3 aggressive

4 approximately

5 assume

6 axis

a. behaving in an angry, threatening way, as if you want to fight someone

b. the imaginary line around which a large round object, such as the Earth, turns

c. to think that something is true, although you do not have definite proof

d. to change something dramatically

e. close to the exact number, amount etc, but could be a little bit more or less than it

f. to shout or scream something, or speak in a very loud voice

7 Clare _____ in pain as she fell.

8 Jim's voice became _____ as his son didn't listen to him.

9 The plane will be landing in _____ 20 minutes.

10 The Earth rotates on a(n) _____ between the north and south poles.

11 I didn't see your car in front of your house, so I _____ you'd gone out.

Grammar 🧑 기본 문법도 모르면서 독해한다 하지 마!

★ 〈because + 주어 + 동사〉 vs 〈because of + 명사상당어구〉

Darwin was the first to propose that long necks evolved in giraffes **because** *they enabled* the animals to eat the treetop leaves.

다윈은 기린들의 목이 길게 발달한 것이 나무의 윗부분에 있는 잎들을 먹을 수 있도록 하기 위해서라고 제안한 최초의 사람이었다.

★ being이 생략된 분사구문

(*Being*) **Situated** at an elevation of 1,350m, the city of Kathmandu, which looks out on the sparkling Himalayas, enjoys a warm climate year-round that makes living here pleasant.

해발 1,350미터에 위치하고 있으면서, 반짝이는 히말라야 산맥이 내다보이는 카트만두시는 일 년 내내 살기 좋은 온화한 기후이다.

★ [part / some / all / most / half / a lot / the rest / 비율 / 분수] + of + 명사 → 명사에 따라 단수 or 복수 결정

Some of *the information* **needs** to be downloaded to be opened.

몇몇 정보는 열어보려면 다운로드를 받아야 한다.

Most of *English learners* **want** to know the differences between British and American English.   대부분의 영어를 배우는 사람들은 영국영어와 미국영어의 차이점을 알고 싶어 한다.

∷ Mini Quiz

1   다음 문장에서 틀린 부분을 찾아 바르게 고치시오.

We study philosophy because the mental skills it helps us develop.

2   다음 괄호 안에서 알맞은 것을 고르시오.

They all reached the beach two hours late, [exhausting / exhausted] but safe.

3   다음 괄호 안에서 알맞은 것을 고르시오.

Nearly half of Tajikistan's population [is / are] under 14 years of age.

[1] Great thinkers and philosophers have disagreed on many matters, but they mostly agree on one point: "We become what we think about." Ralph Waldo Emerson once said, "A man is what he thinks about all day long." [2] The Roman emperor Marcus Aurelius put it this way: "A man's life is what his thoughts make of it." In the Bible we find, "As a man thinks in his heart, so he is." One day, an old man was visiting his son's house. [3] As he was taking a nap, his grandson put a piece of stinky-smelling cheese on his grandfather's mustache just as a joke. Soon, the grandfather awoke and yelled, "This room stinks." So he examined every room of the house in order to see **if** the other rooms smelled too. Every room smelled the same. So he left the house, but the stinky smell did not go away. Desperately, he yelled "the whole world stinks!" We are just like the old man when we have negative thoughts. [4] Everything we experience and every person we see, carries the scent we hold in our mind.

1 **What is one thing that great thinkers and philosophers agree on?**

① They agree that we don't become what we think about.
② They agree that we become what we think about.
③ They agree that we want to be what we think about.
④ They agree that negativism fills our mind.
⑤ None of the above.

2 **What is this passage trying to explain?**

① We have to confirm everything before making any decisions.
② Bear in mind that thinkers and philosophers are always accurate.
③ It's very important to consider things.
④ We are guided by our minds.
⑤ Don't make fools of others, otherwise you will be paid back in the same way.

단어 조사해 오셔~ **Word**

thinker

philosopher

disagree on

matter

agree on

put it this way

take a nap

stinky-smelling

mustache

yell

examine

go away

desperately

scent

🍴 Drill 1 Grammar

명사절 if

if가 이끄는 절은 문장 안에서 명사의 역할을 할 수 있기 때문에 명사절이라 한다. whether와 같은 의미로 '~인지 아닌지'로 해석한다. 현대 영어에서 whether는 보통 문장 맨 앞에 쓰고, if는 보통 동사 표현 다음에 와서 목적어나 보어 역할을 한다.

- I think that websites should say **if** they are private or public.

  내가 생각하기에 웹사이트들은 개인의 정보를 보호하는지 아니면 공개하는지를 밝혀야 한다.

- Please let me know **if** you agree to my plan. 당신이 제 계획에 동의하는지 아닌지 저에게 알려 주세요.

---

1 Certainly, Asians smile to try to be polite even when they are sad, but it is doubtful if such a behavior is unique to them.

   해석 ◐ _____

2 I will come if she comes tomorrow, but I don't know if she will come.

   해석 ◐ _____

3 소방관들은 불이 지하실에서 났는지 아니면 부엌에서 났는지 몰랐다.
   (The fire fighters, the kitchen, start, fire, the basement, know, if)

   영작 ◐ _____

🍴 Drill 2 Translation

1 1번 문장 ◐ _____

2 2번 문장 ◐ _____

3 3번 문장 ◐ _____

4 4번 문장 ◐ _____

¹ The truth is that people desire not only what is necessary in order to survive; most people in our culture are greedy: greedy for more food, drink, possessions, power, and fame. It is well-known that overeating, which is one form of greed, is frequently caused by states of depression; or that compulsive buying is one attempt to escape from a depressed mood. ² The act of eating or buying is a symbolic act of filling the inner void and, thus, overcoming the depressed feeling for the moment. Greed is a passion, that is to say, it is charged with energy and relentlessly drives a person toward the attainment of his goals. In our culture, greed is greatly reinforced by all those measures that tend to transform everybody into a consumer. ³ Of course, the greedy person does not need to be aggressive, provided he has enough money to buy what he desires. ⁴ However, a greedy person who does not have the necessary means must attack if he wants to satisfy his desire. The most drastic example of this is the drug addict who is possessed by his greed for the drug. The many who do not have the money to buy drugs rob, assault, or even kill in order to get the necessary means.

1 이 글의 주제로 가장 적절한 것은?

① 욕구불만이 개인생활에 미치는 영향
② 명성에 탐욕을 부리는 현대인의 욕망
③ 억압된 감정을 극복하는 방법
④ 욕구가 충족되지 못한 인간의 위험성
⑤ 마약 중독의 위험성

2 이 글의 내용과 일치하는 것은?

① 우리 문화에서 대부분의 사람들은 욕심이 너무 적다는 것이다.
② 돈이 충분하더라도 필요한 욕구를 위해 공격적이 될 수 있다.
③ 과식은 탐욕의 형태로 볼 수 없고 단지 불만족일 뿐이다.
④ 필요한 수단이 없는 탐욕스러운 사람은 욕구만족을 위해 끔찍한 범죄를 저지를 수 있다.
⑤ 재산, 권력, 그리고 명성과 같은 것은 인간의 탐욕과는 거리가 멀다.

단어 조사해 오세요~ **Word**

possession

depression

compulsive

depressed mood

that is to say

relentlessly

attainment

reinforce

measure

transform

necessary means

drastic

drug addict

assault

Drill 1 Grammar

전치사의 목적어

전치사의 목적어로는 명사, 대명사, 동명사, 명사절 등이 쓰인다. 전치사 뒤에는 명사가 오는 것이 기본이지만 '행위'를 표현하려면 동사를 반드시 -ing 형태로 만들어 전치사 뒤에 두어 '~것'으로 해석한다.

- There was no evidence of his having killed the dog. 그가 그 개를 죽였다는 것의 아무런 증거도 없었다.
- At first, he refused the money on account of my having helped him, but I insisted on his taking it. 처음에 그는 내가 그를 도와주었다는 이유로 그 돈을 거절했지만, 나는 그가 그 돈을 받을 것을 고집했다.

---

1 A habit is a way of doing a thing without thinking about it. A habit is learned, or formed, after you have done a thing many times. Nearly everything that you do without thinking is a habit.

해석 ○ _____

2 Trying to understand physics is like trying to grow wings and fly.

해석 ○ _____

3 외국어를 배우는 것은 직장을 구하는 것에 도움이 된다. (find, helpful, a job, foreign, learning)

영작 ○ _____

Drill 2 Translation

1 1번 문장 ○ _____

2 2번 문장 ○ _____

3 3번 문장 ○ _____

4 4번 문장 ○ _____

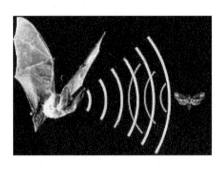

[1] In the world, there are at least 1,000 different species of bats. Bats are in the order Chiroptera. (a) Many of the world's bats live throughout the North American continent. (b) [2] The United States is known to have approximately 44 species which comprise 15 genera of bats. Bats are the only mammals in the world capable of flying. (c) [3] In addition, most species of bats have evolved a system of acoustic orientation, often referred to as 'bat radar.' The technical term for such a system is echolocation. Some bats, comprising 11 genera and more than 18 species, live in the southwestern deserts. (d) Most Big Free-tailed Bats, of which the common name is Mastiff Bats, inhabit the southern Sonoran and Chihuahuan deserts, but they are found on other continents, too. [4] They are also known as Bulldog Bats because of their facial resemblance to bulldogs. (e) Bulldog bats eat insects that many people may consider pests. There are about 85 species of bats in the family.

1 **Which information does the passage mainly contain?**

① Explanation of bats' habitation
② Movements of bats
③ Description of species of bats, including Bulldog Bats
④ Bats' body structure
⑤ Protection of endangered species

2 (a)~(e) 중, 이 글의 흐름상 어색한 것은?

① (a)   ② (b)   ③ (c)   ④ (d)   ⑤ (e)

단어 조사해 오세요~ **Word**

order

Chiroptera

approximately

comprise

genera

mammal

capable of

evolve

acoustic

orientation

refer to

technical term

echolocation

inhabit

pest

 **Drill 1** Grammar

there be 구문의 특징

be동사의 특징은 대표적으로 linking verb와 existence verb의 역할 두 가지로 나눌 수 있다. there와 함께 쓰일 때는 언제나 '존재'를 표현하게 된다. 이때 수의 일치 및 시제를 물어 보는 문제로 구성할 수 있으니 정확히 이해해 두어야 한다. 특히 be동사 자리에는 1형식 동사가 모두 들어갈 수 있다는 것도 유의해야 한다.

• **There is** an old deserted house on the top of the mountain. 산꼭대기에는 오래된 흉가가 하나 있다.

• **There are** four suitcases sitting on the front porch. 4개의 가방이 앞쪽 현관에 놓여 있다.

---

1   To some people, trying to talk over a cell phone in a foreign language seems difficult. There is a good reason for this difficulty.

해석 ○ _____

2   There was a little boy, maybe four years old, standing in the corner of the cell sucking his thumb. I felt sorry for him. "What are you here for?" I asked. "Freedom," he said. He couldn't even say freedom but he was in prison for it.

해석 ○ _____

cell 감방 ｜ prison 감옥

3   한 쪽 양말만을 신는 한 남자가 있다. (wear, one sock, only, a man)

영작 ○ _____

Drill 2 Translation

1   1번 문장 ○ _____

2   2번 문장 ○ _____

3   3번 문장 ○ _____

4   4번 문장 ○ _____

The claim that we have recently entered the information age is misleading. Flooded by (a) <u>cellphones</u>, the Internet, and television, we incorrectly imagine that our ancestors inhabited an innocent world where the news did not travel far beyond (b) <u>the village</u>. It may not be valid to (A) consume / assume that the media make our time distinct from the past, because we know relatively little about (B) how information was shared / how was information shared in the past. _____, the Olympics celebrate the memory of (c) <u>the Greek soldier</u> who brought the news of the Athenian victory over the Persians. Most of us could come up with many other examples – (d) <u>message drums</u>, smoke signals, church bells, ship flags. But their primitiveness would only confirm our sense that we live in a fundamentally different world, one of constant, instant access to information.

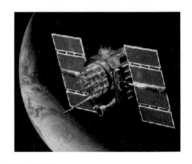

All ages have had <u>a means of sharing information</u>. What makes our time distinct is not the density of the data we take in. It is the technology that does the transmitting. Thanks to (e) <u>satellites</u>, we can find out instantly about events that occur on the other side of the world. It usually took five weeks for Benjamin Franklin in Paris to receive a letter sent from Philadelphia. But the news was still new and (C) surprised / surprising to people there.

(기출)

1 이 글의 요지로 가장 적절한 것은?

① The value of information depends on speed.
② We are entering a new age of information.
③ Even old information can benefit all of us.
④ Every age is in fact an age of information.
⑤ We are flooded by incorrect information.

2 (a)~(e) 중, 밑줄 친 a means of sharing information에 해당하지 <u>않는</u> 것은?

① (a)　　② (b)　　③ (c)　　④ (d)　　⑤ (e)

3 Choose the correct answer that fits most appropriately in this passage.

	(A)		(B)		(C)
①	consume	⋯	how information was shared	⋯	surprised
②	consume	⋯	how was information shared	⋯	surprising
③	consume	⋯	how information was shared	⋯	surprising
④	assume	⋯	how information was shared	⋯	surprising
⑤	assume	⋯	how was information shared	⋯	surprised

4 Choose the best answer to fill in the blank.

① Eventually
② However
③ In fact
④ Therefore
⑤ A few days later

claim

recently

information age

misleading

flood

ancestor

inhabit

innocent

valid

assume

distinct

relatively

come up with

primitiveness

confirm

fundamentally

density

transmit

satellite

instantly

Why do some countries have four seasons while some others have only one season? How do day and night change? As we know, the Earth circles around the Sun. Since _____, the distance between the Earth and the Sun is measured differently depending on where you are. When the Earth is on the left side of the Sun, the northern hemisphere is farther

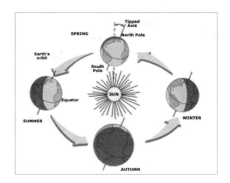

from the Sun than the southern hemisphere; when the Earth is on the right side of the Sun, the southern hemisphere is farther from the Sun than the northern hemisphere. Thus, when summer occurs in the northern hemisphere, people in the southern hemisphere have winter.

While the seasonal changes are caused by the Earth's orbiting motion around the Sun, the rotation of the Earth on its own axis gives us day and night. In order to better understand, let's do a simple scientific experiment. First, you need to prepare a lamp, an apple and a knitting needle. If you are ready, put the lamp in the middle of the room. The lamp represents the Sun and the apple represents the Earth. Now stick the knitting needle in the apple so that the needle represents the axis of the Earth.

Now spin the knitting needle so that the apple can spin on the needle. It shows how the Earth rotates on its axis. The Earth spins on its axis every day which lets most of the Earth have sunlight for a certain amount of time everyday. While one side of the Earth has sunlight, the other side cannot receive any. That is why longitudinal difference causes a time difference. However, remember that the axis of the Earth is tilted slightly. If you circle the apple around the lamp while letting the needle lean to one side at an angle of $23.5°$ from the perpendicular, you will be able to notice that at one side of the room the lamp keeps shining on the top of the apple, while the bottom of the apple remains in darkness continuously; and vice versa at the other side of the room. Thus, if you are at one of the poles, you will be in total darkness for half of the year, but in continuous daylight for the other half of the year.

1 **Choose the most suitable answer to fill in the blank.**

   ① the Earth has been created by something

   ② we can't measure the exact distance

   ③ the Sun is hot enough to push the Earth

   ④ the axis of the Earth is slightly tilted

   ⑤ the circulation of the Earth is irregular

2 **Choose the reason why we have days and nights.**

   ① the revolving around the Sun

   ② the rotation of the Earth on its axis

   ③ the lunar eclipse

   ④ the solar eclipse

   ⑤ the Earth's orbit

3 **What could happen if the axis of the earth was not tilted?**

   ① There would only be two seasons year-round.

   ② Seasons would change irregularly.

   ③ The temperature would be about 23° C most of the time.

   ④ The Earth would rotate faster.

   ⑤ The northern hemisphere and the southern hemisphere could have the same seasons.

4 **What is this passage trying to explain?**

   ① Clarifying the difference between the northern hemisphere and the southern hemisphere

   ② Importance of the Sun and how it affects us

   ③ How to prepare for an experiment on the Earth's rotation

   ④ How to prepare for an experiment on the Earth briefly

   ⑤ The repetition of day and night, and why there are four seasons

단어 조사해 오세요~ **Word**

circle around

measure

northern hemisphere

southern hemisphere

seasonal

orbit motion

rotation

knitting needle

represent

stick

an amount of

longitudinal

perpendicular

vice versa

axis

tilt

A **Translate into English.**

1 철학자 _____

2 낮잠 자다 _____

3 콧수염 _____

4 사라지다 _____

5 극복하다 _____

6 열정 _____

7 만족시키다 _____

8 마약 중독자 _____

9 적어도 _____

10 진화하다 _____

11 전문 용어 _____

12 해로운 것 _____

13 범람하다, 가득 차다 _____

14 조상 _____

15 근본적으로 _____

16 즉각적으로 _____

17 기울다 _____

18 계절에 따른 _____

19 경도의 _____

20 반대로, 거꾸로 _____

B **Translate into Korean.**

1 agree on _____

2 thinker _____

3 matter _____

4 examine _____

5 relentlessly _____

6 measure _____

7 compulsive _____

8 assault _____

9 refer to _____

10 acoustic _____

11 resemblance _____

12 inhabit _____

13 distinct _____

14 confirm _____

15 primitiveness _____

16 satellite _____

17 orbit motion _____

18 rotation _____

19 represent _____

20 circle around _____

C **Choose the correct answers to each question.**

1 In the world, there are at least 1,000 different _____ of bats.
① species   ② mammals
③ inhabit   ④ resemblance

2 Bats are the only _____ in the world capable of flying.
① genera   ② orientation
③ species   ④ mammals

3 The _____ changes are caused by the Earth's orbit around the Sun.
① perpendicular   ② rotation
③ longitudinal   ④ seasonal

D **Translate into English or Korean.**

1 Bottles can reveal their contents without being opened.

_____

2 Parents should take care when they send their children to a sports camp, and should talk with the sports coaches to see if they will respect the children's wishes.

_____

_____

_____

3 우리가 영어를 공부해야 하는 몇 가지 이유들이 있다. (several reasons, why)

_____

we should study English.

E **Choose the correct words to fill in the blanks.**

1 Can you tell me _____ she has any experience in the staging field at all?
① if   ② so   ③ and   ④ but

2 It seems that they just don't like or don't have time for _____.
① to exercise   ② exercised
③ be exercising   ④ exercising

3 _____ nothing better than a fresh roasted head of garlic with a warm loaf of French bread for breakfast.
① This is   ② These are
③ There is   ④ There are

F **Choose the proper word for each sentence.**

1 The system [transforms / transmits] information over digital phone lines.

2 The fairy [transformed / transmitted] the pumpkin into a carriage.

3 Someone with [compulsive / impulsive] buying disorder has urges to shop and spend which are hard to control.

4 Rosa was [compulsive / impulsive] and sometimes regretted things she'd done.

CHAPTER 10	DATE	SELF CHECK	TEACHER	PARENTS
Preview				
Unit 1				
Unit 2				
Unit 3				
Unit 4				
Unit 5				
Review				

아시아 최고의 프리미어리거! 박지성!

박지성은 서울에서 태어나 수원에서 자랐습니다. 박지성은 가난한 집안에서 태어났다고 합니다. 정육점을 하셨던 아버지는 집안 형편이 그리 좋지 못해서 좋은 축구화 하나 못 사주셨다고 합니다. 어려서부터 축구에 대한 대단한 열정 때문에 부모님께 몹시 졸라서 산남초등학교 축구부에 들어갔답니다. 하지만 그 축구부는 1년 이상 지속되지 못하고 폐부되어 박지성에게 실망을 안겨줍니다. 그 후 박지성은 세류초등학교로 전학을 가게 됩니다. 박지성은 어려서부터 축구도 잘하고 예의바른 학생이었다고 합니다. 세류초등학교 6학년 때 쯤에 박지성은 차범근 어린이 축구상을 받았습니다. 그리고 중학생이 되어서 안용중학교에서 축구부 활동을 계속했습니다. 안용중학교는 그다지 축구로 잘 알려지지 않은 학교였는데 박지성 선수가 안용중학교 축구부를 상위권 팀으로 끌어올렸다고 합니다. 그 후 수원공업고등학교 들어갑니다. 박지성은 당시 감독님께 많은 것을 배웠다고 합니다. 고등학교를 마친 후 박지성은 체격조건이 맞지 않아 거절당하던 중 명지대 축구부의 빈자리를 메꿀 수 있는 기회가 옵니다. 결국 대학교 축구부에 간신히 들어간 박지성은 열성적인 태도와 그의 숨은 잠재력을 발휘해 일본 J-리그의 시미즈 에스펄스에서 이적제의가 들어왔으나 연봉협상에서 문제가 생겨 결국 결렬됩니다. 그리고 그다음 교토 퍼플상가에서 이적제의가 들어옵니다. 박지성은 그리하여 일본 J-리그로 진출합니다. 올림픽 선수로 뛰고, 일본 J리그로 뛰다가 2002 월드컵, 박지성이 날개를 달게 됩니다. 히딩크 감독은 박지성이 잠재력이 아주 많은 가능성 있는 선수라고 판단하고 그를 월드컵 예선, 본선 경기들에 꾸준히 출전시킵니다. 월드컵이 끝난 후 히딩크는 박지성을 스카웃해 PSV 아인트호벤에서 뛰게 합니다. 박지성은 PSV의 핵심선수가 되면서 그의 활약을 본 유럽의 여러 팀들이 박지성에 대해 관심을 갖기 시작했습니다. 그 후 유럽의 여러 명문팀에서 박지성을 영입하려고 시도했습니다. 대표적으로 토트넘, 리버풀, 첼시, 맨유 등으로 이러한 엄청난 팀들이었습니다. 결국 박지성은 첼시에서 내건 천만 파운드보다 좀 적은 500만~700만 파운드 정도의 금액으로 맨유행을 결정합니다. 박지성은 떠나면서 자신을 키워준 히딩크에 대한 감사의 표시로 이적료 중 10%를 PSV 아인트호벤의 유소년 축구에 기부합니다. 그리고 맨유에 도착한 박지성은 같은 PSV 출신인 루드 반 니스텔루이와 친하게 지냅니다. 같은 PSV 출신이라서 박지성선수에게 아주 잘해 주었습니다. 박지성선수와 반니스텔루이는 같이 자주 어울리는 그런 아주 친한 친구 사이였습니다. 박지성은 또 루니, 에브라, 반데사르, 네빌, 스콜스, 호나우두, 사하, 긱스, 실베스트르 같은 스타플레이어들과도 아주 친해졌습니다. 맨유 구단 사람들도 박지성의 친근하고 예의 있는 인간성 때문에 그를 아주 좋아한다고 합니다.

CHAPTER

11

Word 🏠 단어도 모르면서 영어 한다 하지 마!

- ☐ **isolation** *n.* 격리, 고립, 고독, 차단
- ☐ **cure** *v.* 치료하다 *n.* 치료(법), 해결책
- ☐ **despair** *n.* 절망, 자포자기 *v.* 단념하다
- ☐ **invisible** *a.* 안 보이는, 구별이 잘 안 가는
- ☐ **preserve** *v.* 보호하다, 유지하다, 저장하다
- ☐ **sea level** *n.* 해발
- ☐ **monk** *n.* 수도사, 수사
- ☐ **locate** *v.* (장소를) 정하다, (위치를) 알아내다
- ☐ **recite** *v.* 낭독하다, 암송하다
- ☐ **accuse** *v.* 고발(고소)하다, 비난하다

- ☐ **stimulus** *n.* 자극, 격려
- ☐ **reflex** *a.* 반사의 *n.* 반사 *v.* 휘게 하다
- ☐ **subsequently** *ad.* 그 후에, 그 결과로서
- ☐ **rapid** *a.* 빠른, 가파른 *n.* 급류
- ☐ **outline** *n.* 윤곽, 개요 *v.* 윤곽을 그리다
- ☐ **poisonous** *a.* 유독한, 유해한
- ☐ **benefit** *n.* 이익, 구제 *v.* 이익을 얻다
- ☐ **roam** *v.* 돌아다니다, 둘러보다 *n.* 배회
- ☐ **range** *n.* 열, 산맥, 범위 *v.* 정렬시키다
- ☐ **frequency** *n.* 빈번, 회수, 주파수

:: Mini Quiz

Draw a line from each word on the left to its definition on the right. Then, use the numbered words to fill in the blanks in the sentences below.

1 control

2 destroy

3 protect

4 dense

5 technology

6 reveal

a. the study, development, and application of devices, machines, and techniques for manufacturing and productive processes

b. to make known something that was previously secret or unknown

c. to damage something so badly that it no longer exists or cannot be used

d. to make someone or something do what you want

e. to keep someone or something safe from harm, damage, or illness

f. made of or containing a lot of things or people that are very close together

7 The cover _____ the machine from dust.

8 When you are angry, you need to have _____ over your temper.

9 Advances in science and _____ have brought us many benefits and convenience.

10 She may be prosecuted for _____ secrets about the security agency.

11 The building was completely _____ by fire.

12 The fog was so _____ that nothing could be seen even an inch in front of our noses.

Grammar 기본 문법도 모르면서 독해 한다 하지 마!

★ one of the 최상급 + 복수명사 → 단수취급

One *of the greatest benefits of this* **is** that it lets in light and provides protection from the weather at the same time.
이것이 주는 가장 큰 혜택 중 하나는 빛을 받아들이는 동시에 기상으로부터 보호한다는 것이다.

★ [feel like / cannot help / have difficulty / be busy / It is no use] + 동명사

Joe, who was on a diet, **couldn't help** *eating* cookies even though his family tried to keep them away from him.
Joe는 다이어트 중이었는데, 그의 가족이 쿠키를 숨겨두려고 노력했음에도 불구하고 쿠키 먹는 것을 참을 수 없었다.

★ 강조구문 [It is[was] not until ~ that]

It was not until *today* **that** I learned something new, that the happiest moments in life do not necessarily involve money.
오늘이 되어서야 나는 인생에서 가장 행복한 순간이 돈과 꼭 관련되지 않는다는 새로운 사실을 배웠다.

:: Mini Quiz

1   다음 문장에서 <u>틀린</u> 부분을 찾아 바르게 고치시오.

One of the most annoying things about using computers are the database problem.

2   다음 괄호 안에서 알맞은 것을 고르시오.

They were busy [to clean / cleaning] up their tent and they didn't see the bear.

3   다음 괄호 안에서 알맞은 것을 고르시오.

[It / This] was not until we actually arrived that we learned of our destination, a small village near the river.

[1]One of the toughest parts of isolation is a lack of an expressive exit. With anger, you can get mad at someone and yell. With sadness, you can cry. [2]But isolation feels like being in a room with no way out.

(A) For people who cannot push themselves, however, support groups are a good cure for isolation. They offer the opportunity for connection in a safe and controlled way.

(B) [3]And the longer you get stuck there, the harder it becomes to share the pain and sorrow. In isolation, hope disappears, despair rules, and you can no longer see a life beyond the invisible walls that imprison you.

(C) Some people find it helpful to work gently at driving themselves back into the world. [4]In one case, a woman reported that after four miserable forced lunches with friends, she suddenly enjoyed the fifth one as she found herself laughing at a joke. (기출)

1 주어진 글 다음에 이어질 글의 순서로 가장 적절한 것은?

① (A) - (B) - (C)
② (A) - (C) - (B)
③ (B) - (C) - (A)
④ (C) - (A) - (B)
⑤ (C) - (B) - (A)

2 Choose the best title for the passage.

① Mixing with Good Company
② Methods of Mind Control
③ The State of Isolation and How to Cure it
④ Expressing One's Feelings
⑤ Disadvantages of Constraint

단어 조사해 오셔~ **Word**

tough

isolation

expressive exit

with no way out

support group

cure

opportunity

connection

control

despair

invisible

imprison

drive

miserable

🍴 Drill 1 Grammar

the + 비교급 ..., the + 비교급 ...

비교급을 활용한 표현으로 〈the + 비교급 (+ S + V), the + 비교급 (+ S + V)〉가 있다. 앞의 표현이 원인에 해당이 되며, 뒤이어 나오는 것은 그에 따른 결과에 초점이 맞춰져 있다. '~하면 할수록, 더욱 더 …하다' 로 해석한다. 〈all + the + 비교급 ~〉은 '더욱 더 ~하다' 의 비슷한 표현의 비교급 표현도 있다.

- The faster he drove, the more nervous I became. 더 빨리 그가 운전할수록, 더욱 더 나는 불안해졌다.

- They became all the better friends because they entered the same college.
  그들은 같은 대학에 들어갔기 때문에 더욱 더 좋은 친구가 되었다.

- The higher we go up, the colder it becomes. 우리가 높이 올라가면 갈수록, 더욱 더 추워진다.

---

1 The more we learn about animals, the more we realize how marvelously they are fitted for the life they have to lead.

해석 ◯ _____

2 It seems that the more money we have, the more we spend. No matter how much money we have, we always wish for more.

해석 ◯ _____

3 그가 샤워하기를 더 오래 동안 기다릴수록 그는 더욱 더 냄새가 난다.
   (long, wait, smelly, become, take a shower)

영작 ◯ _____

🍴 Drill 2 Translation

1 1번 문장 ◯ _____

2 2번 문장 ◯ _____

3 3번 문장 ◯ _____

4 4번 문장 ◯ _____

The building which now protects the wooden blocks was built in 1488. Since then Haein Temple has experienced two fires. (a) [1] Each time the fire destroyed every building of the temple except the one containing the 80,000 wooden blocks. Can you believe it? (b) The building is located at 750 meters, mid-way between sea level and the top of Mt. Kaya at 1,500 meters. (c) As a result, cold air from the mountain top and warm air from the valley floor meet and mix, making very good conditions for preserving the wooden blocks. In recent years, a new building was built to keep the blocks. (d) [2] This building used modern science to try to improve on the old one. (e) Great was the old building.

1 (a)~(e) 중, 글의 흐름으로 보아 주어진 문장이 들어가기에 가장 적절한 곳은?

[3] However, tests showed that the old building that the monks had planned hundreds of years ago without any modern scientific knowledge, was better than the new one.

① (a)   ② (b)   ③ (c)   ④ (d)   ⑤ (e)

2 Choose the best main idea of the paragraph.

① 해인사는 불에 견딜 수 있는 사원으로 건설되었다.
② 팔만대장경 보관 건물은 조상의 놀라운 보존능력을 보여 준다.
③ 최신 과학을 이용한 사원은 전 세계의 주목을 받고 있다.
④ 낡은 건물의 복원은 불가피한 상황이다.
⑤ 팔만대장경은 독일의 인쇄 기술보다 훨씬 이전에 이루어졌다.

단어 조사해 오셔~ **Word**

as a result

valley floor

good condition

preserve

wooden block

destroy

be located

mid-way

sea level

monk

Drill 1 Grammar

도치구문

보어가 문장 맨 앞머리에 나오면 동사가 주어 앞으로 위치하게 된다. 이를 도치구문이라 하고, 보어를 강조 하고 싶을 때 보어를 문장 맨 앞으로 보내는 것뿐이다. 즉, 〈보어 + 동사 + 주어〉의 어순이 된다.

- **Happy** *are* **those** who know the pleasure of doing good. 좋은 일을 하는 즐거움을 아는 사람들은 정말로 행복하다.

- They found hundreds of Greek and Roman jars. Some were still unopened, and in them was wine more than two thousand years old. **Deeper** still at the bottom of some coral *was* **the ship itself.** 그들은 수백 개의 그리스와 로마의 항아리들을 발견했다. 어떤 것들은 아직 개봉되지 않았다. 그 중에는 2,000년 이상이 된 포도주 도 있었다. 산호층 바닥의 더 깊은 곳에는 배 본체가 있었다.

---

1 Happy are those children who have enough food to eat and a safe place to call home. Around the world, many children dream about having the things that these children take for granted.

해석 ◐ _____

2 Great was my mother's happiness when I told her that I would be home on Christmas day. After three years apart, we were finally going to meet on such a special day.

해석 ◐ _____

3 최선을 다하지 않은 사람들은 슬퍼한다. (those who, do their best, sad are)

영작 ◐ _____

Drill 2 Translation

1 1번 문장 ◐ _____

2 2번 문장 ◐ _____

3 3번 문장 ◐ _____

There are many home remedies to get rid of hiccups. [1] In England, to stop the hiccups, a person wets the index finger of the right hand with spit, and crosses the top of the left shoe three times, reciting the Lord's Prayer backwards. In India, people used to surprise or frighten the person who had hiccups by accusing him of stealing something. [2] A hiccup occurs as the result of an action one's organs take to protect themselves. Inside a human body, there are many parts, such as the blood vessels, the nerves, intestines, stomach, lungs, etc. [3] Most body parts move or work with the help of a system which enables those parts to respond to certain stimulus. The responses of those parts are called 'automatic reflexes.' Automatic reflexes occur in all different body organs, but they always work in the same way; they can't happen without stimulus. [4] Sometimes, when a stimuli is given differently or by mistake (for example, water or food go in the windpipe), a reflex corresponding to the stimuli helps the body correct the problem. However, when the reflex fails to correct it, we have the hiccups.

1 **When do hiccups occur?**

① when the body is frightened or surprised
② when the human body tries to protect itself
③ when people wet their index finger of the right hand with spit
④ when blood vessels can't circulate properly
⑤ all of the above

2 다음 중 이 글에서 언급되지 <u>않은</u> 것은?

① 딸꾹질은 멈추는 방법 중에는 주기도문을 거꾸로 외우는 방법도 있다.
② 대부분의 몸 부위는 자극을 받으면 반응을 한다.
③ 인도에서는 상대방의 딸꾹질을 멈추기 위해 그 사람의 물건을 훔쳤다.
④ 기관으로 물이나 음식이 들어가면 딸꾹질이 일어난다.
⑤ 몸의 자동적인 반사작용이 진행되지 못할 때 딸꾹질이 일어난다.

단어 조사해 오세요~ **Word**

home remedy
get rid of
hiccup
spit
Lord's Prayer
recite
accuse
blood vessel
nerve
intestine
lung
respond
stimulus
reflex
windpipe

 **Drill 1** Grammar

2형식 수동태

⟨be + p.p.⟩ 다음에 보어가능어(명사, 형용사, to do, -ing, -ed/en)가 오는 형태이다.

5형식 문장을 수동태로 고칠 경우 2형식 수동태가 되는데, 3·4형식의 수동태 문장과는 구별해서 정확히 이해할 수 있어야 한다. 2형식 수동태의 동사는 linking verb의 역할을 한다. 군이 해석하자면 '~로, ~라고'를 붙여 해석한다.

- Human laws had **been considered** *unchangeable* in primitive times.
  인간의 법은 원시 시대에는 변화될 수 없는 것으로 여겨졌었다.
- A child whose parents are dead **is called** *an orphan*. 부모님이 죽은 아이를 고아라고 부른다.

---

1 Koreans have been proved to be the first people to use movable metal type in the world. Koreans began using metal type some 200 years before Gutenberg invented his in 1450.

해석 ◯ _____

metal type 금속활자

2 He is called cheap because he never spends any money.

해석 ◯ _____

3 This apartment building is called hell because it is so dilapidated.

해석 ◯ _____

4 그녀는 대부분의 사람들에 의해 아름답고 매력적인 것으로 생각되어진다. (think, charming, by most people)

영작 ◯ _____

Drill 2 Translation

1 1번 문장 ◯ _____

2 2번 문장 ◯ _____

3 3번 문장 ◯ _____

4 4번 문장 ◯ _____

Africa is a huge continent surrounded by the Atlantic and Indian Ocean and the Mediterranean and Red Sea. (a) It is the only continent through which the Equator passes. Subsequently, the Tropic of Cancer and the Tropic of Capricorn pass through the continent, also.

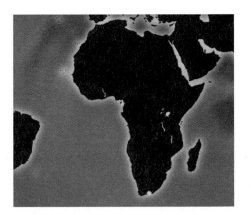

Explorers have always found it challenging to travel in Africa. Two deserts, the Sahara Desert in the North and the Kalahari Desert in the South, spread far and wide. (b) It would take a long time to explore these two deserts because of their climate. The thick and dense forests of Africa, in which numerous poisonous insects and wild animals live, are everywhere throughout the continent. (c) The rivers have many rapids and waterfalls. Therefore, not many explorers succeeded in exploring this continent, and that was _____ (A) _____ Africa 'The Dark Continent.'

(d) In the fifteenth century, for the first time, the outline of Africa was mapped by European sailors. In 1497, Vasco da Gama rounded the Cape of Good Hope on his way to India. (e) However, it was not until 1930 that the whole continent of Africa was explored. Nevertheless, there were brave explorers _____ (B) _____ between those times, such as Mungo Park who tried to trace the course of the Niger River; Burton Speke and Grant who found Lake Tanganyika and Victoria; David Livingstone who tried to discover the sources of the Nile River; and Rene Caille who was the first European to visit Timbuktu.

1 What does the underlined word 'which' in the second paragraph stand for?

① Rivers

② Desert

③ Forests

④ Lakes

⑤ Continent

2 이 글에서 전체 흐름과 관계 없는 문장은?

① (a)　　　② (b)　　　③ (c)　　　④ (d)　　　⑤ (e)

3 What is the main idea of this passage?

① hardship of explorers exploring Africa

② comparison of Africa's past and present

③ size of the Dark Continent

④ report of sightseeing in Africa

⑤ description of Africa and its exploration

4 Choose the correct pair that fits most appropriately in this passage.

	(A)		(B)
①	why called Europeans	⋯	who Africa explored successfully
②	why the reason European called	⋯	successfully explored Africa
③	why Europeans called	⋯	who successfully explored Africa
④	when European called	⋯	which successfully explored Africa
⑤	when called European	⋯	to which successfully explored Africa

단어 조사해 오세~ **Word**

huge continent

Atlantic Ocean

Indian Ocean

Red Sea

Equator

subsequently

Tropic of Cancer

Tropic of Capricorn

dense

numerous

poisonous

rapid

waterfall

outline

Cape of Good Hope

nevertheless

(A)

These new technologies have another benefit for biologists by allowing them to gain access to the unknown world of communication between animals. For centuries, biologists believed giraffes were the silent giants of Africa. In recent years, however, biologists have been able to listen more carefully by means of these technologies and have realized that giraffes may talk, though not in a way that we can hear.

(B)

Communication through infrasound is not limited to giraffes. Over the last few decades, biologists have found that whales, elephants, and some other animals _____. This infrasound, as a means of communication, has a special merit: it can travel a greater distance than higher-pitched noise. Such long-distance communication is a must for animals such as giraffes or elephants that roam over wide areas.

(C)

Infrasound is a low-pitched sound, whose frequency is far below the range of human ears. Scientists, however, have been able to discover the existence of infrasound by using special technologies. These new technologies have revealed that many things can produce infrasound, from earthquakes and thunderstorms to trains and underground explosions, thus making possible the warning of earthquakes and the monitoring of underground nuclear-explosion tests.

기출

1 (A), (B), (C)를 이어 하나의 글로 구성할 때 가장 적절한 순서는?

① (A) - (B) - (C)

② (A) - (C) - (B)

③ (B) - (A) - (C)

④ (C) - (A) - (B)

⑤ (C) - (B) - (A)

2 이 글의 내용을 바탕으로 다음 문장을 완성할 때, 빈칸 (a)와 (b)에 들어갈 말로 알맞은 것끼리 짝지은 것은?

> Some animals ____(a)____ with each other using infrasound that travels ____(b)____ than higher-pitched sounds.

	(a)		(b)
①	communicate	...	more frequently
②	communicate	...	farther
③	interact	...	more frequently
④	compete	...	farther
⑤	compete	...	faster

3 Choose the most suitable answer to fill in the blank.

① also use this extremely low-pitched sound to communicate

② also like to move in an enormous herd

③ are still developing their own methods of communication

④ are endangered due to scarcity of food

⑤ can communicate each other even though they're different kinds

4 Write T if the statement is true or F it it's false.

(1) _____ The new technologies may notify people before disasters.

(2) _____ Biologists knew that giraffes could talk from the beginning.

(3) _____ Higher-pitched noise travels further than infrasound.

A **Translate into English.**

1 치료 _____

2 괴로운, 비참한 _____

3 가두다 _____

4 고립, 격리 _____

5 위치하다 _____

6 해발 _____

7 목판 _____

8 그 결과 _____

9 반사 _____

10 자극, 자극하는 것 _____

11 자택 요법 _____

12 딸꾹질 _____

13 급류 _____

14 적도 _____

15 그 후에, 그 다음에 _____

16 밀집한, 빽빽한 _____

17 주파수 _____

18 밝히다 _____

19 생물학자 _____

20 돌아다니다, 떠돌다 _____

B **Translate into Korean.**

1 connection _____

2 expressive exit _____

3 despair _____

4 invisible _____

5 good condition _____

6 mid-way _____

7 valley floor _____

8 preserve _____

9 recite _____

10 accuse _____

11 nerve _____

12 intestine _____

13 outline _____

14 Tropic of Capricorn _____

15 Atlantic ocean _____

16 poisonous _____

17 range _____

18 extremely _____

19 long-distance _____

20 infrasound _____

C Choose the correct answers to each question.

1 Two scientists from the National University believe they have found a(n) _____ for a disease which has crippled many children.
① isolation   ② cure
③ despair   ④ invisible

2 A hiccup occurs as a _____ of an action one's organs take to protect themselves.
① rid   ② result
③ nerve   ④ reflex

3 A recent survey _____ that three-quarters of CEOs in nonprofit organizations earned less than $100,000 last year.
① unknown   ② range
③ revealed   ④ benefit

D Translate into English or Korean.

1 The more contact a group has with another group, the more likely it is that objects or ideas will be exchanged.

_____

_____

2 Happy are those who do what they want to do in the future.

_____

3 그는 부드럽고 용감한 사람이라고 불린다.
(call, gentle, courageous, man)

_____

E Choose the correct words to fill in the blanks.

1 _____ they become, the more obstacles and monsters they can overcome until they eventually beat the game.
① Stronger   ② Strong are
③ Strong   ④ The stronger

2 _____ those who have dreams and are ready to pay the price to make them come true.
① They are happy   ② Happy
③ Happy is   ④ Happy are

3 Twice a month, we _____ to work around the clock.
① was made   ② make
③ made   ④ were made

F Choose the proper word for each sentence.

1 We must [conserve / observe] our woodlands for future generations.

2 Scientists have [conserved / observed] a drop in ozone levels over the Antarctic.

3 Thousands of people blocked the street, [protecting / protesting] against the new legislation which they don't like.

4 Physical exercise can [protect / protest] you against heart disease.

CHAPTER 11	DATE	SELF CHECK	TEACHER	PARENTS
Preview				
Unit 1				
Unit 2				
Unit 3				
Unit 4				
Unit 5				
Review				

Nike, 처음부터 큰 회사는 아니였다구요~~

나이키의 창립자인 필 나이트(Phil Knight)는 신화적인 비즈니스를 이루었으며 본인 자신도 억만장자가 되었습니다. 필 나이트는 오레곤 주립대학, 스탠포드 경영학교를 졸업했어요. 일본을 여행하는 도중 필은 '타이거' 라는 신발 회사 사장에게 자신을 운동 경기용품 회사의 미국 영업 대리자로 소개했는데, 사실 그것은 거짓이었습니다. 그 후 그는 BRS(Blue Ribbon Sports)를 만들었고, 경기 이벤트 때 트럭으로 러닝화를 팔았습니다. 그리고 얼마 후 필은 자신이 만든 제품을 생산하기 시작했습니다. 그는 회사의 이름을 나이키로 바꾸었고 첫 해에 판매는 8천 달러, 그리고 250달러의 이익을 보았죠. 필은 자신의 제품을 홍보이자 실험을 위해 대학시절 그의 코치였던 빌 바우어만(Bill Bowerman)에게 도움을 청하여 그의 선수들에게 신발을 신겨보고자 하였습니다. 그 후 어느날 그는, 그의 부인의 와플 다리미의 형태를 보고 아이디어를 얻어 연구했어요. 그는 기계에 고무 화합물을 넣었고, 그리고 고무 와플을 직접 구워 냈죠. 그리고 나서 그것들을 자르고 신발 밑바닥에 붙여 보았습니다. 선수들에게 사용해 보고 난 후 그들의 결과가 좋아진 것을 발견했습니다. 마찰력만 향상 된 것이 아니라 쿠션 효과도 생겼어요. 이렇게 해서 나이키 와플 트레이너가 탄생되었습니다. 1970년은 나이키가 신발 역사의 한 획을 그은 때였습니다. 나이키를 뭔가 다른 것으로 차별화시키게 된 것이죠. 필은 당시 테니스계의 이단아 죤 맥켄로(John McEnroe)를 스폰서해서 확실한 홍보효과를 얻었습니다. 그 이유는 죤 맥켄로는 게임 도중 심판에게 욕을 퍼부어 사람들의 시선을 집중시켰기 때문이었어요. 그 후 1979년까지 나이키는 뜨거운 인기를 끌었습니다. 하지만 그럼에도 불구하고 리복(Reebok)에 의해 추격을 당하기 시작했어요. 리복은 에어로빅 분야를 공략하여 성장하였습니다. 결국 신발 판매량에 있어서 나이키를 능가했어요. 나이키는 그들의 특화된 신발을 포함하여 신발 다자인을 다양화시켜 리복에 맞섰습니다. 그러던 중 결정적으로 바로 마이클 조던(Michael Jordan)이 등장했어요. 나이키는 노쓰 캐롤라이나(North Carolina) 대학의 마이클 조던과 계약했습니다. 나이키는 마이클을 위한 신발을 디자인했고, 그것을 Air Jordan X라고 불렀습니다. 결국 80년대 말 나이키는 매출은 연간 8억 7천만 달러에서부터 40억 달러로 급격히 뛰어올랐죠. 그 이유는 Air Jordan X 때문이 아니라 시장을 정확하게 읽는 나이키의 마케팅 능력에 있었을 거예요.

CHAPTER

12

CHAPTER 12

Preview

Word 🏠 단어도 모르면서 영어 한다 하지마!

define *v.* 정의를 내리다, 한정하다	**investigator** *n.* 조사자, 연구자, 수사관
treat *v.* 대우하다, 치료하다	**scene** *n.* 장면, 무대, 경치, 정세
prevalence *n.* 유행, 보급, 널리 퍼짐	**conduct** *n.* 행실, 지도 *v.* 수행하다
influence *n.* 영향, 효과, 세력	**debate** *v.* 논쟁(토론)하다 *n.* 토론
guarantee *v.* 보증하다 *n.* 보증	**morality** *n.* 도덕, 윤리, 교훈
analysis *n.* 분석, 해석, 분해	**penalize** *v.* 유죄를 선고하다
aspect *n.* 관점, 면, 양상	**subdue** *v.* 정복하다, 억제하다, 완화하다
categorize *v.* 분류하다, 범주에 넣다	**collapse** *v.* 무너지다, 붕괴시키다
preserve *v.* 보존하다, 저장하다	**statement** *n.* 진술, 성명서
authority *n.* 권위, 권력, 당국	**overthrow** *v.* 뒤엎다, 폐지하다 *n.* 타도

⁘ Mini Quiz

Draw a line from each word on the left to its definition on the right. Then, use the numbered words to fill in the blanks in the sentences below.

1 meditation   **a.** to send out radio or television programs

2 vital   **b.** continuing, or continuing to develop

3 contact   **c.** very strong and powerful, or very big and impressive

4 ongoing   **d.** extremely important and necessary for something to succeed or exist

5 broadcast   **e.** the practice of emptying your mind of thoughts and feelings, in order to relax completely

6 mighty

   f. to write to or telephone someone

7 Regular exercise is _____ for your health.

8 The discussions are still _____.

9 Give the names of two people who can be _____ in an emergency.

10 The interview was _____ live across Europe.

11 The authority of the once _____ king rotted away.

12 Yoga involves breathing exercises, stretching, and _____.

Grammar 👤 기본 문법도 모르면서 독해한다 하지마!

★ 명사절 접속사 that (that은 생략 가능)

They fear **that** these climbers may try to climb the biggest and tallest trees if they learn their exact locations.

그들은 이 나무 타는 사람들이 그것들의 정확한 위치를 알게 되면 가장 크고 가장 높은 나무들에 오르려고 할지도 모른다고 걱정한다.

★ 전치사의 목적어로 쓰이는 동명사

Music covers the whole range of emotions: it can make us feel happy or sad, helpless or energetic, and some music is capable *of* **overtaking** the mind until we forget all else. 음악은 감정의 전 범위를 아우른다. 그것은 우리를 기쁘게 혹은 슬프게, 무기력하게 혹은 기운 넘치게 만들 수 있으며, 어떤 음악은 그밖의 모든 것을 우리가 잊을 때까지 정신을 압도할 수 있다.

★ anything but vs nothing but (결코[전혀] ~아닌 vs ~외에는, 단지 ~일 뿐)

Their plans for the village are **anything but** down-to-earth.
마을에 대한 그들의 계획은 현실적인 것이 못된다.

I'm going to spend two weeks doing **nothing but** watching DVDs.
나는 2주 동안 아무것도 안 하고 DVD만 볼 것이다.

:: Mini Quiz

1   다음 문장에서 that이 생략된 부분을 찾으시오.

One of the greatest benefits of this is it lets in light and provides protection from the weather at the same time.

2   다음 각 괄호 안에서 알맞은 것을 고르시오.

In my hometown, nobody would buy melon without [to feel / feeling] it and [to smell / smelling] it; and nobody would dream of [to buy / buying] chicken without [to know / knowing] which farm it came from and what it ate.

3   다음 우리말에 맞게 괄호 안에서 알맞은 것을 고르시오.

He is [anything / nothing] but a pretty face.

그는 잘생긴 얼굴은 결코 아니다.

[1] Buddhists believe that they can find inner peace within themselves. And they think that meditation and karma will lead them to Nirvana. Karma can be defined as the rewards or punishments for past actions. Karma simply explains that what exists now has resulted from what was before. [2] A happy person who <u>treats</u> others with kindness and respect will meet people who respect him. This is called good karma. A person who mistreats others will be mistreated. This is called bad karma. Buddha did not wish his beliefs to replace other faiths. However, today there are over three hundred million Buddhists all around the world.

[3] Even though Buddha was born an Indian prince, Buddhism lost its influence in India by the 8th century, partly because of the prevalence of Hinduism, and partly because of the rise of Islam. Nevertheless, his ideas and beliefs are worshiped mostly in China, Korea, Japan, and Southeast Asia. [4] Buddhism is one of the major religious and moral forces in the world.

---

1 다음 중, 이 글의 밑줄 친 <u>treats</u>와 같은 의미로 쓰인 것은?

① It is my family's turn to <u>treat</u> this time.
② The patient was <u>treated</u> with new drugs.
③ My mom <u>treated</u> me to a hamburger.
④ He was upset by the way he was <u>treated</u>.
⑤ I gave some <u>treats</u> to my dog for behaving so well.

2 **Write True or False.**

(1) _____ By the 8th century, Buddhism lost its influence in India.

(2) _____ Buddhists believe that mistreating others and karma will lead them to Nirvana.

(3) _____ Today, there are over three million Buddhists all around the world.

단어 조사해 오세요~ **Word**

Buddhist

meditation

karma

Nirvana

define

deed

mistreat

Buddha

influence

prevalence

Buddhism

Hinduism

worship

moral

force

 **Drill 1** Grammar

양보의 부사절 even though, even if

부사절 even though는 문장 맨 앞에 위치하는 것이 보통이며, even though의 절 내용은 '사실'의 내용을 전달하고, 해석상 의미는 같지만 even if는 '가정'의 표현을 담고 있다.

- He is a great athlete. Even though he has cancer, he did well in the soccer game.

  그는 훌륭한 운동선수이다. 비록 그는 암에 걸렸지만, 그는 축구경기에서 능숙하게 했다.

- Even if the sun were to rise in the west, I would not change my mind.

  비록 태양이 서쪽에서 뜬다 할지라도, 나는 내 마음을 바꾸지 않을 것이다.

---

1   Childhood is an age of adventure. This is still true today, even though today the opportunities of adventure are considerably fewer than they used to be.

    해석 ◯ _____

2   It is difficult to know who are your good friends when everything is going well in your life, but good friends and faithful companions will not leave you even if you find yourself in the most difficult of situations.

    해석 ◯ _____

3   비록 귀신이 방안으로 들어왔는데도 불구하고, 우리는 비명을 지르지 않았다.
    (come, scream, into the room, the ghost)

    영작 ◯ _____

Drill 2 Translation

1   1번 문장 ◯ _____

2   2번 문장 ◯ _____

3   3번 문장 ◯ _____

4   4번 문장 ◯ _____

[1] The introduction of unique products alone does not guarantee market success. [2] Another vital factor is increasing one's responsiveness to the markets by providing products suited for the local communities that make up the market. This means understanding that each country, community and individual has unique characteristics and needs; it requires

_____. [3] In other words, one of the challenges is to avoid a one-size-fits-all strategy that places too much emphasis on the "global" aspect alone. Even categorizing countries as "developed" or "emerging" is dangerous. [4] Upon closer analysis, "emerging" countries are not only vastly different from one another, they are also composed of numerous unique individuals and communities. 기출

---

1 **Choose the best answer to fill in the blank.**

① global markets that expand rapidly

② employment of a one-size-fits-all strategy

③ sensitivity to regional and individual differences

④ resources that make the challenges meaningful

⑤ individual competition to raise productivity

2 **Choose the best main idea of the paragraph.**

① Local communities make up most of the global market.

② People should learn more about the customs of other countries.

③ The one-size-fits-all strategy has given a great success to the global marketing.

④ The idea of marketing should always be adaptable depending on individuals and communities.

⑤ Global marketing is a hard task for an ordinary company to begin.

단어 조사해 오세요~ **Word**

introduction

unique

guarantee

vital

responsiveness

make up

characteristic

needs

require

one-size-fits-all strategy

place emphasis on

aspect

categorize

analysis

vastly

be composed of

numerous

Drill 1 Grammar

관계사 that

관계대명사 that은 바로 앞에 있는 명사(선행사)를 꾸미는 형용사절 역할을 한다. 이때 '~하는, ~했던, ㄴ + 앞의 명사'로 해석하는데, 이러한 순서로 오는 that은 해석상 의미가 없다. 단지 기능상 꾸며 주는 역할을 하는 장치에 불과하다.

• Most parents punish their children in the same way that they were punished by their parents.   대부분의 부모들은 그들이 자신의 부모들에 의해 벌을 받았던 같은 방식으로 자녀들을 벌준다.

• Although this may sound like an obvious first step, it is a step that many people ignore.
비록 이것이 명백한 첫 단계처럼 들릴지라도, 그것은 많은 사람들이 무시하는 단계이다.

---

1   Talking with people that have different backgrounds from your own can help broaden your conversational repertoire and your thinking.

해석 ◯ _____

2   In choosing your occupation, the first thing that you have to consider is whether you are fit for it or not.

해석 ◯ _____

3   황금알을 낳는 거위는 죽이지 마라. (the goose, the golden eggs, lay, kill)

영작 ◯ _____

Drill 2 Translation

1   1번 문장 ◯ _____

2   2번 문장 ◯ _____

3   3번 문장 ◯ _____

4   4번 문장 ◯ _____

Grammar 👤 기본 문법도 모르면서 독해한다 하지 마!

★ 접속사 + 분사구문

Also, **when chatting** with friends, some teenage girls are too expressive, talking and laughing loudly, playing to their unreal audiences.

또한, 십대 소녀들이 친구들과 얘기를 할 때면, 그들은 과장되게 표현하거나, 크게 웃고 얘기하며 가상의 청중들이 있는 것처럼 행동한다.

★ [현재완료 vs 과거] 현재완료는 지금 현재의 상태를 기준으로 해서 과거의 한 시점으로부터 현재까지의 일을 나타낸다. 대부분 〈for + 기간〉이나 〈since + 과거의 한 시점〉과 함께 쓰인다.

Former U.S. President Jimmy Carter, who promotes Habitat for Humanity, **has toured** various countries since 1994.

사랑의 집짓기(HFH)를 추진했던 전 미국 대통령인 지미 카터는 1994년부터 여러 나라들을 방문해 왔다.

★ sensible 분별 있는 / sensitive 민감한 / sensual 육감적인 / senseless 감각이 없는, 무의식의

Hence, the time spent on regular examinations is a **sensible** investment in good health. 따라서 정기검진에 쓰는 시간은 건강을 위한 현명한 투자다.

:: Mini Quiz

1 다음 괄호 안에서 알맞은 것을 고르시오.

Many workers learn new skills while [keeping / to keep] their regular jobs.

2 다음 각 괄호 안에서 알맞은 것을 고르시오.

She [waited / has waited] for her favorite actor to come out since he [went / has gone] into the building.

3 다음 괄호 안에서 알맞은 것을 고르시오.

The homeroom teacher must be [senseless / sensitive] to a child's needs.

(A) [1] It's true that the human body has developed millions of nerves to be highly aware of what goes on both inside and outside of it. This helps us adjust to the world. Without our nerves we wouldn't know what's happening. However, we pay for our sensitivity. We can feel pain when the slightest things

are wrong with any part of our body. Thankfully, there is a way to handle pain. Look at the Indian monk who sits on a bed of nails. They can put a needle right through an arm, and feel no pain. [2] The ability that some humans have developed to handle pain should give us ideas about how the mind can deal with pain.

(B) A moment's drilling by the dentist may make us nervous and upset. Many of us cannot stand pain. [3] To avoid the pain of a drilling procedure that may last perhaps a minute or two, we demand the needle that deadens the nerves around the tooth.

(C) The big thing in withstanding pain is our attitude toward it. If the dentist says, "This will hurt a little," it helps us to accept the pain. By staying relaxed, and by treating the pain as an interesting sensation, we can handle the pain without falling apart. [4] After all, although pain is an unpleasant sensation, it is still a sensation, and sensations are the stuff of life.

---

1   (A), (B), (C)를 이어 하나의 글로 구성할 때 가장 적절한 순서는?

   ① (B) - (A) - (C)   ② (B) - (C) - (A)

   ③ (A) - (B) - (C)   ④ (C) - (B) - (A)

   ⑤ (C) - (A) - (B)

2   이 글의 요지로 알맞은 것을 고르시오.

   ① 고통을 두려워하는 치과 환자들이 늘고 있다.

   ② 통증을 통제하는 방법은 다양하다.

   ③ 신경을 통해 우리 몸의 변화를 알 수 있다.

   ④ 통증에 대한 태도에 따라서 통증을 통제할 수 있다.

   ⑤ 통증은 신경발달에 영향을 끼칠 수 있다.

단어 조사해 오서~ **Word**

highly aware

adjust

pay for

handle

deal with

drilling

stand

deaden

withstand

fall apart

sensation

stuff

🍴 Drill 1 Grammar

문장 맨 앞에 오는 to부정사

문장 맨 앞에 to부정사가 위치하여 콤마(,)로 분리되는 경우 콤마(,)옆에 있는 명사(즉, 주어)를 꾸며 주면서 '~(하기) 위하여'와 같은 역할을 하게 된다. 물론 실제 영자신문과, 소설, 수필 등에서는 콤마(,)로 구분해 주지 않는 경우가 있으니, 많은 영문을 통해 확실히 이해해 두어야 한다.

> To do ~ ...... ,　　　S (명사) + V ~ ......
> └──────────────→ S를 꾸며 주면서 '~위하여' 로 해석한다.

- **To learn English**, it is not always best to go to America.
  영어를 배우기 위하여, 미국에 가는 것이 항상 최선은 아니다.

- **To become healthy**, you should eat only healthy foods and exercise frequently.
  건강해지기 위해서, 당신은 오직 건강식만 먹고 자주 운동을 해야 한다.

1　To join the armed forces, the man had to take a physical and mental exam.

　　해석 ◉ ＿＿＿＿＿＿＿＿＿＿＿＿＿＿＿＿＿＿＿＿＿

2　To travel around the world, Jeff must work hard and save a lot of money.

　　해석 ◉ ＿＿＿＿＿＿＿＿＿＿＿＿＿＿＿＿＿＿＿＿＿

3　여자 친구의 선물을 사기 위해서, Chris는 새로운 백화점에 쇼핑을 갔다.
　　(at the new department store, went shopping, buy, gift)

　　영작 ◉ ＿＿＿＿＿＿＿＿＿＿＿＿＿＿＿＿＿＿＿＿＿

🍴 Drill 2 Translation

1　1번 문장 ◉ ＿＿＿＿＿＿＿＿＿＿＿＿＿＿＿＿＿＿＿

2　2번 문장 ◉ ＿＿＿＿＿＿＿＿＿＿＿＿＿＿＿＿＿＿＿

3　3번 문장 ◉ ＿＿＿＿＿＿＿＿＿＿＿＿＿＿＿＿＿＿＿

4　4번 문장 ◉ ＿＿＿＿＿＿＿＿＿＿＿＿＿＿＿＿＿＿＿

Newton was the first to point out _____, and that consequently color has to occur inside our brains. He wrote, "The waves themselves are not colored." [1] Since his time, we have learned that light waves are characterized by different frequencies of vibration. [2] When they enter the eye of an observer, they set off a chain of neurochemical events, the end product of which is an internal mental image that we call color. [3] The essential

point here is: What we perceive as color is not made up of color. [4] Although an apple may appear red, its atoms are not themselves red.

기출

neurochemical 신경 화학의

---

1 **What is the best title of this paragraph?**

① Differences in Color Names

② Frequencies of Vibration

③ Light Waves of an Object

④ Atoms of an Apple

⑤ Perception of Color

2 **Choose the best answer to fill in the blank.**

① the numbers of colors

② the structure of a human's eyes

③ the significance of colors

④ that colors affect humans in many ways

⑤ that light is colorless

단어 조사해 오세요~ **Word**

point out

consequently

characterize

frequency

vibration

observer

set off

a chain of

neurochemical

perceive

be made up of

 **Drill 1** Grammar

문장 맨 앞에 오는 what

문장 맨 앞에 what이 올 경우 '~것'과 비슷한 역할을 한다. 단, 문장 맨 뒤에 questions mark(?)가 있으면 '무엇'이라는 뜻이 된다. what은 선행사를 포함한다는 점에서 선행사를 수식하는 다른 관계대명사와 구별된다.

- **What** is learned in the cradle is carried to the grave.
  요람에서 배운 것은 무덤까지 간다. (세살 버릇 여든까지 간다.)

- **What** the textbooks do not teach you is when to apply the knowledge.
  교과서가 당신에게 가르쳐 주지 않는 것은 언제 그 지식을 적용하느냐이다.

---

1   What they seek is not so much profound knowledge as quick information.

   해석 ◎ _____

2   What you need to do immediately is eat less and exercise regularly if you want to reduce your body weight.

   해석 ◎ _____

3   역사가 우리에게 가르쳐 주는 것은 매우 중요하다. (teach, very important, history)

   영작 ◎ _____

🍴 **Drill 2** Translation

1   1번 문장 ◎ _____

2   2번 문장 ◎ _____

3   3번 문장 ◎ _____

4   4번 문장 ◎ _____

¹ Salt was man's first food seasoning, and it so dramatically altered his eating habits that it is not at all surprising that the action of spilling the precious ingredient _____.

Following an accidental spilling of salt, a superstitious nullifying gesture such as throwing a pinch of it over the left shoulder became a practice of the ancient people.

² The veneration of salt, and the foreboding that followed its spilling, is poignantly captured in Leonardo da Vinci's *The Last Supper*. Judas has spilled the table salt, foreshadowing the tragedy – Jesus' betrayal – that was to follow.

³ Historically, though, there is no evidence of salt having been spilled at *The Last Supper*. Leonardo wittingly incorporated the widespread superstition into his interpretation to further dramatize the scene. The classic painting thus contains two ill-boding omens: the spilling of salt, and thirteen guests at a table.

---

1 **Choose the best answer to fill in the blank.**

① became illegal behavior
② became a part of superstition
③ became equal to bad luck
④ changed moral standards
⑤ became more common

2 **Choose the best conclusion of this paragraph.**

① 소금을 만들기 위해서는 많은 공정 과정을 거쳐야 한다.
② 불길한 미신이 발생할 정도로 소금은 옛날부터 귀하게 여겨졌다.
③ '최후의 만찬' 논쟁에 대한 진실을 알아야 한다.
④ 불길한 일이 발생할 수 있으므로 사람들은 소금을 엎지르지 말아야 한다.
⑤ 소금은 인간의 첫 양념이므로 역사가 매우 깊다.

단어 조사해 오셔~ **Word**

spilling

nullify

tourist attraction

veneration

foreboding

poignantly

foreshadow

incorporate

further

ill-boding

omen

Drill 1 Grammar

분사구문 -ing

분사구문은 실제 영문에서 차지하는 비중이 많으므로 정확하게 이해해야 한다. 분사구문을 흔히 현재(-ing)와 과거(-ed/en) 분사구문으로 나누어 문장에서 시간, 이유, 조건, 양보, 동시동작, 연속동작 등을 나타낸다고 하는데, 이는 실제 영어를 활용 하는 데에 크게 중요하지 않을 때가 많다. 영어는 순서에 의해서 결정된다고 하였다. 문장 맨 앞에 -ing가 나와 콤마(,)로 분리될 경우 콤마(,)옆에 있는 명사(즉, 주어)를 꾸며 주면서 우리말 '~하는, ~한, ~ㄴ'을 붙여 해석하면 된다. 현대 영어에서는 〈관계대명사 +be동사〉의 생략을 크게 의식하지 않는다.

- Admitting what you say, I'm still against the plan.
  네가 말하는 것을 받아들이기는 했지만 나는 여전히 그 계획에는 반대한다.

- Suffering along with our anxieties and sorrows, we receive some pleasure from the experience. 걱정과 슬픔에 괴로워하는 우리는 그 경험으로부터 즐거움을 얻는다.

---

1 Lies are a part of our everyday social life. Not wanting to hurt the feelings of others, we frequently tell lies.

   해석 ◯ _____

2 Having examined my sister's pulse, the doctor said that there was nothing serious to worry about.

   해석 ◯ _____

3 공원을 걷고 있던 나는 우연히 그녀를 만났다. (meet, happened, park, walk)

   영작 ◯ _____

 Drill 2 Translation

1 1번 문장 ◯ _____

2 2번 문장 ◯ _____

3 3번 문장 ◯ _____

(A)

(a) Some psychologists believe that the experiences that include words and actions of others in our childhood affects our self-image and self-evaluation; for instance, whether we feel worthy or unworthy of respect and love, and whether we feel competent or useless. (b) The way we behave and think is likely to be influenced by what is stored in our memory banks. (c) For example, one father noticed that he became impatient with his children

whenever he had visitors in his house. (d) While discussing this with me, he discovered that his problem was not caused by fear of rejection by the visitors if his children misbehaved. (e)

(B)

Janet told me that she usually disbelieved Bill, her husband, when he praised her. (i) She had difficulty accepting his positive statements. (ii) It troubled Bill as much as Janet. (iii) One day, she ignored his praise, and she suddenly realized why she could not accept his compliments. It had started in her childhood. (iv) Her parents told her not to believe others' positive statements about her, because those people just wanted to take advantage of her in some way. (v) This past experience blocked her ability to accept others' love and care.

1 **What does the writer try to explain through (A) and (B)?**

① You always have to be careful when dealing with others.
② You will be rewarded if you behave well.
③ Positive thinking will bring about good results.
④ Your present behavior are affected by prior experience.
⑤ Love and understanding can resolve any problem.

2 (A)의 글의 흐름으로 보아, 다음 주어진 문장이 들어가기에 가장 적절한 곳은?

> This fear originated from his past experiences of rejection.

① (a)　　② (b)　　③ (c)　　④ (d)　　⑤ (e)

3 **Which statement in (B) relates to the underlined part 'what is stored' in (A)?**

① (i)　　② (ii)　　③ (iii)　　④ (iv)　　⑤ (v)

4 **Which best describes the mood or personality of the father in (A), and Janet in (B)?**

	Father		Janet
①	insane	⋯	disposed
②	irritated	⋯	incredulous
③	insulting	⋯	iniquity
④	strict	⋯	senseless
⑤	harassing	⋯	tense

단어 조사해 오셔~ **Word**

psychologist

self-image

self-evaluation

competent

be likely to

influence

memory bank

rejection

misbehave

praise

have difficulty -ing

positive statement

compliment

take advantage of

block

Along with zodiac signs and a constellation, the belief in blood types is very popular in modern Japan. The idea that blood types explain different personality types is relatively new. In 1916, a Japanese doctor wrote, "Blood type A people are mild-tempered and intellectual. Blood type B people are the opposite to type A." After that, the Japanese became very interested in blood types. Even today, Japanese ask each other about their blood type when they first meet. They find it difficult to understand that most foreigners don't know their own blood type. Most Japanese are type A while most Westerners are type O. Women's magazines generally give information about which types match which and what personality those blood types will have. According to Japanese researchers, certain personality characteristics are related to specific blood types.

People with blood type A are calm and serious. They have a firm character, and are reliable and trustworthy. They think things over and make plans carefully, and try to make themselves more like their own idea of what they should be. They like harmony, peace and organization. They work well with others and are sensitive, patient and affectionate. Their weaknesses are stubbornness and an inability to relax.

People with blood type B are curious and are often enthusiastic about something one minute and something else the next moment. B types tend to excel in things rather than just be average, but they can be so involved in something as to neglect other things. They have the image of being bright and cheerful, full of energy and enthusiasm. However, some people think that they are really quite different on the inside. They tend not to want to have much real contact with others. They are straightforward and like to do things their own way. Creative and flexible, they adapt easily to any situation. However, their insistence on being independent can sometimes go too far and become a weakness.

O types are generally loved by all and their image is of being peaceful, carefree, generous and big-hearted. They are easily influenced by other people or by what they see on TV. They appear to be clear thinkers and to be trustworthy, but often make big mistakes because they don't pay attention. They also have a stubborn and strong-willed side. They want to be leaders, and when they see something they want, they work hard to achieve their goal. Their weaknesses are vanity, jealousy and a tendency to be too competitive.

People with blood type AB are said to be considerate of other people's feelings and are careful when dealing with them. However, they are strict with themselves and those close to them. So they seem to have a dual personality in some cases. They can become sentimental, and tend to think too deeply about things. Cool and controlled, they're generally well-liked and have a lot of friends. However, sometimes they can be blunt and have difficulty making decisions.

1 **Choose the best title of this passage.**

① Blood types and immune system
② Personalities based on blood types
③ Four different kinds of blood types
④ Origins of blood types

2 **What can be inferred from this passage about blood types in Japan?**

① In Japan, blood type has influenced peoples lives in unexpected ways.
② Most Japanese believe specific blood types are related to personalities.
③ The westerners have finally noticed the potential of blood typing.
④ In Japan, everyone apparently knows his or her own blood type and want to know each other about their blood types.

3 **Complete the table by matching the sentences below. Match them to the blood type to which they relate.**

① They are said to be considerate of other people's feelings. _____ Blood type A

② They have the image of being bright and cheerful, full of energy and enthusism. _____ Blood type B

③ Their weaknesses are vanity, jealousy and a tendency to be too competitive. _____ Blood type AB

④ They make plans carefully, and try to make themselves more like their own idea of what they should be. _____ Blood type O

단어 조사해 오셔~ **Word**

zodiac signs

constellation

mild-tempered

specific

trustworthy

affectionate

weakness

stubbornness

enthusiastic

excel

straightforward

do things one's own way

adapt

insistence

big-hearted

strong-willed

vanity

tendency

deal with

dual personality

sentimental

blunt

make decision

A **Translate into English.**

1   신경 _____

2   통제를 잃다 _____

3   다루다 _____

4   대가를 치르다 _____

5   지적하다 _____

6   유발하다 _____

7   연쇄적인 _____

8   느끼다, 지각하다 _____

9   양념 _____

10 불길한 예감 _____

11 해석 _____

12 관광명소 _____

13 심리학자 _____

14 자기평가 _____

15 거절, 거부 반응 _____

16 ~을 이용하다 _____

17 온화한, 상냥한 _____

18 융통성 있는 _____

19 허영심 _____

20 감상적인, 다감한 _____

B **Translate into Korean.**

1   adjust _____

2   highly aware _____

3   deaden _____

4   withstand _____

5   observer _____

6   frequency _____

7   consequently _____

8   characterize _____

9   practice _____

10 nullify _____

11 veneration _____

12 incorporate _____

13 be likely to _____

14 misbehave _____

15 positive statement _____

16 praise _____

17 dual personality _____

18 big-hearted _____

19 excel _____

20 strong-willed _____

C Choose the correct answers to each question.

1 We have learned that light waves are _____ by different frequencies of vibration.
　① observer　　② a chain of
　③ point out　　④ characterized

2 According to Japanese researchers, certain personality characteristics are related to _____ blood types.
　① specific　　② zodiac
　③ weakness　　④ tendency

3 Mr. and Mrs Simpson seemed devoted to each other and were openly _____.
　① insistence　　② stubbornness
　③ excel　　④ affectionate

D Translate into English or Korean.

1 To get good grades, you have to believe in yourself and in your abilities.

_____

2 The essential point here is: What we perceive as color is not made up of color.

_____

_____

3 거리를 따라 걸어가면서, 나무을 인식하지 못할 수도 있지만, 한 새로운 연구에 따르면, 나무는 그늘을 제공하는 것보다 더 많은 일을 한다. (walk down)

_____,

you may not even notice the trees, but, according to a new study, they do a lot more than give shade.

E Choose the correct words to fill in the blanks.

1 _____ become a singer, you should learn to sing with a nice voice by using correct techniques.
　① So　　② To　　③ It　　④ Being

2 _____ is considered a status symbol will differ among countries, based on the states of their economic and technological development, and common status symbols will change over time.
　① What　② Which　③ That　　④ It

3 _____ at an angle in the water, the leaf fish is carried along by the currents until it comes near a smaller fish.
　① Hanging　　② To be hung
　③ Hang　　④ To hang

F Choose the proper word for each sentence.

1 He [conceived / perceived] a small figure in the distance.

2 She had [conceived / perceived] the idea of a series of novels.

3 Stern also studies and [deserves / observes] the behaviour of babies.

4 These people [deserve / observe] to make more than the minimum wage.

CHECK BOX

CHAPTER 13	DATE	SELF CHECK	TEACHER	PARENTS
Preview				
Unit 1				
Unit 2				
Unit 3				
Unit 4				
Unit 5				
Review				

학창시절 껌 좀 씹었니? — 네! 많이 씹었습니다!

껌은 우리에게 너무나도 친숙하고 부담없이 즐길 수 있는 기호식품이죠. 껌의 역사는 매우 오래되었다고 합니다. 늘 먹고 마시기만 하던 인간은 이외에도 항상 무언가를 씹고자 하는 충동을 느꼈으며 이러한 습관은 기원전부터 있었던 것으로 추측됩니다. 기원전 2세기경 멕시코의 마야족 동굴벽화에서 무언가를 씹는 그림이 발견되었으며 마야족 멸망 이후 아메리카 인디언들 사이에서 나무의 수액으로 껌과 비슷한 것을 만드는 방법이 전수되어 왔다고 합니다.

오늘날의 껌과 같은 제품은 1880년대 미국의 토머스 아담스(Thomas Adams)에 의해 상품화되었는데 멕시코에서 자라나는 사포딜라 나무의 라텍스인 치클을 뜨거운 물속에 넣어 부드럽게 한 다음 손으로 둥글게 만들어서 약국에서 판매한 것이 최초였습니다. 껌이 본격적으로 생산된 것은 1890년대 초반 윌리엄 위그리(William Wrigley)가 회사를 설립해 미국 전역에 판매하면서부터죠. 그의 판매 전략은 이익의 대부분을 무조건 광고에 투자하여 소비자들에게 위그리 츄잉껌(Wrigley's Chewing Gum)을 인식시키는 것이었습니다. 이러한 판매전략 덕분에 오늘날까지도 이 회사는 전 세계 껌시장의 최강자 위치를 지키고 있습니다. 1928년에는 회계사인 월터 다이머(Walter Diemer)가 분홍색 색소를 첨가한 풍선껌을 개발해 그 당시 대단한 인기를 모아 껌을 대중화시키는 데 막대한 영향을 끼쳤습니다. 군인들에게도 사랑을 받은 껌은 한국전쟁 당시 미국연합군이 들어오면서 우리나라에서도 대중화되기 시작했고 1956년에는 해태제과에서 순수 우리기술로 껌을 제조하게 되었습니다.

빠르고 정확한 독해를 위한

Just
READING

정답

3

신석영 지음

CHAPTER 01

Preview

Word • Mini Quiz

1. c	2. a
3. d	4. f
5. b	6. e
7. dictionary	8. mixture
9. pharmacist	10. appearance
11. recent	12. talent

Grammar • Mini Quiz

1. had	2. had played
3. will catch → catch	

Unit 1

Answers

1. ②　　　　　　　2. ②

Word

botanist 식물학자
identify 확인하다, 동일시하다
instead of ~대신에
native language 모국어
similarly 유사하게, 비슷하게
zoologist 동물학자
expert 전문가
behavior 행동
agree to ~에 동의하다
misunderstanding 오해, 분쟁
confuse 혼란시키다
refer to 말하다, 부르다
dictionary 사전
look up 찾아보다

Drill 1 • Grammar

1. 제3세계에서 소비되는 나무의 10분의 9는 취사와 난방용으로 사용된다.
2. 성공적인 학교를 만드는 데 있어서, 우리는 학교 공동체에 관련되어 있는 사람들 사이의 관계를 반드시 고려해야 한다.

3. The book borrowed from the library was uninteresting.

Drill 2 • Translation

1. 식물학자들은 식물들과 꽃들을 감정할 때, 그들의 모국어 대신에 라틴어를 사용한다.
2. 만약 과학자들이 라틴어를 사용하는 것에 동의하지 않는다면, 여러 나라 출신의 과학자들이 서로 이야기를 할 때 많은 오해가 있을 것이다.
3. 때때로, 같은 언어를 사용하는 사람들 사이에 같은 이름으로 불리는 동물이 한 종류 이상일 때는 더 혼란스러울 수 있다.
4. 하지만 각각의 사전을 찾아보면, 그것들은 세 종류의 다른 새들을 나타낸다는 것을 알게 될 것이다.

Unit 2

Answers

1. ⑤　　　　　　　2. ③

Word

volunteering 자원봉사
provide 제공하다
opportunity 기회
meet 충족시키다
commitment 의무, 책임
on the part of ~의 입장에서
talent 재능
insight 통찰력
career possibility 경험의 가능성
enhance 높이다, 강화하다
be impressed 감명 받다
intangible 무형의
barrier 장벽, 장애
issue 관심사, 문제점
satisfaction 만족감

Drill 1 • Grammar

1. 그녀는 거의 아무것도 모르는 주제에 대하여 글을 썼다.
2. 언어는 사람들이 다른 사람들과 함께 의사소통하는 수단이다.
3. There are special classes in which people learn how to control their fear.

Drill 2 • Translation

1. 자원봉사란 당신 자신과 당신이 살고 있는 지역사회와 세상에 대해서 배우면서, 사람들의 필요를 충족시키기 위해 시간과 에너지를 제공할 수 있는 기회를 당신에게 부여해 주는 경험이다.

2. (자원봉사를 통해서) 당신의 특별한 재능을 여러 가지 명분에 맞게 매우 다양한 형태로 사용할 기회가 많다.

3. 자원봉사는 당신이 (얻었던 것을) 사회에 환원하거나, 오해나 두려움의 장벽을 깨뜨리거나, 개인적인 관심사를 탐색하도록, 또 나아가서 재미를 갖도록 도와줄 수 있다.

4. 덧붙이자면, 당신의 자원봉사는 개인의 만족감을 증가시킬 뿐만 아니라 더 나은 사회를 건설하는 데 효과를 보게 될 것이다.

Unit 3

Answers

1. ③　　　　　　　　2. ①

Word

survey (설문)조사
mobile phone 핸드폰, 휴대전화
conflict 싸움, 분쟁
political 정치(학)의
struggle 싸움, 다툼
politician 정치가
prosecutor 검사, 검찰관
a majority of 대다수의
car-related accident 자동차 관련 사고
noise pollution 소음공해
regardless of ~와 관계없이, ~에 개의치 않고
disturbingly 방해가 되는, 불안하게 하는
disturb 방해하다
reflect ~을 반영하다, ~을 나타내다
endless 끝없는

Drill 1 • Grammar

1. 그 학생은 다리가 짧고 강하지 않기 때문에 우수한 축구 선수가 되는 것은 어렵다. 그 결과, 그는 골프와 탁구를 배우고 있다.

2. 로마를 여행하는 동안 우리가 보기를 희망했던 모든 경치를 보는 것은 어려웠다. 다만 시간이 충분하지 않아서 우리는 미래에 다시 가기를 바란다.

3. It is wrong to give children everything they want.

Drill 2 • Translation

1. 최근 정치가들과 검사들 사이의 정치적 갈등에서 양측은 핸드폰으로 문제를 해결할 수 있었다.

2. 요즘 차와 관련된 사고의 대다수는 운전 중 또는 붐비는 길을 건너는 동안 핸드폰 통화를 하는 사람들에 의해 일어났다.

3. 한국에서는, 시간과 장소를 불문하고 핸드폰 통화를 하는 아이들뿐만 아니라 노인들을 보는 것이 매우 흔한 일이다.

4. 핸드폰에 의해 야기되는 그러한 문제들은 다른 사람들과 연결되고자 하는 한국 사람들의 끝없는 욕구를 반영한다.

Unit 4

Answers

1. ③　　　　2. ⑤　　　　3. ⑤　　　　4. ①

Word

drunken man 술 취한 사람
sidewalk 인도
companion 동행인
park 주차하다
pass 추월하다, 앞지르다
whizz by 씽하며 날아가다
properly 적절히, 적당히
over-simplification 지나친 단순화
speeder 속도광, 속도위반자
overcome 극복하다
prejudice 편견
limit 제한하다
judge 판단하다
appearance 외모
no longer 더 이상 ~않다
pay attention to ~에 주의를 기울이다
widen ~을 넓히다
horizon 한계, 범위
delightful 몹시 유쾌한
maintain 유지하다
original judgment 원래(본래)의 판단

Unit 5

Answers

1. ⑤

2. (c) is the original shape of the coca cola bottle
   → was the original shape of the coca cola bottle

3. ①

4. ③

Word

pharmacist 약제사
Atlanta 애틀란타 (조지아 주의 도시)
extract 추출물
coca 코카잎(나무)
cola nut 콜라 열매
mixture 혼합물
contain 함유하다, ~이 들어있다
cocaine 코카인(코카잎에서 뽑아낸 마취제)
pharmacy 약국
legally 합법적으로
treat 치료하다
headache 두통
come up with ~을 생각해내다
distinctive 독특한
script 서체
be inspired by ~에 의해 영감을 받다
gourd-shaped 호리병박 모양의
pod 꼬투리
accountant 회계원(사)
mass-produce 대량 생산하다
unique 독특한, 훌륭한
interestingly 재미있게(도)
spread throughout the world 전 세계에 퍼지다
provide 공급하다, 제공하다
local resident 지역 주민
fight against ~에 반대하여 싸우다
original taste 본래의 맛

5. 기회 6. 충족시키다
7. 무형의 8. 의무, 책임
9. 대다수 10. 싸움, 다툼
11. ~와 관계없이 12. 성가시게 하다
13. 판단하다 14. 몹시 유쾌한
15. 지나친 단순화 16. 적절히, 적당히
17. 회계사 18. 치료하다
19. 공급하다, 제공하다 20. 재미있게(도)

C.

1. ② 2. ① 3. ④

D.

1. 나는 부상당한 한 여자가 응급실로 옮겨지고 그녀의 가족들이 그 옆에서 울고 있는 것을 보았다.
2. 나는 그가 아무것도 아는 바가 없는 프로젝트를 지원하는 것을 본 적이 없다.
3. It is impossible to ask Jim not only to come to pick us up but also to drive us to the airport.

E.

1. ③ 2. ④ 3. ① 4. ①

F.

1. accept / permit 2. occasion / chance
3. appear / emerge 4. ceaseless / constant
5. expand / broaden

Review

A.

1. zoologist 2. native language
3. misunderstanding 4. identify
5. volunteering 6. insight
7. issue 8. enhance
9. at least 10. recent
11. usefulness 12. selfishness
13. companion 14. overcome
15. maintain 16. whizz by
17. extract 18. pharmacy
19. mass-produce 20. local resident

B.

1. 공유하다 2. 식물학자
3. 말하다, 부르다 4. 유사하게, 비슷하게

CHAPTER 02

Preview

Word • Mini Quiz

1. e	2. c
3. d	4. a
5. f	6. b
7. mature	8. huge
9. orbit	10. available
11. landed	12. attentive

Grammar • Mini Quiz

1. appear
2. ③ on → at
3. others see you → how others see you

Unit 1

Answers

1. ④   2. ②

Word

huge 거대한
creature 생물, 동물
newborn 새로 태어난, 신생의
full-grown 충분히 성장한
mammal 포유동물
warm-blooded animal 온혈동물
womb (고래의) 자궁
breathe 숨을 쉬다, 호흡하다
gill 아가미
surface 수면
zoologist 동물학자
ancestor 조상
used to do ~하곤 했(었)다
evolve 진화하다, 발전하다
fishlike 물고기 같은

Drill 1 • Grammar

1. 우리 사회에서 가장 많이 교육받은 대다수의 사람들이 우리나라의 역사를 거의 모른다는 것은 매우 놀라운 일이다.
2. 사람들이 늘 휴일을 갖고 싶어 하는 것은 당연하다.
3. It is not clear that God created the whole world.

Drill 2 • Translation

1. 흰긴수염고래는 100피트까지 자랄 수 있으며, 새로 태어난 흰긴수염고래는 다 자란 코끼리보다 더 크다.
2. 고래는 항온동물이고 새끼가 어미의 자궁에서 태어나고 어미젖을 먹기 때문에 포유동물이다.
3. 고래는 포유동물이기 때문에, 그들은 호흡을 위해 아가미를 사용하는 물고기들과 달리 폐를 통해 호흡한다.
4. 동물학자들에 의하면, 고래의 조상은 고대에 육지에서 살았지만 진화하여 물속에서 살기 시작한 이후로 물고기 같아졌다고 한다.

Unit 2

Answers

1. ②   2. ①

Word

adolescents 사춘기 남녀들
tremendous 엄청난
growth spurts 폭발적인 성장변화
mature 성숙하다
puberty 사춘기
in sequence 차례로
trunk 몸통
awkward 이상한
shape 몸매, 체격
magazine ads 잡지 광고
limit 한계
appearance 외모
focus A on B B에 A를 집중하다

Drill 1 • Grammar

1. 문제는 그가 그의 아버지가 다녔던 대학에 가기를 원하지 않는다는 것이다.
2. 비록 어렸지만 Franz는 독일이 프랑스와 잔인한 전쟁을 했었다는 것과 그의 조국 프랑스가 패했었다는 것을 알았다.
3. The fortune teller advised that the couple should not get married.

Drill 2 • Translation

1. 어떤 청소년들은 4, 5학년 때 엄청난 변화를 겪지만 어떤 다른 청소년들은 고등학교 때까지도 성장이 시작되지 않기도 한다.

2. 소녀들에게 성장변화는 사춘기 초기에 시작되지만 소년들은 사춘기 중반이나 후반기에 시작된다.

3. 당신의 몸이 너무 늦거나 너무 빨리 변하거나 또는 친구들의 모습이나 텔레비전이나 잡지 광고에서 보는 사람들의 모습과 다르다고 걱정할지도 모른다.

4. 외모에 대해 너무 걱정을 많이 하기보다는 당신의 에너지를 일상생활에서 친구들과 재미있는 활동에 집중해라.

Unit 3

Answers

1. ②　　　　　　2. ③

Word

construct 건설하다, 세우다
material 재료, 원료
fertile region 비옥한 지역
available 이용 가능한, 쓸모 있는
block out 막다, 차단하다
solar radiation 태양 복사열
insulation 단열재, 절연체
durability 내구성(력)
Arctic 북극
access to ~에 접근(출입)하다
be made of ~로 구성되다
bamboo 대나무
palm tree 야자나무
fibrous 섬유의, 섬유가 많은

Drill 1 ● Grammar

1. 그들은 서로 도와주고, 일에 자부심을 느끼며, 유쾌한 작업환경 유지를 조성하는 직원을 찾는다.

2. 사업이나 직업에서 성공하지 못하는 사람들은 집중력이 부족한 사람들이다.

3. A person who has faith in himself can be faithful to others.

Drill 2 ● Translation

1. 예를 들면 비옥한 지역에 사는 사람들은 가장 구하기 쉬운 재료인 진흙과 찰흙을 사용하는데, 그것들은 열과 태양복사열을 잘 차단한다.

2. 반면에 북극 지역에 살고 있는 에스키모인들은 나무가 없는 눈과 얼음의 지역에 살고 있기 때문에 두꺼운 얼음 덩어리로 집을 짓는다.

3. 사람들이 쉽게 삼림에 접근할 수 있는 북유럽, 러시아 그리고 세계의 다른 지역들에서는 집이 보통 나무로 지어진다.

4. 그래서 사람들이 이러한 거칠고 섬유가 많은 식물을 사용하여 그들의 집을 짓는다.

Unit 4

Answers

1. ④　　　　2. ④　　　　3. ③　　　　4. ⑤

Word

rooftop 지붕위의
of use 쓸모 있는
aircar 비행선
ease 천천히 움직이다
swing 흔들리다
crash 요란한 소리를 내다
incredible 믿을 수 없는, 어마어마한
boom 울리다
roar 으르렁거리다
long-range 장거리의
altitude 고도
bang 쾅 소리를 내다
clatter 덜커덕거리다
duration 지속
power up 동력을 증가시키다
deck 갑판
orbit 범위, 궤도
long for 동경하다
irresistible 억누를 수 없는
urge 충동

Unit 5

Answers

1. ①　　　　2. ⑤　　　　3. ①　　　　4. ②

Word

stick to ~을 고수하다, 얽매이다
emergency situation 응급상황
overly 과도하게, 지나치게
attentive 세심한, 주의 깊은
procedure 절차, 행위, 조치
supervise 감독하다, 관리하다
under control 지시(감독) 하에
priority 우선 순위
struggle 버둥거리다, 허덕이다
larger objective 커다란 목표
fit (into) ~에 적합하다
route 항로, 진로

land (on) ～에 착륙하다
adjustment 조절, 조정
achieve 달성하다, 성취하다
undertake (일을) 맡다, 책임지다

Review

A.

1. full-grown	2. creature
3. zoologist	4. ancestor
5. mature	6. awkward
7. appearance	8. shape
9. material	10. Arctic
11. fibrous	12. durability
13. aircar	14. orbit
15. altitude	16. long-range
17. stick to	18. under control
19. supervise	20. fit (into)

B.

1. 수면, 표면	2. ~하곤 했다
3. 포유동물	4. 아가미
5. 폭발적인 성장	6. 한계

7. 엄청난 8. 사춘기 남녀들
9. 단열재, 절연체 10. 야자나무
11. ~에 접근하다, 출입하다 12. 태양 복사열
13. 덜커덕거리다 14. 지속
15. 믿을 수 없는 16. 쓸모 있는
17. 조절, 조정 18. 치료하다
19. (~에) 착륙하다 20. 절차, 행위, 조치

C.

1. ② 2. ④ 3. ③

D.

1. 아무도 나서서 그 할머니를 도와주려 하지 않았다는 사실은 놀라웠다.
2. 그는 2010년에 전쟁이 일어나는 것뿐만 아니라 누가 이길 것인지도 예언했다.
3. The rule of this game is that people ask questions and then other people who know the answers explain them.

E.

1. ④ 2. ① 3. ② 4. ③

F.

1. d / h 2. a / f 3. c / i
4. b / j 5. e / g

CHAPTER 03

Preview

Word • Mini Quiz

1. b	2. e
3. a	4. c
5. d	6. necessary
7. unreasonable	8. convenient
9. friendly	10. native

Grammar • Mini Quiz

1. makes 2. myself 3. latest

Unit 1

Answers

1. ② 2. ④

Word

seem ～처럼 보이다
influence 영향
gloomy 우울한, 침울한
depress 우울하게 하다
negative feeling 부정적인 감정
indoor 실내의
lighten 기운나게 하다, 기쁘게 하다
energetic 원기(왕성)한

tend to do ～하는 경향이 있다
friendly 친절한
be willing to 기꺼이 ～하다
receive 받다
affect ～에 영향을 끼치다

Drill 1 • Grammar

1. 사실, 연구는 나이가 신체 상태보다는 정신 상태라는 일반적인 지혜를 확인시켜 준다.
2. 현재 우리의 많은 곤경과 스트레스는 시간이 충분치 않다라는 우리의 생각에서 온다.
3. The old man always thanked God for the fact that he was still alive.

Drill 2 • Translation

1. 어떤 사람들은 하늘이 흐려지면 침울해지고 심지어 어떤 사람들은 우기 동안 우울해진다.
2. 비 또는 먹구름은 이유 없이 사람들을 슬프고 우울하게 만드는 것처럼 보인다.
3. 나쁜 날씨 동안 사람들은 실내에서 너무 오랫동안 지내야 하기 때문에 이러한 부정적인 감정을 가질 수 있다.
4. 날씨가 우리 기분에 영향을 미친다는 가장 흥미로운 사실은 사람이 얼마나 많이 밖에 있는지와 그것이 어떤 계절인지 사이의 연관성이다.

Unit 2

Answers

1. ②

Word

point 요점
diffident 자신이 없는
unsuccessful 성공하지 못한
failure 실패
focus on ～에 초점을 맞추다
constantly 계속하여
no mater where ～어디에 있든지 간에
wallow 파묻히다
miserable 비참한
potential 잠재적인
accept 받아들이다
necessary 없어서는 안 될

Drill 1 • Grammar

1. 그것이 왜 그녀의 얼굴 전체에 주름이 그렇게 깊은지의 이유이다.
2. 사람들이 산에 가는 것을 좋아하는 여러 가지 이유가 있다.

3. Angela said (the reason) why she was late for that meeting.

Drill 2 • Translation

1. 나의 요점은 지금 당신이 실패한 것만 들여다보고 그것에 초점을 맞추기 때문에 당신이 자신이 없고 멍청하고 성공하지 못한다는 것이다.
2. 당신이 간파하지 못하고 있는 것은 성공을 하고 자신 있는 사람에게조차 상황은 잘못 돌아간다는 점이다.
3. 자신 있는 사람들은 문제를 파고들어 다시 세우고 전진해나간다.
4. 지금 당신이 미래의 성공에 대한 잠재력을 보지 않고 대신 실패한 것을 들여다보고 있기 때문에 자신 없기를 택하고 있는 것이다.

Unit 3

Answers

1. ③　　　　　　　2. ④

Word

almanac 책력(일출 시각 · 월령 · 조석 등을 기록), 천문력
maroon (사람을) 무인도에 버리다, 귀향 보내다
native 원주민, 현지인
hostile 적의 있는, 비우호적인
refuse 거절하다
total eclipse (of the moon) 개기월식
threaten 협박하다, 위협하다
hide 감추다, 숨기다
occur 발생하다, 일어나다
be terrified 무서워하다, 겁먹다
feed 음식을 주다
in return 답례로, 그 대신에
prophet 예언자
supernatural 초자연적인

Drill 1 • Grammar

1. 부모들은 자녀들이 영향을 받을 수 있는 좋은 행동의 귀감(모델)이 되어야 한다.
2. 그녀는 반 친구들과 함께 불렀던 노래를 흥얼거리기 시작했고, 눈물이 뺨을 타고 흘러내렸다.
3. The strange letters the novelist Poe was reading were found in her attic.

Drill 2 • Translation

1. 1504년에 콜럼버스는 몇 주 동안 자메이카의 무인도에 유배되었다.
2. 어느 날, 콜럼버스는 책력에서 배운 것을 기억해냈다. 그것은 1504년 2월 29일에 개기월식이 있을 것이라는 것이다.
3. 그래서 콜럼버스는 원주민들이 그에게 양식을 주지 않으면 달을 숨겨

버리겠다고 위협했다.

4. 하지만 2월 29일 밤에, 개기일식 정말로 일어났고 모든 자메이카인들은 겁을 먹었다.

Unit 4

Answers

1. ⑤   2. ①   3. ②   4. ③

Word

astronomy 천문학

principle 원리

unreasonable 불합리한, 비이성적인

not because A but because B A 때문이 아니라 B 때문이다

alien 외계인

suspect 의심하다

byproduct 부산물

star formation 별의 형성

originate 발생하다

suitable planet 생존에 적합한 행성

admit 인정하다

populate 사람이 ~에 거주하다

spacecraft 우주선

intelligent life 지적 생명체

planetary system (우리 지구와 같은) 행성 체계

orbit 궤도를 돌다

laws of physics 물리학의 법칙

far apart 멀리 떨어져

Unit 5

Answers

1. ①   2. ②   3. ④   4. ⑤

Word

ordinary 일상적인, 보통의

technology (과학)기술

search for ~을 찾다

select 선택하다

palm-sized 손바닥 크기의

user-friendly (시스템이) 사용하기 쉬운

convenient 편리한

communicate with ~와 의사소통을 하다

no matter where 어디에서 ~하더라도

latest 최신의

device 장치, 설비

home appliance 가전제품

drown out 사라지게 하다, 잠식시키다

addictive 중독성이 있는

electromagnetic field 전자기장

leave ~ behind ~을 뒤에 남겨 두다

turn off 끄다

Review

A.

1. seem	2. depress
3. lighten	4. energetic
5. point	6. accept
7. constantly	8. wallow
9. occur	10. in return
11. threaten	12. prophet
13. byproduct	14. principle
15. orbit	16. admit
17. ordinary	18. device
19. home appliance	20. turn off

B.

1. 영향	2. ~하는 경향이 있다
3. ~에 영향을 끼치다	4. 기꺼이 ~하다
5. 실패	6. 어디에서 ~하더라도
7. 잠재적인	8. 자신이 없는
9. 개기일식	10. 초자연적인
11. 원주민, 현지인	12. 적의 있는, 비우호적인
13. 사람이 ~에 거주하다	14. 행성 체계
15. 의심하다	16. 불합리한, 비이성적인
17. ~을 찾다	18. ~와 의사소통을 하다
19. 최신의	20. ~을 뒤에 남겨두다

C.

1. ④   2. ②   3. ④

D.

1. 대학입학시험을 보지 않아도 된다는 소문은 사실이 아니었다.

2. 숙제를 끝내는 것이 네가 해야 할 첫 번째 일이다.

3. Psychologists studied the reasons why video games are hard to give up.

E.

1. ②　　　2. ②　　　3. ③　　　4. ①

F.

1. b / g　　　2. e / j　　　3. a / d
4. c / i　　　5. f / h

CHAPTER 04

Preview

Word • Mini Quiz

1. d　　　　　　　2. a
3. f　　　　　　　4. b
5. c　　　　　　　6. e
7. peel　　　　　8. recipe
9. evidence　　　10. wealth
11. armor　　　　12. purpose

Grammar • Mini Quiz

1. does　　　2. remain　　　3. misplaced

Unit 1

Answers

1. ①　　　　　　　2. ②

Word

merchant 상인
nomadic 유목민의
Tartars 러시아의 타타르족
soften 부드럽게 하다
saddle 말 안장
pound 빻다
bit 작은 조각
scrape (고기 조각을) 문지르다
season 양념하다
find one's way 길을 찾아가다
refer to A as B B를 A의 이름으로 부르다
recipe 조리법
broil (불에) 굽다
term 용어
ground beef 갈은 쇠고기

Drill 1 • Grammar

1. 그는 몇 년 동안 거기에 살았던 것 같다.
2. 풍경을 빨리 지나치는 것은 전혀 여행하지 않은 것과 같다.
3. He is happy to have finished his homework yesterday.

Drill 2 • Translation

1. 1800년대 초 아시아로 여행을 하던 어느 독일 상인이 타타르 유목민들이 고기를 말안장 밑에 깔고 앉아서 고기를 부드럽게 만드는 것을 보게 되었다.
2. 타타르인들은 그것을 함께 문지른 다음 양념을 해 먹었다.
3. '햄버거'라는 말은 1834년 뉴욕의 델모니코 식당의 메뉴에 나타났던 것으로 믿어진다.
4. 그렇지만 그 왕좌에 대한 또 다른 주장도 있다.

Unit 2

Answers

1. ③　　　　　　　2. ④

Word

heartfelt 진정어린, 진심에서 우러난
act 행위
appreciation 감사
be amazed at ~에 놀라다
purpose 목적
express 표현하다
gratitude 감사(하는 마음)
be good at -ing ~하는 것을 잘하다
attention 주의, 주의력
be touched 감동을 받다
grateful 감사하는, 고마워하는
whereby 그리고, 그것으로 인하여

Drill 1 • Grammar

1. 벤치에서 잠을 자고 있는 남자들은 그들을 돌볼 가족이 없다.

2. 그 코너에 서 있는 남자는 영어로 된 신문을 읽고 있는 중이었다.

3. The woman holding a knife in her hands is waiting for the ghost.

Drill 2 • Translation

1. 그렇게 하기 위해 매주 몇 분 시간을 내는 것은 당신에게 많은 도움을 준다.

2. 일단 이런 시도를 하기로 결정하면, 당신은 얼마나 많은 사람들이 당신의 목록에 올라오는지를 보고 놀라게 될 것이다.

3. 이런 짧은 편지를 쓰는 행위는 당신 삶 속에서 무엇이 옳은지에 대해 당신의 주의를 집중시킬 뿐만 아니라 그것을 받는 사람은 감동을 받고 감사할 것이다.

4. 흔히 이런 간단한 행위가 일련의 사랑을 시작한다, 그리고 그것으로 인해 당신의 편지를 받은 사람은 다른 사람에게 똑같은 일을 하고 싶은 마음이 들 것이다, 또는 아마도 다른 사람에 대해 한층 사랑을 느끼고 그 사랑을 실천하게 될 것이다.

Unit 3

Answers

1. ③   2. ④

Word

great talker 수다쟁이, 잘 지껄이는 사람
poetry 시
word 말
be carried away 날아가다
Mediterranean 지중해
fragment 단편
philosophical 철학의
literary 문학의
criticism 비평
in the sense of ~의 의미에서
refuse 거절하다
naive 순진한, 소박한
evidence 증거
overly 너무, 지나치게
honey-mouthed 입에 사탕발림을 한, 그럴싸하게 들리는 아름다운 말을 하는
unfaithful 불충실한, 성실하지 않은

Drill 1 • Grammar

1. 벌새는 또한 가장 아름다운 새들 가운데 하나이다. 벌새는 너무도 아름다워서 날아다니는 꽃이라 불려왔다.

2. 그에게는 너무도 사나운 개가 있어서 아무도 감히 그의 집 근처에 가지 못했다.

3. The stone was so heavy that I could not move it.

Drill 2 • Translation

1. 그리스인들은 굉장한 수다쟁이들이었기 때문에 그래서 다른 것들도 그렇겠지만 시에 대해서도 틀림없이 말을 많이 했을 것이다.

2. 플라톤 이전에는 시인들 작품 속에 한두 줄 또는 철학적 저서들 중에서 약간의 단편적인 것들을 제외하면 문학이론이라는 의미에서 진정한 문학비평이라는 것은 존재하지 않았다.

3. 그래서 문학에 관한 일반적인 이론으로 출발하려고 한다면 우리는 플라톤에서부터 시작해야 한다.

4. 너무 순진한 연인들처럼 스스로의 눈으로 보는 증거조차 믿기를 거부한 것이다.

Unit 4

Answers

1. ③   2. ⑤   3. ①

4. The use of detergent to clean the fruit can also cause additional water pollution.

Word

nonetheless 그럼에도 불구하고, 그래도, 역시
nutritious 영양분이 많은
peel 껍질, 껍질을 벗기다
essential 없어서는 안 될
dietary fiber 식이섬유
blood sugar 혈당
diabetes 당뇨병
organic 유기체의, 유기 농법의
pesticide 살충제, 농약
contribute to ~에 공헌하다
roughness 거칠음
detergent 세제

Unit 5

Answers

1. ⑤   2. ④   3. ③   4. ③

Word

combatant (격)투사, 싸우는 사람

brutal 잔인한

gladiator （고대 로마의）검투사

Etruscan 에트루리아의(인)

prior to ～에 앞서, 먼저

foundation 건설

force 강요하다

adopt 채택하다

funeral ceremony 장례식

entertainment 오락, 즐거움

arena 원형 투기장

wealth 부

fame 명성

armor 갑옷

have a mock fight 싸우는 척하다

a variety of 여러 가지의

fate 운명

after a while 얼마 후에, 이윽고

Review

A.

1. merchant
2. saddle
3. bit
4. recipe
5. act
6. be touched
7. heartfelt
8. purpose
9. great talker
10. unfaithful
11. criticism
12. naive
13. nonetheless
14. essential
15. detergent
16. organic

17. gladiator
18. wealth
19. arena
20. adopt

B.

1. 유목민의
2. (불에) 굽다
3. 양념하다
4. 왕좌
5. 주의, 주의력
6. 감사하는, 고마워하는
7. 감사
8. 표현하다
9. 입에 사탕발림을 한
10. 거절하다
11. 철학의
12. 문학의
13. 영양분이 많은
14. 당뇨병
15. 식이 섬유
16. 혈당
17. 운명
18. 싸우는 척하다
19. ～에 앞서, 먼저
20. 건설, 설립

C.

1. ①
2. ④
3. ④

D.

1. 돌에 새겨진 글씨는 날씨에 의해 닳아진 듯 보인다.
2. 데이터를 분석하는 이 소프트웨어는 최신이다.
3. The musical was so terrible that we walked out in the middle.

E.

1. ②
2. ②
3. ③
4. ④

F.

1. b / d
2. f / i
3. a / e
4. h / j
5. c / g

CHAPTER 05

Preview

Word • Mini Quiz

1. d
2. b
3. e
4. a
5. f
6. c
7. detergent
8. pretend
9. regretted
10. vocabulary.

11. expression
12. nausea

Grammar • Mini Quiz

1. ③
2. would have seen
3. which

Unit 1

Answers

1. ③   2. ①

Word

mailbox （개인의） 우편함
label 꼬리표, 라벨
awesome 굉장한, 아주 멋진
content 내용(물)
stomachache 복통, 위통
as a matter of fact 사실은, 실제로
detergent 세정제, 세제
advertise 광고하다, 선전하다
get over ～에서 회복하다

Drill 1 • Grammar

1. 많은 과학자들이 지구가 무언가에 의해 창조되었다고 믿는다.
2. 그녀는 다시는 이와 같은 기회가 다시 없을 것이라는 것을 알고 있다.
3. Most college students know good jobs are hard to find.

Drill 2 • Translation

1. 병의 라벨에 "신선한 레몬 쥬스 함유"라는 말과 함께 2개의 레몬 그림이 있었다.
2. 사실, 그 병은 세제회사에서 보낸 무료 샘플이었다.
3. 라벨에 "신선한 레몬 쥬스 함유"라고 되어 있었던 것은 그 회사에서는 세제가 좋은 냄새가 난다고 광고하고 싶었기 때문이었다.
4. 대부분의 사람들은 복통을 일으켰지만 몇 시간 후에 회복이 되었다.

Unit 2

Answers

1. ①   2. ②

Word

value 가치관, 가치기준
determine 결정하다
forbid 금하다
force 억지로 시키다
beverage 음료
thrive 자라다
taboo 금지, 금제
refuse to ～하기를 거부하다
eat one's fill 실컷 먹다

rattlesnake 방울뱀
nausea 구역질, 혐오
vomit 구토
helping 음식 한 그릇
delicacy 진미, 별미

Drill 1 • Grammar

1. 시는 우리에게 우리의 삶 속에서 사라진 것을 제공한다 - 상상의 즐거움의 경험을.
2. 경찰은 누군가를 체포할 때 용의자에게 그 사람의 권리가 무엇인지를 말해야 한다.
3. Nobody knows what will happen in the future.

Drill 2 • Translation

1. 우리의 가치관은 부모에 의해 결정되며 더 큰 의미로는 우리가 살고 있는 문화에 의해 결정된다.
2. 예를 들어, 중국의 일부 지방에서는 우유를 마시는 것이 금지되어 있다.
3. 손님들은 어떤 고기인지 궁금해했지만 배가 부르게 먹을 때까지 나는 말해 주지 않았다.
4. 내가 방울뱀을 중국인에게 대접했다면, 틀림없이 한 접시 더 요구했을 것이다. 중국에서는 그 요리가 진미로 평가되기 때문이다.

Unit 3

Answers

1. ⑤   2. ⑤

Word

difference 차이점
seem like ～처럼 보이다
pronunciation 발음
tend to ～하는 경향이 있다
consonant 자음
articulate 똑똑히(또렷하게) 발음하다
drop 탈락되다, 없어지다
bonnet 덮개, 커버

Drill 1 • Grammar

1. 풍력은 미래에 사람들이 의존할 수 있는 에너지원이다.
2. 오직 64명만을 태우는 Sea Cloud호를 타고 여행하는 것은 특별한 경험이다.
3. My girlfriend always bought me presents which were cheap.

Drill 2 • Translation

1. 하지만 영국 영어와 미국 영어 사이에는 중요한 차이점이 있어서 때때로 그들은 완전히 다른 언어인 것처럼 보인다.
2. 둘째로, 영국과 미국 영어는 종종 같은 의미에 다른 어휘를 사용한다.
3. 미국 사람들은 특정한 종류의 길을 명명하는 데 highway를 사용하지만 영국 사람들은 같은 길을 motorway라고 부른다.
4. 미국 사람들은 차 앞부분을 hood라고 부르지만 영국 사람들은 bonnet이라고 부른다.

Unit 4

Answers

1. ②　　　2. ①　　　3. ①　　　4. ⑤

Word

talent 재능
painting 그림
tempt 마음을 끌다
fame 평판, 명성
well-known 잘 알려진
acknowledge 인정하다
possibility 가능성
be sure 확신하다
overconfident 지나치게 자신을 가지는
frequently 자주, 여러 번
penniless 빈털터리의, 무일푼의
regret 후회하다

Unit 5

Answers

1. ②　　　2. ③　　　3. ④　　　4. ③

Word

screw up 망치다
be punished 벌 받다
miss (학교, 수업 등을) 빠지다
pretend ~인 체하다
as usual 평상시대로
wry 얼굴을 찡그린
stomach cramp 위경련
concern 걱정
deceive 속이다

expression 말, (얼굴의) 안색
awful 몹시 나쁜
appetite 식욕
a couple of shots 두서너 대의 주사
immediately 즉시, 바로
never mind 괜찮다, 걱정하지 마라

Review

A.

1. label	2. advertise
3. detergent	4. get over
5. value	6. force
7. taboo	8. nausea
9. difference	10. consonant
11. beverage	12. vomit
13. well-known	14. acknowledge
15. regret	16. fame
17. screw up	18. concern
19. awful	20. appetite

B.

1. 굉장한, 아주 멋진	2. 내용물
3. 복통, 위통	4. 사실은, 실제로
5. 금하다	6. 결정하다
7. 진미, 별미	8. 자라다
9. ~처럼 보이다	10. 똑똑히 발음하다
11. 탈락되다, 없어지다	12. ~하는 경향이 있다
13. 발음, 발음법	14. 지나치게 자신감 있는
15. 가능성	16. 무일푼의, 빈 털털이의
17. 속이다	18. 괜찮다, 걱정하지 마라
19. 두서너 대의 주사	20. 위경련

C.

1. ①　　　2. ②　　　3. ①

D.

1. 아이들은 수영장에 근무하고 있는 응급 구조대가 없는 것을 걱정했다.
2. 그들은 크리스마스 전에 그들의 부모님으로부터 무엇을 받을지를 알고 싶어 했다.
3. The shape of Korean kites are based on scientific principles which enable them to make good use of the wind.

E.

1. ②   2. ③   3. ③   4. ①

F.

1. b / g   2. d / i   3. a / e
4. h / j   5. c / f

CHAPTER 06

Preview

Word • Mini Quiz

1. b   2. d
3. f   4. a
5. c   6. e
7. satisfaction   8. immediately
9. intend   10. courageous
11. ruler

Grammar • Mini Quiz

1. speaking   2. doesn't
3. than → of

Unit 1

Answers

1. ③   2. ③

Word

Confucius 공자
thinker 사상가, 사색가
in one's time ~의 시대에
suffer from ~로부터 고통을 겪다
poverty 빈곤, 가난
dutiful 성실한, 충실한
obedient 순종하는
prudent 신중한, 분별 있는
thoughtful 사려 깊은
studious 학문을 좋아하는
obey 따르다, 응하다, 복종하다
ruler 통치자, 지배자
mature 분별 있는, 성숙한
be similar to ~와 비슷하다

Confucianism 유교

Drill 1 • Grammar

1. Vicky는, 두꺼운 겨울 외투를 입고 있는데, 내일의 연극 발표회를 위해서 그녀의 고등학교 무대에서 연습을 하고 있다.
2. 이를 그대로 드러내면서 웃는 Susan의 미소는 항상 큰데, 그녀의 치아는 여전히 상태가 좋다.
3. The girl liked the ghost, who played with her.

Drill 2 • Translation

1. 공자는 위대한 사상가인데, 그는 기원전 557년에 태어났다.
2. 공자가 성인이 되었을 때, 그는 신중하고 사려 깊고 학문을 좋아하는 사람이 되었다.
3. 공자는 다른 사람들이 더 나은 삶을 살도록 도와줄 수 있다고 생각해서 가족을 떠났다.
4. 후에, 많은 사람들은 공자를 따랐고 그의 사상과 믿음은 유교라고 불리는 공자학파가 되었다.

Unit 2

Answers

1. ③   2. ②

Word

advertise 광고하다
advertiser 광고주
exclusively 오로지, 독점적으로
be likely to ~할 것 같다
product 제품, 상품
relatively 비교적, 상대적으로
inform (~에 관하여) 알리다
cost-effective 비용 효율이 높은
manufacturer 제조업자
intend to ~하려고 생각하다

Drill 1 • Grammar

1. 우리 선생님은 그것을 5번씩 다시 쓰게 하셨다.
2. 여전히 다른 뱃노래들은 선원들이 그들의 고된 일을 불평하도록 허락한다.
3. I will have Mark fix my bicycle.

Drill 2 • Translation

1. 게다가, 설령 회사가 텔레비전에 광고하는 데 많은 돈을 쓴다 할지라도, 그들은 충분한 고객들이 광고를 볼거라는 보증이 없다는 것이다.
2. 문제는 그들이 사람들의 눈을 광고에 고정시킬 수 없다는 것이다. 왜냐하면 텔레비전은 많은 채널을 가지고 있기 때문이다.
3. 게다가, 제품을 구매할 것 같은 사람들에게 독점적으로 광고를 보내는 것은 불가능하다.
4. 게다가, 광고를 하기 위해 비디오테이프를 사용하는 것이 훨씬 비용 면에서 효율적인데, 왜냐하면 제조업자들이 정말로 그들의 제품을 구매하려는 사람들에게 비디오 광고를 보낼 수 있기 때문이다.

Unit 3

Answers

1. ④　　　　　　　　　　2. ③

Word

set the pace 앞장서다, 모범을 보이다
mightily 매우, 대단히, 심히
unbecoming 안 어울리는
endanger 위험에 빠뜨리다
slaughter 도살
excuse 변명하다
standard 기준, 표준
judgment 판단
disapprove 찬성하지 않다
have the courage to ~할 용기를 갖다, 용기를 내서 ~하다
bow out 절을 하고 물러서다, 손을 빼다
gracefully 점잖게, 정숙하게
satisfaction 만족(감)
stand on one's feet 자신의 발로 일어서다

Drill 1 • Grammar

1. 그 소녀는 거리에 침을 뱉었을지도 모른다. 경찰관은 그녀를 세우고 거리에 침을 뱉는 것은 법에 위배되는 것이라고 말했다.
2. 그녀는 아주 행복하게 보였으므로 나는 그녀에게 좋은 일이 생겼음에 틀림없다고 생각했다.
3. Look at her pale face. Something terrible must have happened to her.

Drill 2 • Translation

1. 이 색깔이 절대 어울리지 않는 몇 사람을 제외하고는 이것이 잘못된 것은 없다.
2. 상층부에서 술을 마시거나 시속 100킬로로 차를 모는 것이 멋있다고 결정한다면 상황은 위험해질 수도 있다
3. 사실, 한두 번쯤, 당신은 잘못인 줄 알면서 했을 가능성도 있을 것이다.
4. 만일 사람들이 당신이 찬성하지 않은 일을 계획하고 있는 것을 알면 용기를 내서 점잖게 물러나라.

Unit 4

Answers

1. ④　　　　　　2. ②　　　　　　3. ①　　　　　　4. ③

Word

temperature 온도, 기온
carbon dioxide 이산화탄소
atmosphere 대기
release 방출하다
iceberg 빙산
consequently 결과적으로
reduce 줄이다, 감소시키다
emission 방사, 방출
alternative energy 대체 에너지
fossil fuel 화석 연료
acre 에이커 (약 1,224평)
cut down 축소하다, 줄어들다
deforest 벌채하다
cattle ranching 가축 방목
provide A with B A에게 B를 제공하다
be gone 사라지다
deforestation 산림 벌채, 산림 개간
current rate 현재 비율

Unit 5

Answers

1. ③　　　　　　　　　　2. ③
3. (e) William and two men who rescued from the first trip → William and two men who were rescued from the first trip
4. ④

Word

keeper 관리자, 지키는 사람
lighthouse 등대
Northumberland 노섬버랜드 (잉글랜드 북동부의 주)
isolate 고립시키다
steamship 기선, 상선
terrify 무섭게 하다
notify 알리다
immediately 즉시, 당장
set out 시작하다, 착수하다
rescue 구조하다
risk ~을 위험에 내맡기다
worn out 기진맥진한
receive ~을 받다, ~을 수여받다
Royal Humane Society 영국 수난 구조회
courageous 용감한, 용기 있는
humane act 인도적(훌륭한) 행위
tuberculosis 결핵(증)

Review

A.

1. thinker
2. ruler
3. Confucianism
4. poverty
5. advertise
6. manufacturer
7. intend
8. exclusively
9. judgement
10. standard
11. excuse
12. satisfaction
13. temperature
14. deforest
15. current rate
16. alternative energy

17. keeper
18. isolate
19. humane act
20. set out

B.

1. 성실한, 충실한
2. 신중한, 분별 있는
3. 사려 깊은
4. 분별 있는, 성숙한
5. 제품, 상품
6. 비용 효율이 높은
7. ~할 것 같은
8. 알리다
9. 매우, 대단히, 심히
10. 찬성하지 않다
11. 도살
12. 점잖게, 정숙하게
13. 빙산
14. 화석 연료
15. 축소하다, 줄어들다
16. 사라지다
17. 등대
18. 무섭게 하다
19. 기진맥진한
20. 결핵

C.

1. ④
2. ④
3. ④

D.

1. 이 장난감들은 나의 친척들이 준건데, 그들은 나와 함께 산다.
2. 이것은 사람들이 인터넷 서핑을 하고 쇼핑을 하는 동안 자선기관에 기부를 할 수 있게 하는 새로운 방법이다.
3. You may have visited your local public library to complete a school project.

E.

1. ④
2. ④
3. ①

F.

1. b / e
2. c / g
3. a / d
4. f / h
5. i / j

CHAPTER 07

Preview

Word • Mini Quiz

1. e
2. d
3. a
4. f
5. b
6. c
7. method
8. disaster.

9. agree
10. qualified
11. gym
12. explore

Grammar • Mini Quiz

1. where
2. to lock
3. much

Unit 1

Answers

1. ①   2. ②

Word

gym 체육관
dribble (공을) 드리블하다
practice 연습하다, 훈련하다
teammate 같은 팀의 사람
keep practicing 계속해서 훈련하다
work out 잘 해내다, 조절하다
make fun of ~를 놀리다
skill 기술
harsh 거친, 불쾌한
catch up with ~를 따라잡다

Drill 1 • Grammar

1. 길 아래로 뛰어가는 그 남자를 세 명의 경찰관이 뒤따랐다. 얼마 후, 그 남자는 막다른 골목으로 접어들었고, 갈 곳이 없었다.
2. 강에서 수영하고 있는 한 소년이 빠져 죽을 뻔 했다. 그 소년은 옆을 지나가는 여자에게 구해달라고 소리쳤지만, 듣게 할 수 없었다.
3. The man talking on the cell phone is my father.

Drill 2 • Translation

1. 그는 두 다리 사이로, 등 뒤로 드리블하다가 바스켓에 공을 집어넣었다.
2. 사람들은 내가 해낼 수 없을 것이라고 했지만, 나는 개의치 않았다.
3. 나는 배구를 열다섯 살이 되어서야 시작했고, 때때로 다른 소녀들이 내 기량이 자기들만 못하다고 나를 놀렸다.
4. 그러나 힘겨운 노력과 결심으로 나는 프로 배구팀에 입단할 수 있었다.

Unit 2

Answers

1. ⑤   2. ④

Word

addiction 중독
reality 현실
extreme 극심한, 극도의
effort 노력
compulsive 강압적인
resistance 저항
futile 무익한, 헛된, 쓸데없는
intend to ~할 작정이다
think back 상기하다
agree 동의하다

Drill 1 • Grammar

1. 재는 이틀 동안 계속해서 떨어졌고, 폼페이를 완전히 덮어버렸다. 그래서 그 도시는 1,700년간 30피트 두께의 화산재 아래 잠들어 있었다.
2. 그 지진은 막대한 인명과 재산 피해를 일으키며 빠르게 왔다 갔다. 3일 후에도 그 도시는 여전히 정상적인 기능을 할 수 없었다.
3. He read a book, waiting for his son to come home.

Drill 2 • Translation

1. 흡연가의 인생이란 중독의 인생이다.
2. 그리고 금연에 성공한 사람들조차도 비흡연가를 유지하기 위해서는 평생 동안 싸워야 한다.
3. 언젠 담배를 끊을 생각이 있지만, 오늘 그럴 생각은 없다.
4. 그리고 매번 피울 때마다 생각이 나서 처음에 시작을 하지 말 것을 하고 바란다.

Unit 3

Answers

1. ①   2. ⑤

Word

necessarily 부득이, 할 수 없이
material value 물질적인 가치
self-satisfaction 자기만족
composer 작곡가
devote 헌신하다, 바치다
ordinary 평범한, 보통의
achieve 성취하다, 획득하다
goal 목표
explore 탐험하다
mention ~에 대하여 언급하다, 거론하다
means 수단, 방법
amusement 즐거움

Drill 1 • Grammar

1. 그들 자신의 역사와 세계의 역사를 이해하는 사람들은 미래에 일어날 일을 예상하는 것이 더 쉬울 것이다.
2. 물이 풍부한 지역의 사람들은 물이 부족한 지역에 사는 사람들에게 물이 얼마나 귀한 것인지를 모른다.
3. Those who don't help others won't be helped by others.

Drill 2 • Translation

1. 사람들이 왜 일을 해야 하는지에 대한 매우 많은 이유가 있다.
2. 일을 하지 않고 살 수 없었던 사람들 중의 좋은 예는 역사상 가장 훌륭한 작곡가들 중에 한 명인 볼프강 아마데우스 모차르트일 것이다.
3. 미국 작가였던 잭 런던은 인생에서 목적을 성취하기 위해 최선을 다하는 평범한 사람들에 대한 이야기를 쓰기 위해 전 생애를 바쳤다.
4. 그들은 일을 즐거움의 수단으로 생각했다.

Unit 4

Answers

1. ①   2. ①   3. ⑤   4. ⑤

Word

generally 일반적으로
be good at ~에 능숙하다
excel 뛰어나다
end 목적
aptitude 적성
specialize in ~을 전문적으로 연구하다
plenty of 많은
unfair 부당한, 불공정한
expand 확대하다
secondary school 중고등학교
horizon 시야, 시계
range 범위, 영역
graduate school 대학원
generalist 만능인
qualified 자질이 있는
humanity 인문학

Unit 5

Answers

1. ③   2. ②   3. ①   4. ②

Word

claim 주장하다
imagine 상상하다
linguistic 언어의, 언어적인
ability 능력
rely upon ~에 의지하다, 의존하다
available 이용할 수 있는

public service 공공사업, 공공(사회)봉사
operator 운전자, 조작자
strictly 엄격히, 정확하게
disaster 재난, 참사
transportation 운송수단, 교통수단
exchange 교환
merchant 상인, 거래처
merchandise 물품, 제품
prehistory 선사시대
means 방법, 수단

Review

A.

1. gym	2. skill
3. harsh	4. catch up with
5. effort	6. compulsive
7. futile	8. agree
9. necessarily	10. achieve
11. goal	12. means
13. generally	14. expand
15. unfair	16. range
17. claim	18. imagine
19. exchange	20. disaster

B.

1. (공을) 드리블하다	2. 놀리다
3. 계속 훈련하다	4. 같은 팀의 사람
5. 극심한, 극도의	6. 저항
7. ~할 작정이다	8. ~에 대해 생각하다
9. 탐험하다	10. 즐거움
11. 거론하다, 언급하다	12. 헌신하다, 바치다
13. 뛰어나다	14. 목적
15. 대학원	16. 자격이 있는
17. 운전자, 조작자	18. 운송, 교통
19. 상인, 거래처	20. ~에 의지하다, 의존하다

C.

1. ③   2. ②   3. ③

D.

1. 그 다음날 그는 그 소녀가 다른 누군가와 놀고 있는 것을 보고서 멀리 떨어져 있었다.
2. 최근 심각한 질병이 아시아를 강타하면서 몇 백 명을 사망에 이르게 하고 있다.

3. Those who never make it are the ones who quit too soon.

E.

1. ①   2. ④   3. ③   4. ③

F.

1. expand   2. expended
3. explore   4. exploit

CHAPTER 08

Preview

Word • Mini Quiz

1. f   2. c
3. a   4. e
5. d   6. b
7. tournament   8. erupted
9. oxygen   10. rescued
11. occurred   12. sacred

Grammar • Mini Quiz

1. It   2. to be used   3. when

Unit 1

Answers

1. ③   2. ④

Word

lead up 오르막으로 인도하다
steep 가파른 언덕
ridge 산등성이
claw one's way up 기어서 올라가다
eerie 섬뜩한
on oxygen 산소(통)에 의지하여
supreme effort 죽을힘을 다한 노력, 극단적인 노력
pull themselves to the top 정상에 자신들을 끌어다 놓았다
party 일행
crack 기회
far-out 훨씬 더 나가는, 엄청난
chap 사람, 녀석
danger 위험

Drill 1 • Grammar

1. 그가 저녁에 들었던 모든 귀신 이야기들이 지금 그의 기억 속에 떠올랐다.
2. 우리는 다른 방향에서 오는 차와 부딪쳤다는 것을 알았다.
3. I recognized her at once since I had seen her terrible face before.

Drill 2 • Translation

1. 마지막 300피트는 깎아 지르는 듯한 좁은 오르막 산등성이였다.
2. Edmund Hillary와 그의 세르파 안내인 Tenzing Norkay는 에베레스트, 세계의 정상에 올라섰다.
3. Hillary가 하산하자 그 기자가 물어 보았다. "왜 그런 일을 하신 겁니까?"
4. 그렇지만 위험성은 당신이 가지고 있는 모든 것을 내놓게 합니다.

Unit 2

Answers

1. ②   2. ③

Word

religion 종교
official 공식적인
soul 영혼
reluctant 마음이 내키지 않는, 좋아하지 않는
vegan 절대 채식주의자
dairy product 유제품
poultry 가금, 닭고기류
sacred 신성한
wander 어슬렁거리다
purify ~을 정화하다
pilgrimage 순례, 성지 참배

bank 강둑

Drill 1 • Grammar

1. 그 나이든 남자는 들어 주는 누구나에게 프랑스에 관해 말하는 것을 좋아했다. 왜냐하면 그는 제2차 세계대전 동안 젊은 군인으로서 그곳에 있었기 때문이다.

2. 그는 대공황을 거쳐서 살았기 때문에 은행을 신뢰하지 않았다. 그는 그의 모든 돈을 집에 두었고 절대 아무것도 신뢰를 가지고 지불하지 않았기 때문에 자신을 운 좋은 사람이라고 생각했다.

3. It feels like winter, for the temperature is so low.

Drill 2 • Translation

1. 인도에는 이슬람교, 기독교, 시크교, 불교 그리고 많은 다른 종교를 믿는 사람들이 있지만 인도의 공식 종교는 힌두교이다.

2. 몇몇의 힌두교인들은 완전 채식주의자라서 그들은 고기와 치즈, 계란 또는 우유와 같은 유제품도 먹지 않는다.

3. 인도에서 쇠고기를 먹는 것은 불법이다. 왜냐하면 소는 힌두교인들 사이에 신성한 동물로 여겨지기 때문이다.

4. 종종 곧 죽을 사람들은 "부활" 전에 영혼을 정화하기 위해서 그 강으로 온다.

Unit 3

Answers

1. ③   2. ②

Word

creature 생물체
mermaid 인어
upper body 상반신
seduce 유혹하다, 꼬드기다
rescue 구조하다
sailor 뱃사람, 선원
supernatural 초자연의, 신기의
foresee ~을 예견하다
mythical 신화의
exhaust 기진맥진시키다
mirage 망상, 환각
assume 가정하다, 추정하다
fin 지느러미

Drill 1 • Grammar

1. 그는 작은 요트로 혼자서 태평양을 건널 정도로 모험적이다.
2. 프로그램을 다듬고 개선한 후에, 컴퓨터 공학자들은 그것을 마이크로소프트 회사에 제출할 정도로 자신 있었다.

3. Karen was rich enough to tour any country she wished for winter vacation.

Drill 2 • Translation

1. 인어는 상반신은 여성의 그것과 비슷하지만 2개의 다리 대신에 물고기의 꼬리를 가지고 있다.

2. 그들의 아름다운 얼굴과 목소리는 종종 바다로 뛰어든 선원들을 유혹하고 결국에는 물에 빠뜨려 익사시킨다.

3. 사실, 인어는 민속이나 신화에만 존재하는 유니콘과 요정과 같은 신화적인 존재이다.

4. 많은 문화들에서 지친 선원들이 먼 곳에서 신기루나 해양 생물체를 보고 그것이 사람의 얼굴이라고 생각했던 것이라고 믿어지고 있다.

Unit 4

Answers

1. ⑤   2. ③   3. ①   4. ④

Word

in favor of ~에 찬성하여
ridiculous 우스운, 어처구니없는
aside from ~와는 별도로, ~를 제외하고
modify 수정하다
recent 최근의
dominate 지배하다
involving ~를 수반하는
artistry 기교, 예술성
remindful of ~를 연상케 하는
appeal 매력, 호소력
strength 힘
high-tech racket 최첨단 라켓
tournament 대회, 승자 진출전
winning point 결정타

Unit 5

Answers

1. ④   2. ⑤   3. ③   4. ①

Word

destroy 파괴하다
be covered with ~로 덮이다
volcanic ash 화산재

excavate 발굴하다

erupt 분화하다

volcanic activity 화산 활동

dormant volcano 휴화산

extinct 활동을 멈춘

tectonic plate 텍토닉 플레이트 (판상(板狀)을 이루어 움직이고 있는 지각의 표층)

flowing speed 흐르는 속도

lava 용암

steepness 경사면, 가파른 언덕

temperature 온도

gentle 완만한

slope 경사면

molten rock 용암

enormous 거대한

earth's crust 지각

occur 발생하다

fiery blast 화염 폭발

shot out 밖으로 나오다

vent 분출구, 구멍

crashing roar 놀랄 만한(두려울 만한) 굉음

Review

A.

1. steep	2. eerie
3. party	4. danger
5. religion	6. wander
7. sacred	8. soul
9. creature	10. exhaust
11. fin	12. mermaid
13. ridiculous	14. appeal

15. tournament	16. recent
17. erupt	18. extinct
19. lava	20. enormous

B.

1. 오르막으로 인도하다	2. 산등성이
3. 산소(통)에 의지하여	4. 지배하다
5. 유태교	6. 불교
7. 마음이 내키지 않는	8. 정화하다
9. 유혹하다	10. 초자연의, 신기의
11. 신화의	12. 망상, 환각
13. ~에 찬성하여	14. ~와는 별도로
15. 수정하다	16. 기교, 예술성
17. 휴화산	18. 발굴하다
19. 화산재	20. 용암

C.

1. ② 　　　　2. ③ 　　　　3. ①

D.

1. 비서는 다음 프로젝트가 승인받았다고 보고했다.
2. 그녀는 노래를 부르고 있기 때문에 그 소식을 듣고 매우 행복함에 틀림없다.
3. An increasing number of elderly people in Japan are deciding that they are still young enough to keep working.

E.

1. ④ 　　　2. ② 　　　3. ③ 　　　4. ①

F.

1. Dairy	2. daily
3. wandering	4. wondering

CHAPTER 09

Preview

Word • Mini Quiz

1. b	2. a
3. e	4. f

5. c	6. d
7. shortened	8. layer
9. significance	10. extinct
11. injection	

Grammar • Mini Quiz

1. those → that
2. a number of → the number of
3. those → that

Unit 1

Answers

1. ③   2. ③

Word

glow 빛나다, 빛을 내다
scare 겁주다
scary 무시무시한, 두려운
reflect 반사하다
in the distance 먼 곳에서
directly 똑바로, 정확히
light bulb 전구
layer 층
crystalline substance 투명한 물질
the number of ~의 수
blood vessel 혈관
whereas 반면에

Drill 1 • Grammar

1. 아이들은 커다란 거미가 거미줄에 매달려 있는 것을 봤고, 작은 새가 노래하는 것을 들었다.
2. 배 위에 있는 사람들은 아침 7시 약간 지나서 그 소년이 물에 빠지는 것을 아무도 보지 못했다. 나는 사고 전부를 내 눈으로 봤다.
3. I watched her dancing in front of the mirror with a strange-looking woman.

Drill 2 • Translation

1. 어두울 때, 개나 고양이의 눈이 빛나는 것을 봤을지도 모른다.
2. 하지만, 왜 그들의 눈이 빛나는지에 대한 이유를 안다면 그다지 무섭지 않을 것이다. 그들의 눈은 빛이 정면으로 그들을 향해 빛나고 있지 않을 때조차 먼 곳에서 빛을 반사할 수 있다.
3. 이 색깔은 그들 눈에 있는 혈관 숫자에 좌우된다.

Unit 2

Answers

1. ④   2. ③

Word

extinct 멸종한
controversy 논쟁
apparently 분명히, 명백히
spar 다투다
prehistoric 선사시대의
doomsday (공룡에 닥친) 최후의 날
acknowledge 인정하다
fabled 우화의(공룡이 만화, 영화 등으로 표현된 것을 빗대어)
beast 동물, 짐승
trigger 촉발하다
asteroid 혜성
present 제시하다
blast 폭발
disastrous 재난을 일으키는
aftermath 여파, 결과, 후유증
sulfuric acid 황산
collision 충돌
inevitable 피할 수 없는

Drill 1 • Grammar

1. 그의 건강 문제에도 불구하고 그는 노령까지 살았다. 매일 그는 운동했고 좋은 음식을 먹었고 그리고 일찍 잠자리에 들었다.
2. 가난함에도 불구하고 그녀는 자기 자신을 수치스럽게 생각하지 않았다.
3. With all〔In spite of, For all〕his high test scores, he could not go to university.

Drill 2 • Translation

1. 공룡이 멸종한 지 6천 5백만 년이 되었지만, 무엇이 멸종시켰는가에 대한 논쟁은 분명히 그 (논쟁) 자체의 생존기간을 늘려가면서 계속되고 있다.
2. 지난주 공룡 대토론회는 선사시대의 최후의 날에 대한 두 개의 새로운 이론에 대해 과학자들이 다투면서 또 뉴스의 각광을 받았다.
3. 한 쪽은 충돌의 결과로 발생한 황산 구름이 지상의 대부분의 생명체를 파괴했다는 것이다.
4. 다른 한 쪽은 그 충돌이 지구의 반대편에 강렬한 화산 활동을 일으켜 멸종을 피할 수 없는 것으로 만든 이중의 타격을 입혔다는 것이다.

Unit 3

Answers

1. ②   2. ③

Word

shorten 줄이다

celebrate 경축하다, 축하하다
harvest season 수확(추수) 계절
Celtic 켈트족
deceased 고인, 죽은 사람
hold 개최하다
placate 달래다, 위로하다
evil spirit 악령
treat 음식, 먹거리
combination 결합, 짝맞추기
spooky 무시무시한
devoted to ~에 바치는

Drill 1 ● Grammar

1. 언어는 사람들이 서로 의사소통을 하기 위해서 존재한다. 그러나 종종 언어는 두 명의 개인 사이에서 그리고 민족들 사이에서 오해의 소지가 될 수도 있다.
2. 그 선생님은 그가 말한 것을 아이들이 이해할 수 있도록 천천히 말했다.
3. The thief wore black so that the people would not recognize him.

Drill 2 ● Translation

1. 이것은 추수기의 끝을 축하하기 위해 10월 31일에 열리는 축제이다.
2. 켈트족은 10월 31일에 세상의 살아있는 사람들과 죽은 사람들 간의 간격이 사라지고 죽은 사람들이 소생한다고 믿었다.
3. 그래서 그들은 살아있는 희생자들을 찾고 있을지 모르는 유령들과 악령들을 달래기 위해서 밤에 큰 축제를 벌였다.
4. 로마사람들은 또한 과일의 신인 Pomona 여신을 축하하기 위에서 10월 말에 휴일을 보냈다.

Unit 4

Answers

1. ②   2. ③   3. ⑤   4. ②

Word

divide 나누다, 분류하다
clinical 임상의
temporary 일시적인
temperamental 변덕스러운
biological death 생물학적 죽음
vital 생명 유지에 필수인
cease 중지하다, 그만두다
permanent 영구적인
organism 유기체
disintegration 분해

tissue 조직
irreversible 돌이킬 수 없는
irritable 성급한
prolong 연장하다
reanimate 소생하다
narcotic sleep 마취에 의한 수면
metabolism 신진대사
illustrate 설명하다
drain 빼내다
artery 동맥
blood pressure 혈압
respiration 호흡
set in 시작하다, 자리 잡다
artificial respiration 인공호흡
spontaneous 자발적인
specific 특정한
injection 주사
seize 빼앗다
syringe 주사기

Unit 5

Answers

1. ①   2. ④   3. ⑤   4. ③

Word

peer pressure 동료 집단으로부터 받는 사회적 압력
occupation 직업
health status 건강상태
contain 함유하다
nutrient 영양분
carbohydrate 탄수화물
lipid 지방질
balanced diet 균형식
blood pressure 혈압
yield 생산하다
synthesize 합성하다
repair 치료하다
vital cell 생체 세포
consume 섭취하다
constitute ~을 구성하다
membrane 막, 세포막
immune system 면역체계
vast 굉장한, 엄청난
significance 중요성
solvent 용제, 용매

lubricant 윤활유
circulate 순환시키다
ultimate solution 궁극적인 해결책
maintain 유지하다
on a regular basis 정기적으로

Review

A.

1. glow
2. light bulb
3. directly
4. blood vessel
5. controversy
6. aftermath
7. collision
8. acknowledge
9. treat
10. devote (to)
11. deceased
12. placate
13. divide
14. organism
15. prolong
16. drain
17. significance
18. membrane
19. circulate
20. maintain

B.

1. 투명한 물질
2. 먼 곳에서
3. ~의 수
4. 반사하다

5. 촉발하다
6. 다투다
7. 피할 수 없는
8. 제시하다
9. 무시무시한
10. 개최하다
11. 면역체계
12. 줄이다
13. 호흡
14. 시작하다, 자리 잡다
15. 혈압
16. 주사기
17. 용제, 용매
18. 섭취(소비)하다
19. 균형식
20. 건강 상태

C.

1. ①
2. ①
3. ②

D.

1. 나는 내 여동생이 요리를 하면서 부엌에서 플루트를 부는 것을 들었다.
2. 그의 성공과 업적에도 불구하고 그는 여전히 그 자신을 낙오자로 본다.
3. Group leaders must learn this lesson and put it into practice in order to achieve productive and positive results.

E.

1. ③
2. ②
3. ④
4. ②

F.

1. extinct
2. distinct
3. treat
4. threats

CHAPTER 10

Preview

Word • Mini Quiz

1. f
2. d
3. a
4. e
5. c
6. b
7. yelled
8. aggressive
9. approximately
10. axis
11. assumed

Grammar • Mini Quiz

1. because → because of
2. exhausted
3. is

Unit 1

Answers

1. ②
2. ④

Word

thinker 사상가
philosopher 철학자
disagree on ~과 의견이 다르다, 의견이 맞지 않다
matter 문제, 주장, 진술
agree on ~에 공감하다, 동의하다
put it this way 이렇게 말하다
take a nap 낮잠 자다
stinky-smelling 고약한 냄새가 나는, 악취가 나는

mustache 콧수염
yell 소리치다
examine 살피다, 검사하다
go away 사라지다
desperately 절망적으로, 자포자기가 되어
scent 냄새

Drill 1 • Grammar

1. 확실히 아시아 사람들은 그들이 슬플 때조차도 예의를 지키려고 웃지만, 그러한 행동이 그들에게 특별한 것인지 의문이다.
2. 그녀가 온다면 나도 갈 것이지만, 그녀가 올지 안 올지 나는 모른다.
3. The fire fighters did not know if the fire started in the basement or the kitchen.

Drill 2 • Translation

1. 위대한 사상가들과 철학자들은 많은 문제들에 의견이 달랐지만 대부분 한 요점에 대해서는 동의한다: "우리는 우리가 생각하는 대로 된다."
2. 로마의 황제 Marcus Aurelius는 이런 식으로 설명했다, "사람의 인생은 생각으로 이루어져 있다."
3. 그가 낮잠을 자고 있을 때, 그의 손자가 장난으로 할아버지의 콧수염에 지독한 냄새가 나는 치즈 한 조각을 놓았다.
4. 우리가 경험하는 모든 것과 우리가 보는 모든 사람은 우리 생각에 있는 그 향기를 지닌다.

Unit 2

Answers

1. ④   2. ④

Word

possession 재산
depression 억압 (상태)
compulsive 강제적인, 억지의
depressed mood 억압된 기분
that is to say 다시 말하자면
relentlessly 무자비하게
attainment 달성, 획득, 도달
reinforce 강화하다
measure 수단
transform 바꾸다, 변형시키다
necessary means 필요한 수단
drastic 철저한, 과감한
drug addict 마약 중독자
assault 폭행하다

Drill 1 • Grammar

1. 습관이란 어떤 것에 대해 생각하지 않고 그것을 행하는 방식이다. 습관은 어떤 것을 여러 번 행한 후에 습득되고 형성된다. 당신이 생각하지 않고 행하는 거의 모든 것은 습관이다.
2. 물리학을 이해하려고 노력하는 것은 마치 날개를 자라게 해서 나는 것과 같다.
3. Learning a foreign language is helpful in finding a job.

Drill 2 • Translation

1. 진실은 사람들이 살아남기 위하여 필요한 것만 욕심을 낸다는 것이 아니라, 우리 문화에서 대부분의 사람들은 욕심이 많다는 것이다. 더 많은 식량, 술, 재산, 권력, 그리고 명성에 탐욕을 부리는 것이다.
2. 과식이나 (물건을) 사는 행동은 내적 공허감을 채우려는 상징적 행동으로, 이렇게 해서 순간적으로나마 억압된 감정을 극복하려는 것이다.
3. 물론 탐욕스러운 사람은 자기가 욕심내는 것을 살 돈이 충분하다면, 공격적이 될 필요는 없다.
4. 그러나 필요한 수단이 없는 탐욕스러운 사람은 자신의 욕구를 만족시키고 싶다면 공격해야 한다.

Unit 3

Answers

1. ③   2. ⑤

Word

order 〔생물〕 (동식물 분류상의) 목(目)
Chiroptera 익수류(翼手類)
approximately 대략, 대체로
comprise ～으로 이루어지다
genera (genus의 복수) 〔생물〕 속(屬)
mammal 포유류
capable of ～할 수 있는
evolve 진화하다
acoustic 청각의, 음파를 사용하는
orientation 지향, 방위 측정
refer to ～라고 부르다
technical term 전문용어
echolocation 반향 위치 결정법
inhabit 서식하다
pest 해로운 것, 해충

Drill 1 • Grammar

1. 어떤 사람들에게 있어서 외국어로 핸드폰 통화를 하려 하는 것이 어려운 것처럼 보인다. 이러한 어려움에는 상당한(정당한) 이유가 있다.

2. 아마도 4살일 것 같은 어린소년이 엄지손가락을 빨며 감방 구석에 있었다. 애가 안쓰러웠다. "무엇을 위해 여기 있는 거니?"라고 물었다. "자유."라고 꼬마가 말했다. 그는 자유를 말할 수조차 없었지만 그는 그것 때문에 감옥에 있었다.

3. There is a man who wears only one sock.

Drill 2 • Translation

1. 세상에는 적어도 천 가지 다른 종의 박쥐가 있다.
2. 미국에는 15속(屬)의 박쥐로 구성된 약 44종이 있는 것으로 알려져 있다.
3. 게다가 박쥐의 대부분의 종은 청각 지향의 기관을 진화시켰는데, 그것은 종종 '박쥐 레이더'라고 불리기도 한다.
4. 그들은 불독과 얼굴이 비슷하기 때문에 불독박쥐라고도 불린다.

Unit 4

Answers

1. ④   2. ②   3. ④   4. ③

Word

claim 주장
recently 최근에
information age 정보시대
misleading 오해하게 하는
flood 범람하다, 가득 차다
ancestor 조상
inhabit 살다, 거주하다
innocent 단순한
valid 타당한, 정당한
assume 추정하다, 추측하다
distinct 다른, 별개의
relatively 상대적으로
come up with 떠오르다, 생각이 나다
primitiveness 원시성, 원시적인 것
confirm 확인하다
fundamentally 근본적으로
density 밀도
transmit 전하다, 전송하다
satellite 인공위성
instantly 즉각적으로

Unit 5

Answers

1. ④   2. ②   3. ⑤   4. ⑤

Word

circle around 주변을 돌다
measure 재다, 측정하다
northern hemisphere 북반구
southern hemisphere 남반구
seasonal 계절에 따른
orbit motion 공전운동
rotation 회전, 순환
knitting needle 뜨개바늘
represent 상징하다, 나타내다
stick 찔러 넣다, 고정시키다
an amount of 상당한, 상당한 양의
longitudinal 경도의, 경선의
perpendicular 수직선, 수직의 위치
vice versa 반대로, 거꾸로
axis (회전체의) 축
tilt 기울다

Review

A.

1. philosopher   2. take a nap
3. mustache   4. go away
5. overcome   6. passion
7. satisfy   8. drug addict
9. at least   10. evolve
11. technical term   12. pest
13. flood   14. ancestor
15. fundamentally   16. instantly
17. tilt   18. seasonal
19. longitudinal   20. vice versa

B.

1. ~에 공감하다, 동의하다   2. 사상가
3. 문제, 주장, 진술   4. 살펴보다, 검사하다
5. 무자비하게   6. 수단
7. 강제적인   8. 폭행
9. ~라고 부르다   10. 청각의
11. 비슷함   12. 서식하다
13. 다른, 별개의   14. 확인하다
15. 원시성, 원시적인 것   16. 인공위성

17. 공전운동　　　　18. 회전, 순환
19. 상징하다, 나타내다　　20. 주변을 돌다

C.

1. ①　　　　2. ④　　　　3. ④

D.

1. 유리병은 열지 않아도 그 내용물을 보여 줄 수 있다.
2. 부모들이 자식들을 스포츠 캠프에 보낼 때, 부모들은 돌보아야 하고, 코치들이 아이들의 의견을 존중해 주는지 아닌지를 알기 위해 코치들과 이야기를 나눠봐야 한다.

3. There are several reasons why we should study English.

E.

1. ①　　　　2. ④　　　　3. ③

F.

1. transmits　　　　2. transformed
3. compulsive　　　　4. impulsive

CHAPTER 11

Preview

Word • Mini Quiz

1. d　　　　　　2. c
3. e　　　　　　4. f
5. a　　　　　　6. b
7. protects　　　8. control
9. technology　　10. revealing
11. destroyed　　12. dense

Grammar • Mini Quiz

1. are → is　　2. cleaning　　3. It

Unit 1

Answers

1. ③　　　　　　2. ③

Word

tough 힘든
isolation 고립, 격리
expressive exit 표현의 출구
with no way out 출구가 없는
support group 후원 단체
cure 치료

opportunity 기회
connection 교제, 사귐
control 통제하다
despair 절망
invisible 눈에 보이지 않는
imprison 가두다
drive 몰고 가다
miserable 괴로운, 비참한

Drill 1 • Grammar

1. 우리가 동물에 대해 더 많이 배우면 배울수록, 그 동물들이 살아나가야 할 생활에 얼마나 훌륭히 적응하는지를 더욱 더 많이 우리는 이해한다.
2. 우리가 돈을 가지면 가질수록 더 많이 쓰는 것처럼 보인다. 아무리 돈을 많이 가지고 있다고 하더라도 우리는 항상 더 가지고 싶어한다.
3. The longer he waits to take a shower, the smellier he becomes.

Drill 2 • Translation

1. 고립 상태가 주는 가장 힘든 면 중 하나는 표현의 출구가 없다는 것이다.
2. 하지만 고립 상태는 출구가 없는 방 안에 있는 것과 같다.
3. 그리고 그곳에 오랫동안 갇혀 있을수록 고통과 슬픔을 함께하는 것은 더 힘들어진다.
4. 한 사례에서, 어떤 여성은 친구들과 강제로 괴로운 점심식사를 네 번 한 후에 다섯 번째 점심식사에서 어떤 농담을 듣고 갑자기 웃게 되면서 그 식사를 즐기게 되었다고 전했다.

Unit 2

Answers

1. ⑤   2. ②

Word

as a result 그 결과(로서)
valley floor 계곡바닥
good condition 좋은 상태
preserve 보존하다
wooden block 목판
destroy 파괴하다
be located ~에 위치하다
mid-way 중간
sea level 해발
monk 수도승, 수사

Drill 1 • Grammar

1. 먹을 충분한 음식과 집이라 부르는 안전한 곳을 가진 어린이는 행복하다. 세계 주위의 많은 어린이들은 이들 어린이들이 당연하다고 생각하는 것들을 가지는 것에 관해 꿈을 꾼다.
2. 내가 어머니에게 크리스마스에 집에 갈 것이라고 말했을 때 어머니의 기쁨은 굉장했다. 3년을 떨어져 있다가, 우리는 그런 특별한 날에 마침내 만나려 했다.
3. Sad are those who do not do their best.

Drill 2 • Translation

1. 그때마다 화재는 8만 개의 목판을 보유하고 있는 건물을 제외한 모든 건물들을 파괴해버렸다.
2. 이 건물은 옛날 건물을 개량하기 위해 최신 과학을 이용했다.
3. 그렇지만 실험에 의하면 수백 년 전 스님들이 과학적 지식도 없이 계획했던 낡은 건물이 새것보다 더 낫다는 것을 보여 주었다.

Unit 3

Answers

1. ②   2. ③

Word

home remedy 자택요법
get rid of ~을 제거하다, 없애다
hiccup 딸꾹질
spit 침
Lord's Prayer 주기도문
recite ~을 암송하다, 낭독하다

---

accuse 비난하다, 책망하다
blood vessel 혈관
nerve 신경
intestine 창자, 장
lung 폐
respond (자극 등에) 반응하다
stimulus 자극, 자극하는 것
reflex 반사작용
windpipe 기관, 숨통

Drill 1 • Grammar

1. 한국인은 세계에서 움직이는 금속활자를 사용했던 최초의 국민으로 밝혀졌다. 한국인은 1450년 구텐베르크가 그의 것을 발명하기 약 200년 전에 금속활자를 사용하기 시작했다.
2. 그는 결코 어떤 돈도 쓰지 않기 때문에 인색하다고 불려진다.
3. 이 아파트 건물은 너무 헐었기 때문에 지옥이라고 불린다.
4. She is thought beautiful and charming by most people.

Drill 2 • Translation

1. 영국에서는 딸꾹질을 멈추기 위해 오른손 두 번째 손가락에 침을 묻히고 거꾸로 주기도문을 암송하면서 왼쪽 신발 꼭대기에 세 번 십자가를 긋는다.
2. 딸꾹질은 스스로를 보호하기 위해 사람의 조직이 취하는 생리작용의 결과로 일어난다.
3. 대부분의 신체 기관은 그러한 기관이 어떤 자극에 반응하는 것을 가능케 하는 조직의 도움으로 움직이거나 작동한다.
4. 때때로, 자극이 다르게 또는 실수로 (예를 들어 물이나 음식이 기관으로 들어가는 것) 일어날 때 자극에 따른 반사가 신체가 문제를 바로잡는 데 도움을 준다.

Unit 4

Answers

1. ③   2. ②   3. ⑤   4. ③

Word

huge continent 거대한 대륙
Atlantic ocean 대서양
Indian Ocean 인도양
Red Sea 홍해
Equator (지구의) 적도
subsequently 그 후에, 그 다음에
Tropic of Cancer 북회귀선
Tropic of Capricorn 남회귀선
dense 밀집한, 빽빽한

numerous 매우 많은, 엄청난
poisonous 독을 함유한, 독성의
rapid 급류
waterfall 폭포
outline 윤곽, 외형
Cape of Good Hope 희망봉
nevertheless 그럼에도 불구하고

Unit 5

Answers

1. ④   2. ②   3. ①
4. (1) T   (2) F   (3) F

Word

technology 기술
benefit 이점
biologist 생물학자
unknown world 미지의 세계
giant 거인
infrasound 초저주파음파
over the last few decades 지난 수십 년에 걸쳐
extremely 매우, 몹시, 아주
low-pitched sound 저음
higher-pitched noise 고음
long-distance 장거리의
roam 돌아다니다, 떠돌다
frequency 주파수
range 범위, 한도
reveal 밝히다
thunderstorm 천둥
explosion 폭발
warning 경고, 주의, 경보
nuclear-explosion test 핵폭발 실험

Review

A.

1. cure
2. miserable
3. imprison
4. isolation
5. be located
6. sea level
7. wooden block
8. as a result
9. reflex
10. stimulus
11. home remedy
12. hiccup

13. rapid
14. equator
15. subsequently
16. dense
17. frequency
18. reveal
19. biologist
20. roam

B.

1. 연결, 교제, 사귐
2. 표현의 출구
3. 절망
4. 눈에 보이지 않는
5. 좋은 상태
6. 중간
7. 계곡바닥
8. 보존하다
9. 암송하다, 낭독하다
10. 비난하다, 책망하다
11. 신경
12. 창자, 장
13. 윤곽, 외형
14. 남회귀선
15. 대서양
16. 독을 함유한, 독성의
17. 범위, 한도
18. 매우, 몹시, 아주
19. 장거리의
20. 초저주파음파

C.

1. ②   2. ②   3. ③

D.

1. 어떤 집단이 다른 집단과 더 접촉을 많이 할수록, 사물이나 사상이 교환될 가능성이 더 많다.
2. 미래에 자기가 하고 싶은 일을 하는 사람들은 행복하다.
3. He is called a gentle and courageous man.

E.

1. ④   2. ④   3. ④

F.

1. conserve   2. observed   3. protesting
4. protect

CHAPTER 12

Preview

Word • Mini Quiz

1. e
2. d
3. f
4. b
5. a
6. c
7. vital
8. ongoing
9. contacted
10. broadcasted
11. mighty
12. meditation

Grammar • Mini Quiz

1. One of the greatest benefits of this is (that) it lets in light and provides protection from the weather at the same time.
2. feeling / smelling / buying / knowing
3. anything

Unit 1

Answers

1. ④
2. (1) True   (2) False   (3) False

Word

Buddhist 불교도
meditation 명상, 묵상
karma 업보(業報), 인과응보, 숙명
Nirvana 열반, 극락
define 정의를 내리다
deed 행위, 행동
mistreat 혹사하다, 학대하다
Buddha 석가모니
influence 영향력, 세력, 위력
prevalence 보급, 널리 퍼짐
Buddhism 불교
Hinduism 힌두교
worship 숭배하다
moral 도덕적인
force 세력, 집단, 단체

Drill 1 • Grammar

1. 어린 시절은 모험을 할 나이이다. 비록 오늘날 모험의 기회가 예전보다 상당히 줄기는 했지만, 오늘날까지도 이것은 여전히 사실이다.
2. 당신의 삶에서 모든 것이 잘 될 때 진정한 친구가 누구인지 아는 것은 어렵다. 하지만 진정한 친구와 충실한 동료는 비록 당신이 가장 어려운 상태에 있다하더라도 당신을 떠나지 않을 것이다.
3. Even though the ghost came into the room, we did not scream.

Drill 2 • Translation

1. 불교신자들은 마음속에서 영적인 평화를 찾을 수 있다고 믿는다.
2. 다른 사람들을 친절과 존경으로 대하는 행복한 사람은 그를 존경하는 사람들을 만나게 될 것이다.
3. 비록 부처는 인도 왕자로 태어났지만 부분적으로 힌두교의 보급 때문에, 그리고 부분적으로는 이슬람교의 번성 때문에, 불교는 8세기에 인도에서 영향력을 잃었다.
4. 불교는 세계에서 주요한 종교적이고 도덕적인 세력 중 하나가 되었다.

Unit 2

Answers

1. ③
2. ④

Word

introduction 도입
unique 독특한, 특이한
guarantee 보증하다
vital 중요한
responsiveness 반응성
make up 구성하다
characteristic 특성, 특징
needs 필요
require ~을 필요로 하다
one-size-fits-all strategy 모든 것을 하나의 크기로 맞추는 전략
place emphasis on ~을 강조하다
aspect 측면
categorize 범주화하다
analysis 분석
vastly 거대한, 엄청나게 큰
be composed of ~로 구성되다
numerous 매우 많은, 엄청난

Drill 1 • Grammar

1. 당신 자신과 다른 출신 배경을 가진 사람들과 대화를 나누는 것은 당신의 대화 레퍼토리와 생각을 넓히는 데 도움이 될 수 있다.
2. 직업을 고르는 데 있어서, 당신이 고려해야 할 첫 번째 것은 당신이 그 직업에 맞는지 맞지 않는지이다.
3. Don't kill the goose that lays the golden eggs.

Drill 2 • Translation

1. 특이한 상품만을 소개하는 것이 시장에서의 성공을 보장하지 않는다.
2. 또 다른 중요한 요소는 시장을 구성하는 지역 사회에 적합한 상품을 제공함으로써 시장에 대한 반응성을 증가시키는 것이다.
3. 다시 말하자면, 난제들 중의 하나는 단지 "세계적인" 측면만 너무 강조하는 모든 것을 하나의 크기로 맞추는 전략을 피하는 것이다.
4. 좀 더 상세히 분석을 해 보면 "떠오르는" 국가들은 서로 서로 아주 다를 뿐 아니라, 그들은 또한 수많은 독특한 개인들과 공동체들로 구성되어 있다.

Unit 3

Answers

1. ④

Word

corpse 시체, 송장, 사체
crack 빙하나 얼음의 깨진 틈
lost 행방불명의
contact 연락하다
investigating 연구, 조사
authority 당국
scene (사건의) 장소, 현장
in the meantime 그 사이에
ice pick 얼음 부수는 도구
frozen grave 얼어붙은 무덤
investigator 조사가
recently 최근에
best-preserved 가장 잘 보존된
mummy 미라
preserve 보존하다

Drill 1 • Grammar

1. 당신이 할 수 있는 것은 당신의 어머니에게 당신이 어떻게 느끼는지를 말하는 것이다.
2. 나는 야구경기가 끝난 후 어떻게 그들이 그렇게 빨리 집에 왔는지 궁금했다.
3. Where and how he passed away remained a mystery.

Drill 2 • Translation

1. 1991년에 두 명의 등산객이 오스트리아와 이탈리아의 사이에 위치한 알프스 고지에서 죽은 사체를 발견했다.
2. 조사당국이 해발 3,200미터의 현장에 도착하는 데는 나흘이 걸렸다.
3. 마침내 사체가 완전히 발굴되자 조사가들은 최근에 죽은 사람이 아니라는 것을 깨달았다.
4. 곧 세계는 이 아이스맨이, 그렇게 불리게 되었는데, 5,000년도 더 오래 전에 죽은 사람이라는 것을 알게 되었다.

Unit 4

Answers

1. ②　　　　2. ⑤　　　　3. ②　　　　4. ④

Word

cloned life 생명복제
debate 논의하다, 토론하다
morality 도덕성, 윤리성
cloning 복제(미수정란의 핵을 체세포의 핵으로 바꿔 놓아 유전적으로 똑같은 생물을 얻는 기술)
unethical 비윤리적인
nothing but 단지 ~일 뿐(only), ~밖에 없는(아닌)
human reproductive right 인간 생식의 권리
experimentation 실험(법)
conduct 수행하다, 실시하다
fetus 태아
abnormality 비정상
publish 공식적으로 발표하다
andrology 남성병학(남성의 병을 연구하는 학문)
ongoing 진행 중인
infertile 생식력이 없는, 불임의
oppose 반대하다
bill 법안, 의안
House of Representatives (미 의회, 주 의회의) 하원
outlaw 금지하다, 불법화하다
offender 위반자
penalize 유죄로 선고하다, 처형하다

Unit 5

Answers

1. ⑤　　　　2. ④　　　　3. ④
4. (C) attacking → attack으로 고침

Word

subdue 정복하다

hardcore 강경한, 단호한, 타협하지 않는

Muslims 이슬람교

overthrow 굴복(전복)시키다

terrorist 테러리스트, 테러행위자

plot ～을 몰래 계획하다, 음모를 꾸미다

hijack 공중 납치하다

crowded 사람으로 가득찬

collapse 무너지다, 붕괴하다

due to ～ 때문에

opposition 반대, 저항, 야당

Opposition Alliance 야당 연맹

statement 연설, 주장

broadcast ～을 방송하다

subsequently 그 후에

be known by ～에 의해 알려지다

mighty 강력한, 강대한

Review

A.

1. Buddhist
2. mistreat
3. define
4. prevalence
5. introduction
6. responsiveness
7. aspect
8. be composed of
9. crack
10. investigator
11. best-preserved
12. lost
13. cloned life
14. morality
15. experimentation
16. ongoing
17. subdue
18. opposition
19. due to
20. subsequently

B.

1. 대우하다, 취급하다
2. 영향력, 세력, 위력
3. 정의를 내리다
4. 집단, 단체
5. 특성, 특징
6. 보증하다
7. ～을 필요로 하다
8. 필요
9. 장소, 현장
10. 미라
11. 당국
12. 그 사이에
13. 수행하다, 실시하다
14. 생식력이 없는
15. 태아
16. 비윤리적인
17. 음모를 꾸미다
18. 단호한
19. 공중 납치하다
20. 연설, 주장

C.

1. ①
2. ②
3. ③

D.

1. 비록 그는 중대한 범죄를 저질렀지만 그는 이 나라를 위해 많은 일을 했다.
2. 간단히 말해, 우리는 아이들이 양심 즉 그들을 옳은 길로 지켜줄 수 있는 내부의 강한 목소리를 키우기를 원한다는 것이다.
3. Find out how banks keep your money safe, how banks make money, and how to start your own bank.

E.

1. ③
2. ③
3. ②

F.

1. define
2. definite
3. aspect
4. inspect

CHAPTER 13

Preview

Word • Mini Quiz

1. b
3. f
5. c
7. seasoning
9. denied
11. adapt

2. d
4. e
6. a
8. handle
10. vibrations
12. trustworthy

Grammar • Mini Quiz

1. keeping
2. has waited / went
3. sensitive

Unit 1

Answers

1. ①
2. ⑤

Word

highly aware 극도로 예민한
adjust 적응하다
pay for ~에 대가를 치르다
handle 다루다
deal with ~을 다루다
drilling 스케일링, 치과의 드릴로 갈기
stand 참다, 견디다
deaden 누그러뜨리다, 죽이다
withstand 견디다
fall apart 통제를 잃다, 동요하다, 당황하다
sensation 감각
stuff 구성요소

Drill 1 • Grammar

1. 군대에 입대하기 위해서, 그 남자는 신체검사와 지능검사를 받아야 했다.
2. 세계를 여행하기 위해서, Jeff는 열심히 일해야 하고 많은 돈을 저축해야 한다.
3. To buy a gift for his girlfriend, Chris went shopping at the new department store.

Drill 2 • Translation

1. 인간의 신체가 신체의 외부와 내부 모두에서 일어나는 일을 아주 예민하게 알아챌 수 있는 수백만 개의 신경을 발달해냈다는 것은 사실이다.

   해설 be aware of는 '~을 알다, ~을 감지하다'이고, both A and B는 'A와 B 둘 다'이다. 목적격 it은 the human body를 뜻한다.

2. 어떤 사람들이 고통을 다룰 수 있는 능력을 개발했다는 점은 정신이 고통을 어떻게 다룰 수 있는가에 관해 우리에게 아이디어를 제공해 줄 것이다.

   해설 목적격 관계대명사 that은 '~는'으로 해석되며 선행사(The ability)를 수식하고 있다.

3. 아마 1~2분 지속될 스케일링 절차의 고통을 피하기 위해 우리는 치아 주변에 있는 신경을 죽이는 주사바늘을 요구한다.

   해설 To avoid는 목적을 나타내는 to부정사의 부사적 용법으로 '피하기 위하여'로 해석하며 comma(,) 뒤에 오는 문장을 수식한다.

4. 결국 고통이 불쾌한 감각이기는 하지만, 그것도 하나의 감각이며, 감각이란 삶의 구성요소인 것이다.

   어구 after all 아무튼, 어쨌든, 결국

Unit 2

Answers

1. ⑤
2. ⑤

Word

point out 지적하다
consequently 결과적으로
characterize 특징짓다
frequency 주파수
vibration 진동
observer 관찰자
set off 유발하다
a chain of 연쇄적인
neurochemical 신경화학의
perceive 느끼다, 지각하다
be made up of ~로 구성되다

Drill 1 • Grammar

1. 그들이 찾고 있는 것은 심오한 지식이라기보다는 빠른 정보이다.
2. 몸무게를 줄이고 싶다면 당신이 즉시 해야 할 것은 덜 먹고 규칙적으로 운동을 하는 것이다.

3. What history teaches us is very important.

Drill 2 • Translation

1. 그가 살던 시대 이후로 우리는 빛의 파장이 다양한 진동의 주파수로 특징지어진다고 알아왔다.
2. 그 파장은 관찰자의 눈에 들어올 때 연쇄적인 신경 화학적 현상을 유발시키며, 그 현상이 끝날 때 우리가 색깔이라 부르는 내적인 정신적 이미지가 만들어진다.
3. 여기에서 근본적 요점은 우리가 색깔로 인식하는 것은 색깔로 구성되어 있지 않다는 것이다.
4. 사과는 빨갛게 보일지 모르지만 그것을 이루는 원자는 전혀 빨간색이 아니다.

Unit 3

Answers

1. ③   2. ②

Word

spilling 쏟기
nullify 무효로 하다
tourist attraction 관광명소
veneration 존경, 귀하게 여김
foreboding 불길한 예감
poignantly 예리하게
foreshadow ~의 전조가 되다, 슬쩍 비추다
incorporate 짜 넣다
further 좀 더
ill-boding 불길한
omen 징조

Drill 1 • Grammar

1. 거짓말은 우리 일상 사회생활의 한 부분이다. 타인의 감정에 상처를 주고 싶지 않은 우리는 종종 거짓말을 한다.
2. 내 여동생의 맥박을 검진했던 의사는 걱정할 정도로 심각한 것은 아무 것도 없다고 말했다.
3. Walking in the park, I happened to meet her.

Drill 2 • Translation

1. 소금은 인간의 첫 양념이었으며 인간의 음식 습관을 매우 극적으로 바꾸어놓았기 때문에 가장 귀한 양념을 쏟는 행위가 불길한 것과 동등하게 취급되는 것은 전혀 놀라운 일이 아니다.
2. 고고학자들은 기원전 6,500년에는 유럽에 살고 있던 사람들이 유럽 대륙(the continent)에서 발견된 최초의 염광으로 생각되는 오스트리아의 할슈타인과 할슈타트 광상들을 실제로 채굴하고 있었다는 것을 알고 있다.

3. 소금을 귀하게 여기는 마음과 소금을 엎질렀을 때 뒤따르는 불길한 징조는 레오나르도 다빈치의 '최후의 만찬' 속에 예리하게 나타나 있다.
4. 하지만 역사적으로 최후의 만찬에서 소금이 엎질러졌다는 아무런 증거도 없다.

Unit 4

Answers

1. ④   2. ⑤   3. ④   4. ②

Word

psychologist 심리학자
self-evaluation 자기평가
competent 유능한, 능력이 있는
be likely to ~할 것 같다
influence 영향을 끼치다
memory bank (머릿속의)기억 장치
rejection 거절, 거부 반응
misbehave 버릇없는 짓을 하다
praise 칭찬하다
have difficulty -ing ~하는 데 어려움을 겪다
positive statement 긍정적인 표현
compliment 칭찬하는 말
take advantage of ~을 이용하다
block 막다, 방해하다

Unit 5

Answers

1. ②   2. ②   3. ④, ②, ①, ③

Word

zodiac sings 별자리
constellation 별자리
mild-tempered 온화한, 상냥한
specific 특정한, 구체적인
trustworthy 믿을 수 있는, 신뢰할 수 있는
affectionate 애정 어린, 상냥한
weakness 약점
stubbornness 완고함, 완강함
enthusiastic 열정적인, 열렬한
excel 빼어나다, 탁월하다
straightforward 솔직한, 직접의

do things one's own way 마음대로 하다
adapt 적응하다, 조화시키다
insistence 고집, 주장
big-hearted 관대한, 친절한
strong-willed 강한 의지의
vanity 허영심
tendency 경향
deal with 다루다, 취급하다
dual personality 이중성격
sentimental 감상적인, 다감한
blunt 퉁명스러운, 무뚝뚝한
make decision 결정하다

Review

A.

1. nerves
2. fall apart
3. handle / deal with
4. pay for
5. point out
6. set off
7. a chain of
8. perceive
9. seasoning
10. foreboding
11. interpretation
12. tourist attraction
13. psychologist
14. self-evaluation
15. rejection
16. take advantage of
17. mild-tempered
18. flexible
19. vanity
20. sentimental

B.

1. 적응하다, 조절하다
2. 극도로 예민한
3. 누그러뜨리다, 죽이다
4. 견디다
5. 관찰자
6. 주파수
7. 결과적으로
8. 특징짓다
9. 풍습, 습관
10. 무효로 하다
11. 존경, 귀하게 여김
12. 짜 넣다
13. ~할 것 같다
14. 버릇없는 짓을 하다
15. 긍정적인 표현
16. 칭찬(하다)
17. 이중성격
18. 관대한, 친절한
19. 빼어나다, 탁월하다
20. 강한 의지의

C.

1. ④
2. ①
3. ④

D.

1. 좋은 성적을 받기 위해서 너는 네 자신을 믿고 네 능력을 믿어야 한다.
2. 여기에서 근본적 요점은 우리가 색깔로 지각하는 것은 색깔로 구성되어 있지 않다는 것이다.
3. Walking down the street, you may not even notice the trees, but, according to a new study, they do a lot more than give shade.

E.

1. ②
2. ①
3. ①

F.

1. perceived
2. conceived
3. observes
4. deserve